# Homelessness

# HOMELESSNESS
## PUBLIC POLICIES AND PRIVATE TROUBLES

*Edited by*
*Susan Hutson and David Clapham*

CASSELL

London and New York

Cassell
Wellington House, 125 Strand, London WC2R 0BB, England
370 Lexington Avenue, New York, NY 10017-6550

First published 1999

**British Library Cataloguing in Publication Data**
A catalogue record for this book is available from the British Library.

ISBN 0 304 33895 8 Hardback
    0 304 33896 6 Paperback

**Library of Congress Cataloging-in-Publication Data**
Homelessness: public policies and private troubles/edited by Susan Hutson and David Clapham.
    p.  cm.
  Includes bibliographical references and index.
  ISBN 0–304–33895–8 (hardcover). — ISBN 0–304–33896–6 (pbk.)
    1. Homelessness — Government policy — Great Britain. 2. Housing policy — Great Britain. 3. Great
Britain — Social policy. 4. Great Britain — Politics and government. 5. Great Britain — Social
conditions. I. Hutson, Susan. II. Clapham, David, 1951–
HV4545.A4H68   1998
362.5'8'0941—dc21                                        98—11419
                                                              CIP

Typeset by York House Typographic Ltd, London
Printed and bound in Great Britain by Biddles Ltd, Guildford and King's Lynn

# Contents

# List of figures

# List of tables

# The contributors

**Isobel Anderson** is a Lecturer in the Housing Policy and Practice Unit, Department of Applied Social Science, University of Stirling. Since 1990 she has been engaged on a programme of research on single/youth homelessness; access to housing for low income single people; and housing and social exclusion.

**David Clapham** is Professor of Housing and Director of the Centre for Housing Management and Development at Cardiff University.

**Angela Evans** is Honorary Research Fellow at the Centre for Housing Management and Development, Cardiff University. She is a freelance housing researcher with a particular interest in homelessness and housing need, access to social housing and perceptions of social housing.

**Janet Ford** is the Joseph Rowntree Professor of Housing Policy and Director of the Centre for Housing Policy at the University of York. Her main research interests concern owner occupation and, in particular, the extent to which and ways in which it can be sustained. She has written widely about the housing market and the labour market.

**Suzanne Fitzpatrick** is a researcher at the Centre for Housing Research and Urban Studies, University of Glasgow. She has recently submitted her doctoral thesis on youth homelessness. Her current research interests include housing law, young people's position in the housing market and in urban neighbourhoods and the evolution of housing and homelessness policies in the European Union.

**Bridget J. Franklin** is a Lecturer in Housing at Cardiff University. She has a first degree in Social Anthropology, a higher degree in Sociology, and also possesses the postgraduate Diploma in Housing. After some years working in the voluntary sector she has held various university research posts, and has an interest in research into housing and community care, the role and definition of housing management, and the relationship between people and their physical surroundings.

**Brian Harvey** is a graduate in history from Dublin University (Trinity College). He works as a research consultant in Dublin, specializing in social exclusion and European issues. He was an executive member of FEANTSA from 1988 to 1995 and its president for 1991–5.

**Susan Hutson** is Senior Lecturer in Sociology at the University of Glamorgan. She was previously a Research Fellow at University College, Swansea, where her research focused on young people in relation to homelessness, leaving care, unemployment and part-time working as well as sport.

**Keith Jacobs** is a Senior Lecturer at the School of the Built Environment, University of Westminster. His most recent publication is *The Dynamics of Local Housing Policy* (1999), published by the Ashgate Press.

**Jim Kemeny** is Professor of Urban and Housing Sociology at the Institute for Housing Research and the Department of Sociology, Uppsala University, Sweden. See his home page for further information: http://www.soc.uu.se/staff/jim_k.html.

**Mark Liddiard** is a Lecturer in Social Policy at the University of Kent at Canterbury. To date, most of his research has been in the field of youth homelessness. He is co-author, with Susan Hutson, of *Youth Homelessness: The Construction of a Social Issue* (1994), published by Macmillan. However, his recent research has shifted in focus towards arts and cultural policy, with a particular interest in museums and the mass media.

**Tony Manzi** is a Senior Lecturer at the School of Construction, Housing and Surveying, University of Westminster. He is currently undertaking PhD research into management culture in housing organizations.

**Peter Somerville** is currently Reader in Policy Studies at the University of Lincolnshire and Humberside. He has worked for many years for local housing authorities and has published widely on housing management and housing policy, including homelessness policy.

**Joan M. Smith** is Reader and Head of the Housing and Community Research Unit, Staffordshire University, which was established in 1989. Her research interests include youth homelessness and the housing needs of young people, social exclusion and young people, gendered welfare states and the family as well as community policy and community regeneration.

# Acknowledgements

We would like to thank the School of Humanities and Social Sciences, University of Glamorgan and the Department of City and Regional Planning, Cardiff University. We would also like to thank our families for their encouragement and support, in particular John and Amanda for their work on the final text. We would especially like to thank the contributors for making the editing of this collection such an enjoyable task.

To John, Holly, James, Cynthia, Amanda, Hannah and Elizabeth.

# Introduction

*Susan Hutson*

As the title indicates, this book is centrally concerned with the public policies which surround homelessness. In the first chapter, Jacobs, Kemeny and Manzi point out that much of politics is concerned with establishing a dominant discourse by which an issue is defined and dealt with. The changes in these discourses around homelessness are their concern as well as being a central theme to the book (see Chapters 2 and 6). In terms of public policy, the book also offers a detailed examination of the passing of homelessness legislation (see Chapter 2) and the operation of bureaucratic structures which result from it (see Chapters 7 and 10). Legislation can differentiate access to resources and homelessness legislation places single people in a particularly disadvantaged position. Anderson (Chapter 8) focuses on this while Smith (Chapter 6) addresses the situation of women. Many chapters illustrate the way in which public policies themselves create homelessness and, in this context, the increase in mortgage repossessions in the early 1990s is considered. Within the book, public policies are set in a broader scene. The impact on policy of the media hype which homelessness has attracted is examined by Liddiard (Chapter 4), while the need for a European-wide definition and response is set out by Harvey (Chapter 3). Although many authors deal with specific legislation, in particular the 1977 Housing (Homeless Persons) Act and the 1996 Housing Act, and the period which lies between them, their observations have relevance to wider political processes and public discourses.

The title also indicates that homelessness is experienced, on a day-to-day basis, as a private trouble – a teenager rowing with parents (Chapter 6), a homeless person fearing violence in a hostel (Chapter 11), someone in debt staying in to save money and hiding her situation from others (Chapter 5). Fitzpatrick and Clapham (Chapter 9) show that homelessness is part of a

multifaceted experience and suggest that this can best be seen by constructing individual housing pathways. All these and other chapters show that the
experience of not having a home can fracture social networks and stop
people from participating in society. As Anderson (Chapter 8) comments:

At a time when politicians and others are concerned about the breakdown of the
fabric of society it is surprising that weaknesses in housing policy are not central to
these debates.

The concept of homelessness, as it is understood today, did not exist in the
19th century (Lund, 1996, p. 84). From this time, state intervention can be
divided into two strands. First there were moves, by the state, to improve the
housing conditions for the majority of the population. Second, the state
took measures to provide for and control the dependent and unsettled
poor. State responsibility for housing conditions first began in the 1870s,
with health regulations; then, in 1915, the state intervened directly in the
housing market with the imposition of rent control. From 1919 to the late
1960s, there was a drive to build council houses and to subsidize private
building, particularly after the First World War when 'homes for heroes' was
the slogan and, again, after the Second World War. This led overall to
increasing standards and, by the late 1960s, the number of houses was
broadly equivalent to the number of households (Malpass and Murie, 1994,
p. 71). From then on, and particularly through successive Conservative
governments, the building of social housing came to a virtual standstill.
This, coupled with the drive towards home ownership, has meant that the
state responsibility for the provision of housing has lessened. In separate
chapters, Smith (6), Evans (7) and Anderson (8) document the effect this
has had in increasing homelessness.

   Under the Poor Law Acts, passed through the 19th century, paupers or
the unsettled poor were put to work in the workhouses. Most were seen as
responsible for their position in so far as their poverty was felt to arise from
their idleness and fecklessness. Interestingly they were not referred to as
homeless people but simply as paupers. In the 1990s, homelessness is
associated not with the housing needs of the majority but with a minority
who are still seen as idle and feckless. Public attitudes towards these people
today echo earlier sentiments. This is documented, by Anderson (Chapter
8), in relation to single people, and by Smith (Chapter 6), in relation to
single-parent mothers. Concerns with the housing needs of the majority
have been replaced by moral criticism of the minority who fail to get
themselves housed. There is a call, by many writers in this book (see Jacobs,
Kemeny and Manzi (Chapter 1); Harvey (Chapter 3); Smith (Chapter 6);
Evans (Chapter 7) and Anderson (Chapter 8)), for the state to take on its
responsibility again and acknowledge that 'homelessness', which today is
defined as a minority and pathological problem, should be redefined as one
of ordinary people wanting ordinary houses.

The 1977 Housing (Homeless Persons) Act stands as a landmark in these changing trends and is used as a starting point of many chapters. It was in this Act that 'homelessness' became defined as a distinct term. The Act followed the TV drama documentary *Cathy Come Home* (1966), the launching of Shelter (1966) and the Greve Report (1971), all of which helped to raise the profile of homelessness as a political issue. Homelessness was linked to a shortage of accommodation following slum clearance rather than the actions of individuals. The response, in the Act, was to give certain categories of homeless people a statutory right to housing. Two decades later, the 1996 Housing Act removed this route. By this time, homelessness was seen not to result from a shortage of accommodation but from the behaviour of a marginalized few. Several chapters in this book (Jacobs, Kemeny and Manzi (Chapter 1); Somerville (Chapter 2); Evans (Chapter 7)) look in detail at the passing of these two Housing Acts and at the reasons for a marked shift in policies and attitudes towards homelessness.

These two decades saw a marked increase in homelessness. In terms of homeless households accepted for rehousing, the figures rose from 53,110 in 1979 to 120,200 in 1996 with a peak year in 1991 when the figure was 146,290 (Department of the Environment, Quarterly Returns). These figures do not include single homeless people, but Burrows and Walentowicz (1992) give an estimated figure of 1,712,000 in that year. There are certain clear causes for this rise. Namely, the collapse of traditional manufacturing industries in the 1980s and the resulting unemployment are linked with the increase in welfare dependency. Cutbacks in public spending in the face of a global recession and continuing monetarist policies lay behind cuts for council housing building. The withdrawal of welfarist protection at a time of economic insecurity has led to personal destitution even to the extent of street homelessness which is shocking in a Western economy.

It is ironic that, as homelessness figures have been rising, housing has declined as a social issue of public concern. By the 1997 election, homelessness was not on the agenda and public interest in the restrictions of the 1996 Housing Act was minimal. The effects of government policies on homelessness were hidden, in part, by the gains which many people felt they were making through home ownership. The marginalization of homelessness, through an emphasis on rough sleeping, concealed the wider experience of those without stable or secure homes. Even the rise in mortgage repossessions in 1991, as the housing market collapsed and interest rates rose, was presented by the government as a 'one-off' crisis. Those in debt suffered in isolation and blamed themselves. Ford (Chapter 5) shows how it was interpreted as a personal and a minority problem.

Against this background and the focus on public issues and private troubles, there is a number of themes which run through the chapters.

## Changing discourses

In Chapter 1, Jacobs, Kemeny and Manzi show how homelessness is being continuously contested and defined. Taking a social constructivist approach, they identify two major competing definitions of homelessness which have alternately influenced policies. In the first 'minimalist' definition, homelessness is defined narrowly and extremely as in the case of 'rooflessness'. The problem is seen to be a minority one, marginal to the life of the average citizen. Moreover, in this definition, homelessness is often linked with personal pathology or fecklessness. In the second 'structuralist' definition, homelessness is defined more broadly as housing need and it is seen as a structural problem requiring broad policy intervention by the state.

These two contrasting viewpoints run through a number of other chapters (see Chapters 6 and 7) and there is consensus that the two Housing Acts in 1977 and 1996 are significant landmarks in this change of emphasis. The 1970s saw a rediscovery of poverty and other social problems within the welfare state. The setting up of Shelter was symptomatic of this and its use of the media for campaigning started a trend. In the Housing (Homeless Persons) Act of 1977, the definition of homelessness as a structural problem justifying broad state intervention successfully challenged earlier views, which had been consistent since the passing of the 19th-century Poor Laws linked homelessness with vagrancy and idleness. Through successive Conservative governments, from 1979 to 1997, homelessness became a marginal problem which was pushed well down the policy agenda. With cutbacks in public spending, the sale of council houses and the marginalization of local authorities, a minimalist definition of homelessness was re-established, so that in the 1996 Housing Act, state help for homeless people was limited and temporary.

Somerville (Chapter 2), taking a structural approach, identifies three forces operating between the two Housing Acts of 1977 and 1996. First, *centralization*, or the increased control of the central government over the local authorities – in forcing them to house certain homeless groups in 1977 and, in 1996, removing this separate track for homeless people and enforcing a centralized system of housing allocation. Second, he outlines the *depoliticization* of homelessness from being a national housing issue to a technical specialism dealt with in the homelessness sections of housing departments. Third, he looks at the process of *marketization*, whereby the state is absolved of responsibility for providing housing and the private sector becomes the main provider for homeless people. The state is only expected to give assistance in a crisis. Somerville shows how the government was able to strengthen its power through centralization while defending itself against attack by depoliticizing the issue.

Smith (Chapter 6) looks in detail at the changing discourses around women and welfare. In the 1977 Housing (Homeless Persons) Act, the dominant image of women was as mothers struggling to raise future citizens. By contrast, in the political rhetoric around the 1996 Housing Act, the dominant image was that of a single parent deliberately using her children to gain benefits and housing. This change – from state protection to a moral attack on welfare – was extreme.

## Public policies

A social issue is shaped and defined by legislation and a number of chapters look in detail at the legislative process. Somerville (Chapter 2) looks at the role of political groups in homelessness legislation. Despite increases in centralization, depoliticization and marketization, he finds that these groups and their positions are relatively static. He highlights the dominant and continuing role of the government, or the Department of the Environment, in forcing local authorities to implement national policy. Ironically, in 1977, the local authorities were forced to house certain categories of homeless people. Two decades later, it was these local authorities who were defending the existing homelessness structures against further change.

On the European scene, many of the same factors operate. Cuts in public spending, unemployment, wider home ownership all exacerbate homelessness and reduce the stock of affordable accommodation. Harvey (Chapter 3) calls for the need to make visible the common problem of homelessness across national boundaries. This is hindered by the lack of comparable statistics, differences in specific housing legislation and the local control of housing. For these reasons, housing failed to become part of the agenda for the new treaty of European Union being drawn up at the intergovernmental conference of 1996–7.

A number of chapters refer to the way homelessness is presented in the press. Was it *Cathy Come Home* which first led to public concern about families? Somerville (Chapter 2) suggests that the Department of the Environment pursued its objectives in the 1977 Housing (Homeless Persons) Act, uninfluenced by public concern or the press and points out that the debates which preceded the 1996 Housing Act did not feature in the media. Liddiard (Chapter 4), who looks centrally at the links between the press coverage, public opinion and policy, says it is difficult to trace direct connections. However, he and others (Smith, Chapter 6) feel that media representations are important in influencing public images. In terms of a press agenda, it is easier to present rough sleeping than other aspects of housing need and these images have come to symbolize homelessness. However, such images stress the personal rather than the structural, the pathological rather than the ordinary and, in this way, press coverage has played a role in the current dominance of a minimalist definition.

While the role of the press may be nebulous, public opinion is more so. When *Cathy Come Home* was shown in 1966, slum clearance was affecting many ordinary families and the scandal of 'Rachmanism' was in the news-papers. Why did mortgage arrears, which were affecting many ordinary families, not create a similar response in the 1990s? Ford (Chapter 5) shows how the current situation of mortgage repossessions is seen to be outside government responsibility, although it is the 'entrenched' outcome of a number of government housing and financial policies. Mortgage debt is resolved individually through the courts, by individual lenders rather than by changes in government policies. Those in debt tend to blame themselves and hide their situation, finding their own ways through a personal trouble rather than querying the policies.

**Routes through housing**

Homelessness is the creation of public policies. In responding to home-lessness by legislation, routes are created whereby people do or do not qualify for housing. Several chapters look at the way in which people move through these bureaucratic routes. Smith (Chapter 6) and Evans (Chapter 7) both use survey data to challenge the idea that women have had privileged routes into housing since the 1977 Housing (Homeless Persons) Act. Evans shows that legislation should be seen as a rationing process rather than a passport to housing. She concludes, however, that the bureaucratic processes are inefficient in so far as only one fifth are satisfactorily housed by the end. She shows how people are put off from applying because of the stigma involved, from fear that they will not be treated well or that they will not like the accommodation offered. Although Smith feels that women with children were afforded some protection in terms of housing and benefits in the 1970 Act, she illustrates the moral backlash against single mothers in the 1990s. She fears that the recent emphasis on rough sleeping as qualifying someone as homeless will tend to exclude women who are more likely to present as homeless from staying with parents, friends or relatives rather than from hostels or sleeping on the street.

Anderson (Chapter 8) details the way in which single people have been consistently excluded from these routes into social housing. They are excluded despite their rising numbers and the fact that there is very little difference between 'priority' and 'non-priority' need applicants in terms of their experience of housing need or their ability to find alternative accom-modation. This latter fact is endorsed by Evans' material (Chapter 7). Anderson shows how this disqualification from housing routes leads to their invisibility and, moreover, makes it possible to keep homelessness statistics low.

Much of our information about homelessness comes from static surveys and is statistical in nature. However, homelessness can be better understood when looked at as a process or, as Fitzpatrick and Clapham (Chapter 9) suggest, a pathway in which homelessness may make up shorter or longer episodes. They use qualitative data to show how young homeless people use a mix of informal networks and voluntary sector service provision. They suggest that, while media and public policy tend to focus on young homeless people using city centre services, these young people are atypical in the extremity of their experience and their dislocation from their families and communities. They find that many more young people remain in their local area and are reliant on informal networks. This is also the experience of Hutson (Chapter 11), who suggests that the agency services for homeless young people tend to stress the need for professional support and so play down young people's own lifestyles and informal networks. Fitzpatrick and Clapham suggest that, by using biographical interviewing, individual situations and reactions can be placed alongside structural factors in explaining social exclusion.

## Social exclusion

It is clear that homelessness is caused by exclusion – exclusion from the labour market and welfare, exclusion from the housing market and exclusion from the family. Recession and economic restructuring underlie the current trends in homelessness. The exclusion of under-25s to full social security benefits triggered youth homelessness after 1988. Homelessness among single people results directly from their exclusion from council housing. Anderson (Chapter 8) illustrates that where people do not gain access to housing, they are further excluded from 'wider aspects of well being and social participation taken as "usual" among the majority in society'. In particular, homelessness excludes people from employment and so, often, from good health. Social exclusion can lead to the placing of blame on the individual. For example, Franklin (Chapter 10) points out that if people do not have a home, it is often assumed that there is something wrong with them.

An actual episode of homelessness often follows exclusion from the family. Such family exclusion is explored in this book by Fitzpatrick and Clapham (Chapter 9) as well as by Smith (Chapter 6). Smith shows how family arguments are often provoked by the external environment of crime and drug use. A distinction is drawn between those young people to whom these arguments cause temporary disruption and those where the dislocation from the family is long-term and more deep-seated. Truancy, crime and drug-use may remove young people from mainstream routes and cause major arguments. Hutson (Chapter 11) shows how such elements of lifestyle can cause prejudice in neighbourhoods when such young people are eventually housed. Probationary tenancies can exacerbate this prejudice, which may continue to exclude people from permanent housing.

### Demographic change and a 'risk' society

Running behind the changing discourse and polices, which form the core of the book, lie broader changes in the labour market and the pattern of household formation which some (Beck, 1992) identify as constituting a 'risk' society. Unemployment, part-time working, short-term contracts, increasing participation by women in the labour force, rising divorce rates, cohabitation and later marriage all lead people to take more individuated routes though life. Ford (Chapter 5) links some of these changes with mortgage repossession in so far as the increased casualization of the labour market puts people at risk and the inclusion of the woman's income in the loan drew in more mortgagors from the 1980s. Financial risks and arrears are likely to increase as households dissolve more often.

Anderson (Chapter 8) outlines the growth in single-person households, which have doubled since the 1960s. This shows how housing legislation, in excluding single people, is out of step with the current life course of younger people seeking housing. Across Europe, Harvey (Chapter 3) shows how the majority of homeless people are alone without a partner and that one third are separated or divorced. Smith (Chapter 6) shows that, although the rise in single mothers was due to many factors, in particular increases in divorce, it was the young, never-married mothers who bore the brunt of the remoralization of welfare. She stresses that, although their actions merely reflect the age-old wish to have a family and to look for safe and secure accommodation, assessment of their behaviour lies at the centre of a debate to justify public spending cuts.

### Support

Both Franklin (Chapter 10) and Hutson (Chapter 11) look centrally at the question of the provision of 'support' for single homeless people. This current emphasis on support reflects to the fact than an increasing number of tenants have support needs whether they are housed under community care or homelessness legislation. Hutson links the emphasis on support with the number of support and child-care agencies who have created a new area of professional work within youth homelessness. Franklin shows how support is currently provided on the fringes of two different agencies – housing and social services – and argues that this can lead to inefficiency. Hutson suggests that requests for support come from only a minority of homeless people and finds some mismatch between the support on offer and the lifestyles of some young people.

## Private troubles

The private experience of homelessness runs through a number of chapters. Hutson (Chapter 11) uses private accounts to look at temporary accommodation. The dangers of sharing accommodation with others – who are not known and often feared – is a dominant aspect of such personal accounts, even when the conditions of their accommodation are improved. In terms of support, she suggests some discrepancies in the way in which the experience of homelessness and the need for support is expressed between agency workers on the one hand and homeless people on the other.

In Chapter 9 by Fitzpatrick and Clapham and Chapter 6 by Smith, the experience of homelessness is illustrated by direct accounts in which eviction, high mobility, petty crime and drug use are evident. In both chapters, a distinction is made between, on the one hand, abusive or disrupted families where the family ceases to operate for the young person who may go into care and, on the other hand, families where the family continues to operate but the young person may be evicted on a short-term basis. Here the young person may return or make occasional use of family resources. Smith shows the motivation behind many of the young women starting their own families.

Ford (Chapter 5) shows how, although mortgage debt is created by structural, economic forces, the processes around it are experienced as personally stigmatizing. Moreover, the debt is seen to arise from being a poor manager or, at worst, feckless. This definition is internalized by the debtors who hide their situation.

## Conclusions

The connection which C. Wright Mills (1959) makes between such private troubles and public policies is contained within this well-known statement:

When, in a city of 100,000, only one man is unemployed, that is his personal trouble, and for its relief we properly look to the character of the man. ... But when, in a nation of 50 million employees, 15 million men are unemployed, that is an issue, and we may not hope to find its solution within the range of opportunities open to any one individual. The very structure of opportunities has collapsed.

The numbers experiencing difficulties with housing are more than just a few. Although the public messages about homelessness may include individual blame and social pathology, both the creation and the solution of homelessness lie with public policies. The chapters which follow look in detail at the relationship between public policies and private troubles.

## References

Beck, U. (1992) *Risk Society: Towards a New Modernity*, London, Sage.

Burrows, L. and Walentowicz, P. (1992) *Homes Cost Less Than Homelessness*. London: Shelter.

Greve, J., Page, D. and Greve, S. (1971) *Homelessness in London*, Edinburgh, Scottish Academic Press.

Lund, B. (1996) *Housing Problems and Housing Policy*, London, Longman.

Malpass, P. and Murie, A. (1994) *Housing Policy and Practice*, 4th edn, London, Macmillan.

Wright Mills, C. (1959) *The Sociological Imagination*, London, Oxford University Press.

# 1 The struggle to define homelessness: a constructivist approach

*Keith Jacobs, Jim Kemeny and Tony Manzi*

## Introduction

There is a large secondary literature on the subject of homelessness (see for example Glastonbury, 1971; Greve, 1964; Greve *et al.*, 1971; Watson and Austerberry, 1986). In addition, homelessness has been subjected to intense empirical research, much of it funded by government and charitable organizations (for a small selection see Anderson *et al.*, 1993; Niner, 1989; Pleace, 1995; Thomas and Niner, 1989). Yet in nearly all of this, as in so much of the housing literature, homelessness is usually treated as an objective and objectifiable phenomenon, within the positivist tradition of social enquiry. We argue that the definition of homelessness in Britain has changed over the last 30 years as vested interests have struggled to impose their particular interpretation of policy debates and to push the homelessness issue as they define it either higher up or lower down the policy agenda.

The first part of the chapter outlines the main features of the constructivist perspective on the study of social problems, which treats the dominant definitions of what constitutes a social problem as contested and unstable. We argue that homelessness is a classic example of how the struggle by different vested interests to impose a particular definition of homelessness on the policy agenda is critical to the way in which homelessness is treated as a social problem. The bulk of the chapter then traces in general terms the struggle between the proponents of two major ideological perspectives – defining homelessness as a structural problem requiring broad welfare measures as against the state minimalist definition in which homelessness is principally defined as the result of individual fecklessness and irresponsibility – to impose their particular definitions of homelessness

The chapter traces the changing fortunes of these two ideologies during the post-war period. We show how a minimalist definition, which was dominant during the early post-war period, was successfully challenged during the 1960s and resulted in the 1977 Housing (Homeless Persons) Act which enshrined a broad definition of homelessness and was intended to guarantee the homeless the right to housing. We then trace the counter-challenge by the minimalists during the ensuing Conservative governments which succeeded in narrowing the definition of homelessness to exclude more and more categories of homeless and which pushed the homelessness problem lower and lower down the policy agenda. Finally, we make some observations on the role that research has played in the course of this struggle and comment on the unstable nature of negotiated orders and the definitions of social problems that accompany such processes.


## The constructivist perspective

Constructivist approaches have until recently been almost unknown in housing studies, where short-term political and policy-driven perspectives have meant that the positivist tradition remains the overwhelmingly dominant perspective, with all forms of hermeneutic analysis neglected (but see Kemeny, 1984 and Kemeny, 1988). There is, however, evidence that this is beginning to change. For example, Clapham and Franklin (1997) and Sahlin (1996) both use constructivist approaches to analyse quite detailed issues of housing management and allocation processes while Hastings (1998) carries out a discourse analysis of a planning document. It is therefore appropriate to begin this discussion by contextualizing the homelessness debate within the large constructivist literature on social problems.

Social policy addresses and attempts to ameliorate or eliminate specific social problems. However, problems are too easily taken for granted as a constant and unquestioned backdrop with which social policy must grapple. This view is particularly entrenched in the more positivistic tradition. There is a tendency to adopt a 'taken for granted' stance to the existence of social problems and assume that we all 'know' intuitively which are the important ones. The question of why some issues become social problems at certain points in time and then lose salience at others or even fade away completely is rarely even acknowledged, let alone taken up and problematized.

Social problems are seen as having a more prominent and interactive part to play in social policy in the hermeneutic tradition and particularly in the school of thought that has come to be known as 'constructivist', much of which was inspired by the emergence within sociology of symbolic inter-actionism, phenomenology and ethnomethodology during the 1960s, particularly within the sociology of deviance and medical sociology. Today, the influence of constructivist perspectives remains patchy, varying widely from one field of social enquiry to another. It is particularly influential in the sociology of science with its own journal, *Social Studies in Science*. There has been a renewed interest in constructivist and discourse analyses within many of the basic social science disciplines, particularly following the work of Foucault.

In the constructivist perspective, social problems are seen as being formed by the power of identifiable groups in society to define a certain issue as a 'problem' that needs tackling in a particular kind of way. The ability to define an issue as a social problem then leads to the construction of a policy and the creation of a public or sometimes private organization to deal with the perceived problem, often including the diverting of significant resources to facilitate this. Meanwhile, other interests continue to try to influence policy by attempting to get their particular approach accepted by policy-makers. Social problems are thereby viewed, in this perspective, as being essentially unstable, capable of being redefined and moved up and down policy agendas as different interests succeed in gaining the upper hand in the ongoing struggle to define priorities.

Essentially then, in the constructivist perspective, the study of social problems centrally involves the study of the exercise of power in society. The study of social problems thereby becomes closely associated with theories of power and the study of decision-making, and 'non-decision making' (Crenson, 1971). It also becomes part of the study of social movements (Mauss, 1975; Useem and Zald, 1982). Early pioneering theoretical work in this field is that of Blumer (1969), Spector and Kitsuse (1973) and Kitsuse and Spector (1973). More recent work includes Best (1989) and Sarbin and Kitsuse (1994). One area in which the constructivist perspective has been important is in the contribution of the media to the rise and fall of social problems (Cohen, 1972; Fishman, 1978; Orcutt and Turner, 1993).

Of course, the structure of a society does provide the basis for the emergence of certain kinds of 'problems'. Thus, for example, the fewer resources that are committed to an area like housing, the more homelessness there is likely to be. But this basis only provides latent tendencies. Other conditions need to be fulfilled for homelessness to become defined as a 'problem' which has higher priority on the policy-agenda. This is essentially a definitional matter. Something does not become a problem until enough people have begun first to perceive it and then to define it as such, thus adopting a particular construction of the situation. And for this to take place, enough people, and particularly people in positions of power and influence, have to be persuaded that this is the case. Furthermore, the way in which the 'problem' is defined is critical to determining how the problem is perceived – for example, whether it is a problem that is largely an individual or social welfare responsibility. So latent tendencies become actualized through the formulation and articulation of a 'problem' in a particular way. An early example of research into the rise and fall of an issue as a social problem is Gusfield's (1963) classic study of the changing status of alcoholism in the USA as a social problem.

Much of politics is concerned with the use of propaganda to establish a dominant discourse over problem-defining and the policy-making that is appropriate to deal with the problem as defined. Unemployment, single-parenthood, homelessness and other conditions can, for example, be defined as being the result of personal inadequacy so as to minimize their importance and locate the responsibility for their solution with the individual. Discourses can be strongly emotive and quite vitriolic, as has on occasion been the case around policies towards single parents or immigrants. Alternatively, such issues can be defined as social problems which need universal welfare provision. Policy-making is thereby built up on the basis of assumptions that are made concerning the nature of the condition to be treated. De Neufville and Barton (1987) show how policies are built on myths that provide the emotional impetus for their implementation, and one of the examples they give is in housing, where the myth of 'the independent yeoman' is used to fuel the drive to encourage owner-occupation. The following section therefore examines the construction and implementation of homelessness policies in the United Kingdom from the 1960s to the present.

## The rise and fall of homelessness as a social problem

Homelessness is, of course, a social problem in which journalism has played a key role. The impact of the film *Cathy Come Home* on housing policy is a classic example of media impact on policy (see Chapter 4). This makes it all the more striking that housing researchers have neglected to explore the impact of this film on policy towards homelessness. In order to illustrate the impact of competing interests in the struggles to define homelessness, the following section examines three key episodes in homelessness policy: the discourse surrounding the film *Cathy Come Home*, first broadcast in 1966; the passing of the 1977 Housing (Homeless Persons) Act and the 1996 Housing Act. Together an analysis of these episodes illustrates the struggle between competing definitions and helps to explain the success of minimalist explanations of homelessness in current policy discourse.

*The rise of homelessness as a social problem: critical social policy, pressure groups and the film* Cathy Come Home

In contrast to the contemporary policy environment, the 1950s and 1960s were decades of high employment, economic growth and rising living standards. At the same time, however, there remained large sections of the population who suffered considerable deprivation. Yet the prevailing ethos of the time was one of optimism. Social scientists focused disproportionately on the 'problems' of prosperity, fretting over whether workers were becoming 'bourgeois' (Goldthorpe *et al.*, 1969), how working-class children were coping with the cultural conflict between their middle-class grammar school environment and their working-class origins (Jackson and Marsden, 1962) or how clerical occupations were being seen as a temporary 'bridging occupation' *en route* to executive status and full membership of the prosperous middle classes with their lifetime secure careers (Dale, 1962; Broom and Smith, 1963).

These assumptions gradually became subject to question by the late 1960s with the emergence of debates about the 'rediscovery' of poverty (see Chapter 6). The changing research context enabled new conceptualizations of social problems to be disseminated into media discussion and thereby enter the public domain. Two works were of particular significance in this respect. The study carried out by Abel-Smith and Townsend (1965), which attempted to offer a redefinition of the notion of poverty, had a substantial impact in challenging some of the optimistic assumptions about the capacity of the welfare state (for example Crosland, 1956). In the domain of homelessness policy, Greve's (1964) report precipitated a shift in academic and subsequently media representation of this social problem. What did this transformation consist of?

Campaigning organizations, interested in the issue of homelessness in the 1960s, were anxious to redefine notions of housing need in such a way as to draw attention to issues such as shortage, affordability and fitness of accommodation. For Wilson (1970, p. 19), as the first Director of Shelter:

the aim ... was to relate homelessness to housing scarcity, and not to welfare (in its administrative sense), and get full recognition of the scale of the problem.

Criticisms of official policy were based on two complaints. First, that government statistics failed to acknowledge the extent of homelessness and, second, that policy involved moral assumptions about the character of homeless individuals. As a consequence, it was important to construct the issue in terms of structural explanations that would engender sympathy and understanding rather than blame and judgement. This implied that it was crucial to find a terminology that would redefine the problem in such a way that attention would be drawn towards discussion of the inadequacy of existing state provision. The difficulty was that the popular image of homelessness, prior to *Cathy Come Home*, was constructed on the foundations of the 1948 National Assistance Act. This legislation was predicated upon notions of homelessness as a consequence of vagrancy, alcoholism, destitution, pauperism and unwillingness to work (see Chapter 2). An example of prevailing attitudes is illustrated by an interview with a housing officer in

Glastonbury's study of homeless families (1971, p. 106; also cited in Thompson, 1988):

I have to pay attention to the ordinary standards of decent people. We don't want these dead-legs. They muck up the books and make life a misery for ordinary folk.

If perceptions were to change, it was essential to combat the widespread discrimination and hostility towards such groups. For those advocating change, the screening of *Cathy Come Home* in 1966 marked a turning-point in the representation of homeless people. Some extravagant claims about its impact have been made. For example Berry (1974, p. 63) claims:

For years the whole question of homelessness had been surrounded by callous public indifference, now overnight it was a matter of national concern, widespread and deep.

Such perspectives interpreted the film as precipitating a shift in attitudes away from previous notions of fecklessness, irresponsibility and personal blame towards structural explanations of government failure. According to such explanations, the film helped to raise both the profile of homelessness as a distinctive problem and to focus on responses which justified a solution in terms of 'housing' shortage rather than social service assistance.

However important the film, its significance should not be overstated. *Cathy Come Home* occupies something of a legendary status within the history of UK housing policy, whereby it is often claimed to be responsible for the creation of the pressure group Shelter (Loveland, 1995, p. 55). However, the broadcasting of the play and the formation of Shelter were coincidental, taking place within a few days of each other (Timmins, 1995). The foundation of several London housing associations around this time also contributed to the mythology surrounding the play. The programme clearly served as a convenient symbol for the inadequacies of government policy, but a range of factors helped to change the popular representations of homelessness (see also Chapter 2). Besides the media interest and the new critical research, the growth of single-issue pressure groups was a significant factor in the changing political climate. As we have noted, the aim of the campaigning organizations was to construct a definition of the problem that would compel central government to respond with a statutory framework. It was anticipated that the combination of factually based studies with dramatic media representations would transform public attitudes so that homelessness would not always be perceived as a question of individual culpability.

On a superficial level, the campaigns resulted in a shift in discussion towards a more socially aware and critical approach. This, in turn, led to the acceptance of a new and broader social definition of homelessness. The eventual result was the 1977 legislation and the imposition of a statutory duty upon local authorities to house persons who were broadly defined as homeless. However, it is crucial to note that the attitudinal changes were the result of a combination of factors including the failure of the slum clearance programmes and the decline of the private rented sector. Hostility towards the latter was marked by the growing media interest in the phenomenon of 'Rachmanism', a term associated with harassment and victimization of private sector tenants (Kemp, 1992).

Therefore, the new ideological climate and interest in structural explanations were the result of complex and interdependent processes. The transformation effected by the legislation should also be qualified. While designating a major symbolic policy change, it nevertheless, in practice, imposed severe limitations on the groups to be housed. In contrast to some social policy areas, the attempt to impose universalist and non-judgemental definitions must be seen as unsuccessful. In order to demonstrate this the following section examines the 1977 Act in some detail.

*The zenith and decline of homelessness as a social problem: the 1977 Housing (Homeless Persons) Act and its subsequent interpretation*

There are competing interpretations of the significance of the 1977 Act. As we have noted, many of those involved in the original campaign viewed it as a great success for pressure group activity (Raynsford, 1986). Other perspectives emphasize the extent to which the legislation was a necessary compromise between interest groups and central and local government (Thompson, 1988). The imprecise nature of the Act has also led to the generation of an extensive body of case law. This too had important effects in redefining the concept as a result of bargaining and negotiation between different interest groups and precipitating a large number of different interpretations of homelessness based on legal precedent. Most important, perhaps, has been the influence of an increasingly restrictive financial context determining local authority implementation. The net result has been a conflict between individuals and groups, on the one hand, attempting to include themselves within statutory definitions and, on the other, resource-stretched local authorities attempting to narrow the criteria (Somerville, 1994). The difficulty in reaching agreed definitions is illustrated by Bramley's (1988) construction of a continuum of homelessness – ranging from rooflessness at one end to unsatisfactory accommodation at the other. A recognition of the socially determined nature of homelessness, therefore, requires that the concept can only be analysed by reference to the processes of interdependence and dominance of specific groups at particular periods in time. The definition is therefore highly contingent on power relationships between these conflicting interests and subject to fluctuation at different periods of time and in different localities (see Chapter 2).

The specific character of debates about homelessness in the UK is further complicated by the provisions of the 1977 Housing (Homeless Persons) Act (later consolidated as part III of the 1985 Housing Act). As a result of concerns expressed by local authority associations, the legislation included a series of restrictions upon applicants (Lund, 1996, p. 87). Consequently statutory duties were incumbent upon local authorities only once a series of investigations had been successfully completed. These comprised the establishment of 'homelessness' itself, 'priority need' (including 'vulnerability'), 'intentionality' and 'local connection'. Applicants therefore had to overcome these obstacles before eligibility was determined. These requirements were introduced in order to suppress latent demand and limit the burden upon local authorities. Crucially, the legislation permitted considerable latitude for authorities to construct their own interpretations of these categories. These concepts and their implications for housing policy should be briefly examined in order to understand how contemporary perceptions of homelessness have been formulated.

In establishing housing responsibilities, local authorities had to satisfy themselves that applicants met the necessary initial criteria of 'homelessness'. This has meant a variety of interpretations and ever stricter classification as resources have become more scarce. Significantly, the legislation has been criticized as both restrictive and too broad. Therefore, on the one hand, from the perspective of recent Conservative ministers, the Act enabled groups who were not 'truly homeless' (i.e. 'roofless') to receive priority assistance, such as young expectant mothers living in the parental home (Ridley, 1992; Thatcher, 1994). On the other hand, from the perspective of campaigning groups, the legislation incorporated a definition that was far too narrow. These differing perspectives are important as they show that the definition of a politically sensitive concept such as homelessness will be continually problematic and subject to conflicting pressures.

The second concept of 'priority need' was introduced to dispel concern that entitlement to homelessness assistance would encourage claims from undeserving groups. Therefore access was targeted towards specific needs, including individuals perceived as in some sense 'vulnerable'. This vague concept has led to a wide disparity in interpretation despite attempts at clarification from the Department of the Environment. For example, some authorities interpret 'vulnerability' as including individuals undertaking rehabilitation programmes for drugs or alcohol whereas others apply a much more restrictive definition (Moroney, 1992).

The introduction of the concept of 'intentionality' has, again, proved a site for substantial conflict and negotiation. An example can be given from the London Borough of Tower Hamlets where a decision was taken to determine families arriving from Bangladesh as intentionally homeless despite previous residency in the UK (Commission for Racial Equality,

1988). In this instance, the local authority contrived to explain home-lessness as the result of individual choice. In order to understand this construction the decision taken by the council can be explained by reference to two pressures. First the influence of an indigenous white community who resented what they perceived as favourable treatment in allocations to particular ethnic groups. The second pressure resulted from the difficulties of declining local authority stock, primarily as a result of the right to buy and lack of resources to provide for new council housing. The decisions, taken by Tower Hamlets, provided a notorious example due to the racialized overtones, but similar restrictive definitions were adopted by other inner city authorities in the light of severely constrained resources.

The establishment of a 'local connection' for applicants has aroused controversy in that it provides opportunities for authorities to dispel their duty under the legislation. This has led to disputes between authorities in determining rehousing responsibilities (for example *R.* v. *Slough Borough Council, ex parte* Ealing London Borough Council 1980). This had led some commentators to warn of a 'merry-go-round' effect as authorities attempt to shift their obligation onto other local areas (Arden and Hunter, 1992, p. 199).

The above examples emphasize the preliminary barriers erected to determine eligibility. However, even when successful, applicants are subject to further constraints and opportunities for conflict. The suitability of accommodation offered is a key arena of dispute where the role of the legal establishment in reinterpreting legislation can be clearly seen (for example *R.* v. *Hillingdon London Borough Council, ex parte* Puhlhofer, 1986). An analysis of the discourses of homelessness and power relationships would, therefore, need to consider the impact and significance of legislative interpretation by the courts in further narrowing definitions and circumscribing local auton-omy. By the mid-1990s, the legislation was under severe strain from the combined impact of legal rulings, government hostility and local authority impotence. The effectiveness of homelessness provisions was further brought into question by the 1995 ruling that local authorities could discharge their obligation by the provision of temporary accommodation (*R.* v. *Brent London Borough Council, ex parte* Awua). This latter judgment was cited by government ministers to justify changes to the legislation. In addition, the increasing use of the private rented sector to house the homeless has engendered a reinterpretation of the legislation (London Research Centre, 1995) and demonstrates that the provisions were subject to strain.

Discrepancies in interpretation of their statutory duty and the exercise of discretionary powers have been highlighted in recent research on local authority implementation of homelessness policies. For example, Evans and Duncan (1988), Niner (1989), Bramley (1993) and Mason (1994) have raised concerns about inconsistencies and differential local responses. It is clear that, despite attempts to maintain a standardized framework through the Department of the Environment (1994) Code of Guidance, the homelessness policies are, in practice, subject to competing interpretations and substantial policy variation between local authority areas. In the case of homelessness, what determines these responses is primarily the availability of local resources. Due to the pressures of such constraints, the definition of homelessness, priority need, intentionality, local connection as well as decisions to rehouse and what accommodation to offer, are subject both to high degrees of variability and change as pressures increase on local authority housing stocks.

In addition to resource constraints, local authorities are further subject to the pressures of political demands. The marginalization of homeless groups and their lack of an effective political role explain why attempts to restrict their access to housing meet minimal opposition (Hoggart, 1995, p. 76). As social rented housing is perceived as a limited and residual tenure for an underclass, resistance to change will be minimal. This is crucial to understanding how the ideological environment reinforces the struggle to define homelessness and explains how minimalist interpretations have gained influence since the 1960s.

The drastic decline in new council housing construction since 1979, compounded by the loss of large numbers of houses mainly under the right to buy, put increasing pressure on local authorities and forced a number of them to challenge early interpretations of the meaning of homelessness. There is also a much more restrictive ideological context to the debate. Central government hostility to benefit dependency and media interest in social security 'scroungers' have helped to question local welfare responsibilities (Clarke, 1990). The culmination of various ideological pressures and socio-economic circumstances has been the pressure to change the legislation in order further to limit access to social rented housing. The result has been the 1996 Housing Act.

*The fall of homelessness as a social problem: the 1996 Housing Act*

Interpretation of the law is important and has been discussed in some detail to illustrate how legislation is reconceptualized as a result of competing pressures. A key consideration of the 1996 legislation was the desire of central government to introduce greater uniformity in practice among local authorities. The reforms were premised upon the need for change based on the principle of 'fairness' in homelessness policy. The 1995 White Paper, therefore, expressed concern at the problem of 'queue-jumping' and the 'fast track' allocation to homeless families at the expense of childless couples (see Chapter 6). This was expressed as follows:

When the homelessness legislation was introduced in the late 1970s, it was expected that only a tiny minority of people looking for a rented home would need to use this route into long term social rented housing. In practice, as the courts have interpreted the legislation, it has meant that anyone who is accepted by the local housing authority as statutorily homeless receives priority in the allocation of a life-long tenancy. They gain this priority regardless of the importance of the needs of other people on the housing waiting list. (Department of the Environment, 1995, p. 36)

The implication of this statement is that there is a distinction to be drawn between those receiving assistance under the legislation and other households in need. The Conservative government attempted to establish a clear minimalist criterion for homelessness assistance, namely that help should be only temporary and short-term. It was successful in this objective owing to the substantially changed ideological climate and relative dominance of certain interests. Therefore, in spite of the widespread criticism from pressure groups and professional bodies, the outcome was only minor modifications to the proposals. The residualization of local authority housing and the marginalization of both local authorities and their client groups have resulted in a limited set of policy options and an inevitable restriction in the definition of the social problem of homelessness.

It should be clear, from the discussion of homelessness, that established definitions are contingent on the dominant discourses that prevail (Kemeny, 1988, p. 214). In the UK, it is clear that the current working definition of homelessness has become increasingly narrow and restricted and, as a result, it has been moving closer towards its equation with 'rooflessness'. This again marks a genuine contrast with the debates of the 1960s. The spectre of 'Rachmanism' no longer succeeds as a potent symbol of the failure of the private rented sector. The 1996 Housing Act was therefore able to promote tenure diversity and increasing use of private renting as a solution to housing problems.

We have shown how the 1977 Housing (Homeless Persons) Act can be viewed as a compromise between two competing ideologies of state welfare – the first, a structuralist ideology in which the state should address social need and the second, a minimalist one in which state provision should be limited only to those 'deserving' support, for example families and those with children. The minimalist ideology became especially evident in the early 1990s, for example in the promotion of the Rough Sleepers Initiative. In targeting attention to the most visible manifestations of homelessness, the government was able to construct a policy agenda in which it appeared that it was taking steps to meet real need. This in turn meant that much of the media reporting of homelessness did not establish the integral connection between government economic and social policies and the surge in homeless people sleeping rough on the streets. Local government has also contributed to minimalist definitions of homelessness – principally, though not entirely, motivated by resource constraints.

Over the last few years, there have been more demands for a tighter definition of homelessness that excludes asylum seekers and sets limits on the rights of single parents. The redefinition of the 1977 legislation and the new policies contained within the 1996 Housing Act demonstrate how universalist notions have been consistently undermined. Policies towards the homeless are not simply measures taken to address housing need. Responses to homelessness reflect a far wider range of issues including family ideology, latent racism, resource constraints and practical problems associated with implementation. In the final part of this chapter, we review the construction of what the homelessness problem is and draw some conclusions about the relationship between competing definitions of homelessness and dominant ideologies. Before that, however, the next section considers the research agenda for homelessness policy.

## The research agenda

The proliferation of research on homelessness, now being commissioned by government departments and housing agencies, provides a final example of the struggle to define homelessness. At one level, this proliferation could be interpreted as a concern with policy implementation, in so far as research is required to ensure that the resources, when committed, are effective in minimizing what is recognized as a perceived problem. Yet there are other reasons which explain the willingness to fund and commission research. It certainly has not escaped the attention of observers that research has often been deployed as a smoke-screen to hide policy failure and one which, in the long run, proves far more effective both in resource terms and in fending off criticism. However 'independent' social researchers, employed to undertake work on homelessness, may be, it is an inescapable fact that the control and dissemination of the findings rest with the funding institutions. The research that has emanated from the government has been largely practice-based, the assumption being that administrative remedies can alleviate the symptoms of homelessness. What has been missing, in much of the commissioned research, is an exploration of the political and ideological context in which homelessness is addressed. This has meant that homelessness, in terms of the research now undertaken, excludes both a discussion of the way the concept has been subject to competing ideologies as well as any analysis of the underlying economic causation of homelessness, in particular the contraction in public sector housing provision.

Much of the research on homelessness is contracted out to university research centres. The advantage of this practice to the government is that the research is deemed to be politically neutral and objective. At the same time, the employment vulnerability of contract research staff has made it easy for government ministries such as the Department of the Environment to exercise strict control over what may and may not be published even to the extent of undermining academic autonomy. Academics are themselves under pressure to secure such research contracts, particularly now that the Higher Education Funding Council subsidy is based on research output measures.

It is therefore worth noting that, although there are notable exceptions (see below), the majority of the government-funded research on homelessness excludes any analysis which links homelessness to wider economic policies. Instead, the research is administratively focused, suggesting that local authority bureaucracy and inter-agency working could remedy the plight of the homeless who are so narrowly defined. A clear example of this was the Department of the Environment report (Evans and Duncan, 1988), which, although rigorous, omitted the discussion of the context of homeless policy. Effectively, housing researchers, working on contracts, have adopted the narrow definition of homelessness which its policy-making funders wish to promote. There has, generally, been little attempt to widen the discussion in order to examine broader definitions of homelessness, such as could have been achieved by exploring the distinctions between 'homelessness' and 'housing need'.

There are other private agencies also engaged in housing research which promote an implicit ideological perspective. For example, the Joseph Rowntree Foundation has supported numerous enquiries on homelessness (Greve, 1991; Stockley and Bishopp, 1993; Bevan and Rhodes, 1996). The Foundation shares the government's research agenda in its promotion of practical research and its reluctance to commission theoretical or conceptual discussions of homelessness. There are, of course, academics within the university sector who have discussed homelessness at a conceptual level (see Watson and Austerberry, 1986; Gurney, 1990; Somerville, 1992 and 1994) and this research has been undertaken independently rather than being subject to the restraints inevitably imposed by external funding agencies or the restrictive clauses of much central government-funded research.

Finally, the other main research undertaken on homelessness has been instigated by homeless pressure groups such as Shelter and SHAC who have sought to publicize the gaps in provision. However, as charities, the research undertaken has to be politically neutral and this has affected the type of studies published. The conclusions of such studies usually demand more resources from government in terms of affordable housing or highlight those local authorities who have sought to redefine their responsibilities towards the homeless. Often, the charities engaged in homelessness research rely on a pathological conceptualization of homelessness, as this is the most effective way of attracting donations and effecting a construction of the homelessness problem which seeks to apportion blame on both bureaucracies and policy-makers, thereby removing it from a wider context

(Conway, 1988; Moroney, 1992). Moreover, charities are effectively engaged in competition to attract funds both from the government and individuals. The conception of homeless people as victims deserving our support is an essential construct to safeguard donations. Charities too have a vested interest in promoting views of what it is to be homeless which are often individualized and in line with their own specific aims, and so are relevant to their own particular target groups and definitions of homelessness (MIND, 1987; Age Concern, 1995). The approach often reinforces stereotypical representations and ignores self-definitions that question this construction of what it means to be homeless (see Hutson and Liddiard, 1994).

There are, however, signs that more critical theoretical concerns are appearing in academic publications (Loveland, 1993; Kennett, 1994; Samson, 1994; Hoggart, 1995; Williams, 1995; Burrows *et al.*, 1997). This is, in part, fuelled by the increasing recognition that 'grant capture' must be followed up by independent academic publication, as measured in the research assessment exercises, as much as a growing awareness of the paucity of theoretical and conceptual analysis. In spite of this, it is probably the case that the treadmill of grant applications, which are needed simply to keep insecure research staff in continuous employment, will restrict the output of critical research in this area. It remains to be seen whether or not the re-emergence of this critical research agenda will pave the way for yet one more swing of the pendulum in terms of the definition of homelessness.

## Conclusions

The cursory examination undertaken in this chapter shows how the history of recent housing policy in this area has been primarily a struggle between competing interpretations of homelessness. We can surmise that there are several different interest groups engaged in the struggle to set an agenda for homelessness policy. The most powerful and influential has been central government, which has now established a strict quantifiable definition of homelessness to reinforce its ideological objectives. As we have sought to show, it has taken steps to reduce the responsibility of the state in the resource solutions to homelessness – hence the redefinition of local authority duties within the Housing Act and the downgrading of homelessness to just one of many needs – yet, at the same time, conveying to the wider public that it is willing to tackle the effects of homelessness.

The brief discussion of differing agendas on homelessness illustrates how competing definitions vie with each other within the context of policy discourses. It needs stating that, within each of these agencies, there are conflicts and tensions about the form of research and the policy agenda, and it would be a mistake to suggest that any definition of homelessness remains static. Instead, conceptions of homelessness change over time and are subject to ideological influences, availability of resources and expectations bestowed on government and policy makers. Finally, it is important that future research in this area should be vigilant over the need to identify the complex patterns to the processes involved in the social construction of homelessness. We have attempted to show the value of drawing out the significance of competing accounts – in particular, 'structuralist' and 'minimalist' definitions of homelessness. By taking this approach, we hope to have demonstrated how a constructivist approach can sharpen existing explanations of policy change. At a time when the homelessness debate has again become narrowly focused, the need for critical reflection remains paramount.

## References

Abel-Smith, B. and Townsend, P. (1965) *The Poor and the Poorest*, London: Longman Green.

Age Concern (1995) *We Will Need to Take You in: The Experience of Homelessness in Old Age*, Edinburgh: Scottish Council for Single Homeless/Age Concern.

Anderson, I., Kemp, P. and Quilgars, D. (1993) *Single Homeless People*, London: HMSO.

Arden, A. and Hunter, C. (1992) *Manual of Housing Law*, 5th edn, London: Sweet and Maxwell.

Berry, F. (1974) *Housing: The Great British Failure*, London: Charles Knight.

Best, J. (ed.) (1989) *Images of Issues: Typifying Contemporary Social Problems*, New York: Aldine.

Bevan, M. and Rhodes, D. (1996) *Housing Homeless People in the Private Rented Sector*, York: Joseph Rowntree Foundation.

Blumer, H. (1969) *Symbolic Interactionism: Perspective and Method*, Englewood Cliffs (New Jersey): Prentice Hall.

Bramley, G. (1988) 'The definition and measurement of homelessness', in G. Bramley *et al.* (eds) *Homelessness and the London Housing Market*, Occasional Paper No. 32, School for Advanced Urban Studies, Bristol: University of Bristol.

Bramley, G. (1993) 'Explaining the incidence of statutory homelessness in England', *Housing Studies*, vol. 8, no. 2, pp. 126–47.

Broom, L. and Smith, J. H. (1963) 'Bridging occupations', *British Journal of Sociology*, vol. 14, no. 4, pp. 321–34.

Burrows, R., Pleace, N. and Quilgars, D. (eds) (1997) *Homelessness and Social Policy*, London: Routledge.

Clapham, D. and Franklin, B. (1997) 'The social construction of housing management', *Housing Studies*, vol. 12, no. 1, pp. 7–26.

Clarke, A. (1990) 'Prejudice, ignorance and panic! Popular politics in a land fit for scroungers', in M. Loney, D. Boswell and J. Clarke (eds) *Social Policy and Social Welfare*, Buckingham: Open University Press.

Cohen, S. (1972) *Folk Devils and Moral Panics*, London: Paladin.

Commission for Racial Equality (CRE) (1988) *Homelessness and Discrimination*, London: CRE.

Conway, J. (1988) *A Prescription for Ill Health: The Crisis for Homeless Families*, London: Shelter.

Crenson, M. (1971) *The Unpolitics of Air Pollution: A Study of Non-decision Making in the Cities*, Baltimore: Johns Hopkins University Press.

Crosland, C. A. R. (1956) *The Future of Socialism*, London: Jonathan Cape.

Dale, J. R. (1962) *The Clerk in Industry*, Liverpool: Liverpool University Press.

De Neufville, J. and Barton, S. (1987) 'Myths and the definition of policy problems', *Policy Sciences*, vol. 20, pp. 181–201.

Department of the Environment (1994) *Homelessness Code of Guidance for Local Authorities*, 3rd edn, London: HMSO.

Department of the Environment (1995) *Our Future Homes: Opportunity, Choice, Responsibility*, London: HMSO.

Evans, A. and Duncan, S. (1988) *Responding to Homelessness: Local Authority Policy and Practice*, London: HMSO.

Fishman, M. (1978) 'Crime waves as ideology', *Social Problems*, vol. 25, pp. 531–43.

Glastonbury, B. (1971) *Homeless Near a Thousand Homes*, London: George Allen and Unwin.

Goldthorpe, J., Lockwood, D., Bechhofer, F. and Platt, J. (1969) *The Affluent Worker in the Class Structure*, Cambridge: Cambridge University Press.

Greve, J. (1964) *London's Homeless*, London: Bell.

Greve, J. (1991) *Homelessness in Britain*, York: Joseph Rowntree Foundation.

Greve, J.; Page, D. and Greve, S. (1971) *Homelessness in London*, Edinburgh: Scottish Academic Press.

Gurney, C. (1990) *The Meaning of the Home in the Decade of Owner Occupation: Towards an Experiential Perspective*, Bristol: SAUS Working Paper 88.

Gusfield, J. (1963) *Symbolic Crusade: Status Politics and the American Temperance Movement*, Urbana: University of Illinois Press.

Hastings, A. (1998) 'Connecting linguistic structures and social practices: A discursive approach to social policy analysis', *Journal of Social Policy*, vol. 27, no. 2, pp. 191–211.

Hoggart, K. (1995) 'Political parties and the implementation of homeless legislation by non metropolitan districts in England and Wales 1985-1990', *Political Geography*, vol. 14, no. 1, pp. 59–79.

Hutson, S. and Liddiard, M. (1994) *Youth Homelessness: The Construction of a Social Issue*, London: Macmillan.

Jackson, M. and Marsden, D. (1962) *Education and the Working Class*, London: Routledge.

Kemeny, J. (1984) 'The social construction of housing facts', *Scandinavian Housing and Planning Research*, vol. 1, pp. 149–64.

Kemeny, J. (1988) 'Defining housing reality', *Housing Studies*, vol. 3, no. 4, pp. 205–18.

Kemp, P. (1992) 'The ghost of Rachman', in C. Grant (ed.) *Built to Last: Reflections on British Housing Policy*, London: Shelter.

Kennet, P. (1994) 'Models of regulation and the urban poor', *Urban Studies*, vol. 31, no. 7, pp. 1017–31.

Kitsuse, J. and Spector, M. (1973) 'Toward a sociology of social problems: Social conditions, value judgements and social problems', *Social Problems*, vol. 20, no. 4, pp. 407–19.

London Research Centre (1995) *Housing Homeless Households in the Private Rented Sector: A Permanent Solution?*, London: London Research Centre.

Loveland, I. (1993) 'An unappealing analysis of the public/private divide? The case of the homelessness legislation', *Liverpool Law Review*, vol. XV, no. 1, pp. 39–60.

Loveland, I. (1995) *Housing Homeless Persons: Administrative Law and Process*, Oxford: Clarendon Press.

Lund, B. (1996) *Housing Problems and Housing Policy*, London: Longman.

Mason, P. (1994) 'The figures that flatter to deceive', *Inside Housing*, 30 September.

Mauss, A. (1975) *Social Problems as Social Movements*, Philadelphia: Lippincott.

MIND (1987) *Homelessness and the Plight of Mentally Ill People*, London: MIND.

Moroney, L. (1992) *Homelessness: A Good Practice Guide*, London: Shelter.

Niner, P. (1989) *Homelessness in Nine Local Authorities: Case Studies of Policy and Practice*, London: HMSO.

Orcutt, J. and Turner, J. (1993) 'Shocking numbers and graphic accounts: Quantified images of drug problems in the print media', *Social Problems*, vol. 40, pp. 190–212.

Pleace, N. (1995) *Housing Vulnerable Single Homeless People*, York: Centre for Housing Policy.

Raynsford, N. (1986) 'The 1977 Housing (Homeless Persons) Act', in N. Deakin (ed.) *Policy Change in Government*, London: Royal Institute of Public Administration.

Ridley, N. (1992) *My Style of Government*, London: Fontana.

Sahlin, I. (1996) *On the Border of Housing: Rejection, Repulsion, Special Contracts*, Lund: Arkiv: Lund Studies in Social Welfare XIV.

Samson, C. (1994) 'The three faces of privatisation', *Policy*, vol. 28, no. 1, pp. 79–97.

Sarbin, T. and Kitsuse, J. (1994) *Constructing the Social*, London: Sage.

Somerville, P. (1992) 'Homelessness and the meaning of the home: Rooflessness or rootlessness?, *International Journal of Urban and Regional Research*, vol. 16, no. 4, pp. 529–39.

Somerville, P. (1994) 'Homelessness policy in Britain', *Policy and Politics*, vol. 22, no. 3, pp. 163–78.

Spector, M. and Kitsuse, J. (1973) 'Social Problems: A reformulation', *Social Problems*, vol. 21, no. 2, pp. 145–59.

Stockley, D. and Bishopp, D. (1993) *Young People at Risk of Homelessness*, York: Joseph Rowntree Foundation.

Thatcher, M. (1994) *The Downing Street Years*, London: HarperCollins.

Thomas, A. and Niner, P. (1989) *Living in Temporary Accommodation: A Survey of Homeless People*, London: HMSO.

Thompson, L. (1988) *An Act of Compromise*, London: SHAC/Shelter.

Timmins, N. (1995) *The Five Giants: A Biography of the Welfare State*, London: Harper Collins.

Useem, B. and Zald, B. (1982) 'From pressure group to social movement: Organisational dilemmas of the effort to promote nuclear power', *Social Problems*, vol. 30, no. 2, pp. 144–56.

Watson, S. and Austerberry, H. (1986) *Housing and Homelessness: A Feminist Perspective*, London: Routledge.

Williams, P. (1995) 'The United Kingdom housing context', *Housing Policy Debate*, vol. 6, no. 3, pp. 759–83.

Wilson, D. (1970) *I Know It Was the Place's Fault*, London: Oliphants.

# 2 The making and unmaking of homelessness legislation
## Peter Somerville

## Introduction

In an earlier paper (Somerville, 1994), I provided a historical reconstruction of the 1977 Housing (Homeless Persons) Act, attempting to explain, in a new way, how the Act came into being and how it survived intact until the mid-1990s. Long-term changes in Britain's social structure were identified at one level and it was shown how, to some extent, the political developments responded to these long-term changes. Relying on the detailed information concerning the processes leading up to the passage of the Act, the paper identified the system of institutions and agents which were responsible for homelessness policy in Britain and argued that the relative stability of this system was largely responsible for the enduring nature of the Act's provisions. This chapter reproduces and updates the arguments of that earlier paper and takes the view that the system of agencies remains fundamentally the same as twenty years ago. The radical changes introduced by the Housing Act 1996, therefore, have been caused primarily not by changes in the system of agencies itself, but by wider social structural changes which can be summarized as: centralization, depoliticization, and deregulation/marketization.

## Historical background

Welfare policy in Britain originated in the later Middle Ages as a result of the social disintegration caused by the Black Death. The duty to accommodate those who could not support themselves fell on the local parishes in which these people lived. Such parochial duties were consolidated in the

Poor Law Act 1601, which made it clear that the duty arose only in relation to those who had 'settlement' in the parish, by virtue of birth or apprenticeship or other condition acceptable to the parish as evidence of settlement (Hoath, 1983). Later, following the Industrial Revolution, the Poor Law Amendment Act 1834 transferred the responsibility for poor relief from individual parishes to elected Boards of Guardians representing groups of parishes, and introduced the principle of 'less eligibility', according to which relief was not to be such as to put a recipient in a better position than someone who was not homeless or destitute. The powers of the Boards of Guardians then passed to local authorities under the Local Government Act 1929 (Hoath, 1983, pp. 1–2).

The National Assistance Act 1948 formally repealed the Poor Laws, but the spirit of those laws continued, and persists even today (Somerville, 1994). Throughout the 1950s and 1960s, many local authorities continued to use sex-segregated Poor Law hostels for homeless families, and those without 'settlement' continued to be treated as vagrants by being transported out of the area (Raynsford, 1986, pp. 35–6). The Poor Law tradition was therefore maintained by local authorities in spite of national legislation against it. As a result, for most homeless people, the coming of the welfare state made no difference to their treatment – those who were 'settled' in the area were seen as 'deserving', while those who were deemed 'less eligible' or 'undeserving' were often rejected or removed from the area.

Many writers have commented on the entrenched attitudes of local housing authorities up to the mid-1960s (Greve *et al.*, 1971; Raynsford, 1986, pp. 39–40; Widdowson, 1988, p. 14). The typical stance of these authorities towards homeless people was negative, unhelpful, ignoring, uncaring, moralistic, stereotyping and rejecting. The authorities saw themselves as catering for the needs of the mainstream in society and this tended to mean long-term residents of the area with clearly stable household structures who were prepared to 'wait their turn' on the authorities' lists. In contrast, a significant proportion of homeless people (although not a majority) were relative newcomers to the local authority area with possibly unstable household arrangements and all of these demanded to be rehoused immediately. In the years of extreme housing shortage following the Second World War, therefore, it was probably inevitable that the needs of homeless people would be marginalized.

This historical and bleak picture for the homeless began to change only following the Rent Act in 1957. This Act provided for the de-control of private sector rents and thus led to a sharp increase in homelessness due to evictions by landlords. Many of the families so evicted were identifiably part of the mainstream population which local authorities regarded as 'deserving' of assistance and, as a result of this, public sympathy for the plight of the homeless began to grow. Even so, homelessness did not become a national political issue in its own right until the slum clearance programmes of the

1960s were contributing to the rise in homelessness by displacing people whom the local authorities subsequently failed to rehouse. All this helps to explain why the media, in the shape of *Cathy Come Home* (1966), were able to make the impact upon public opinion which they did (Raynsford, 1986, p. 44; see also Chapter 4). The television play came at a time when the most severe housing shortages (for most people) had largely been overcome, or appeared to be on the verge of being overcome, even though the numbers of homeless were at an all-time high. Significantly, the main causes of homelessness – eviction by private landlords and displacement by slum clearance programmes – were most clearly not the responsibility of homeless people themselves.

Media attention and public sympathy are not, by themselves, sufficient to produce policy change. The 1977 Housing (Homeless Persons) Act in particular represented a clearer, more decisive break from the Poor Law tradition than the 1948 National Assistance Act. For the first time, certain groups said to be in 'priority need' were given a right to permanent housing rather than only an entitlement to welfare assistance. Key processes of change in British society, as well as more enduring ideological and institutional factors, were responsible for the passing of this Act. These processes have been described in detail in Somerville (1994).

Essentially, it was argued that certain categories of people – such as children, elderly people, pregnant women, and women at risk of violence – were more 'vulnerable' within the housing system and therefore more deserving of state assistance, which had not been adequate under the 1948 Act provisions. If local housing authorities were not willing to assume responsibility for housing such people on a permanent basis, then legislation might be necessary to compel them to do so. With the growing prosperity of the post-war years, attitudes had begun to shift away from Poor Law traditions towards forms of familism and welfarism (see Chapter 6). The essentially punitive nature of the earlier Poor Law regime had involved the break-up of nuclear families and the exacerbation of those families' housing problems. This was incompatible with the new emphasis, in social policy, of keeping families together as well as with the claims of the state to be achieving improvements in the welfare of the families concerned.

The institutional factors leading to the 1977 Housing (Homeless Persons) Act related mainly to the agents which were responsible for legislative change. Most accounts of how the Act came into being attach key importance to the role of the Joint Charities' Group in campaigning for legislative reform from 1974 to 1976. Somerville (1994), however, has cast considerable doubt on this interpretation of the historical events, arguing that it was the Department of the Environment, ministers and senior civil servants who played the crucial role, with both public opinion (as expressed through the media) and backbench Members of Parliament being important but secondary influences. Compared to these, the effect of the Joint Charities'

Group on the legislative process was a minor one. The civil servants appeared most responsive to the longer-term changes, with ministers being both receptive to the advice of their servants and, to some degree, sensitive to electoral opinion. Backbench MPs were able to exercise a decisive influence in the parliamentary proceedings of the Bill, although generally their role was limited to that of communicating electoral opinion to ministers. Pressure groups outside government, including the local authority associations as well as the Joint Charities' Group, had relatively little real power or influence which they could bring to bear on government. They could not seriously claim to represent electoral opinion, so their only hope of influence on policy was through informal contacts with Department of Environment ministers and officials, through eliciting sympathy from backbench MPs and through high-profile campaigning in the media. To the extent that such campaigning helped to shape electoral opinion, it is possible, albeit unverifiable, that the Joint Charities' Group did have an important, though indirect, influence. The system of agents as a whole is illustrated in Figure 2.1.

As can be seen from Figure 2.1, there are three distinct levels in the policy process. The first may be called 'agenda setting', in which wider social forces and structural changes influence the agents and institutions which are more directly responsible for decision-making. At this level, the exact causal chains are difficult to determine, but the structural factors certainly include the changing nature of housing markets and long-term trends in the role of the welfare state. These major changes then exert what may be called a 'pattern of influence' at the second level, which is the level at which the key agencies dealing with homelessness operate. From Figure 2.1 it can be clearly seen that the Department of the Environment is at the centre of this 'system of agencies', although local authorities also play a major role. The effects of this system can then be viewed at the third level, namely that of 'policy outcome', which in this case means legislative change. The strong influences worth noting are those which occur at this level, namely the driving force of the Department of the Environment in bringing about the new homelessness law as well as the negative but crucial impact of the local authorities in failing to co-operate with the Department of the Environment which made the move towards legislation necessary.

The 1977 Housing (Homeless Persons) Act was therefore a major achievement. It did not, however, put an end to Poor Law thinking and attitudes. In particular, the amendments which the opposition successfully made to the Act, with respect to intentionality and local connection, echoed the pre-1948 distinction between the 'deserving' and the 'undeserving' poor and were in line with the belief that 'charity begins at home'. Those in priority need, who were deemed to be intentionally homeless, had a right only to temporary accommodation, and a local authority which found that a homeless person in priority need did not have a connection with their

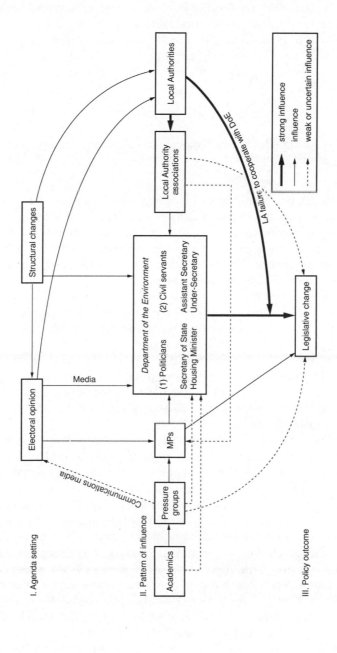

I. Agenda setting

II. Pattern of influence

III. Policy outcome

Structural changes

Local Authorities

Local Authority associations

Department of the Environment

(1) Politicians
Secretary of State
Housing Minister

(2) Civil servants
Assistant Secretary
Under-Secretary

Electoral opinion

Media

MPs

Communications media

Pressure groups

Academics

Legislative change

LA failure to cooperate with DoE

strong influence

influence

weak or uncertain influence

Figure 2.1 The system of agencies involved with homelessness policy in Britain

area, in terms of residence or employment and so on, had a right to refer that person to an authority with which they did have a local connection. This distinction, between priority and non-priority groups, was itself based on an assumption that only the former were deserving of statutory assistance. These underlying themes – of moralism, parochialism and paternalism – cannot be easily reconciled with the Department of the Environment's themes of uniform standards of housing provision, universalism and nationalism, illustrated by nationally defined minimum enforceable rights for all homeless in priority need.

## The 1977 Housing (Homeless Persons) Act in retrospect: a precarious achievement

This Act was made possible by major changes both in society and in public administration. It came to pass mainly as a result of initiatives taken at the higher levels of the Department of the Environment. However, the Act was much more than simply a response to these structural changes. The success of mass housing provision, the role of council housing as a safety net and the growing problem of homelessness generally could all have resulted equally well in a requirement for local housing authorities to secure accommodation for the homeless on a *temporary* basis only. Such a requirement could have met the immediate housing needs of homeless people. It would have been consistent with local authority housing's residual role and this could have been, arguably, an adequate response to the homelessness crisis precipitated by the decline in private renting. In the light of more recent developments, the crucial question perhaps is: what were the factors which prompted the Department of the Environment to opt for a duty to secure *permanent* housing for the homeless?

The first factor was the local authorities' resistance to the Department of the Environment's original proposals from 1974 onwards. The extent and depth of this resistance led the Department of the Environment to conclude that a duty to provide only temporary accommodation would be open to widespread abuse by local authorities and, as a result, homeless people would continue to receive unfair treatment at their hands. There was also a fear that, unless homeless people were given a right to permanent accommodation, they might not receive any such offers at all in some areas.

Second, until the 1970s, there was a perception in government circles – especially Labour governments, but Conservative ones as well – that council housing was 'for life', in line with Aneurin Bevan's phrase: 'from the cradle to the grave'. It therefore seemed reasonable and fair that homeless people should have an entitlement to housing on the same basis as that on which it was offered to everyone else. A duty to secure temporary accommodation only could tend to reinforce long-term discrimination against the homeless.

Third, the private rented sector had traditionally been notorious for its poor physical conditions and bad management. The decline of this tenure was therefore not a matter of great social or political concern – at least until the 1980s. Consequently, in the 1970s there did not appear to be any good reason not to offer homeless people social rented housing on a permanent basis. There was no question, at this time, of a stay in temporary accommodation being followed by a return to a private sector tenancy.

These three factors had one important characteristic in common – namely that they were relatively transient. First local authority resistance, with only a few exceptions, soon crumbled away and, by the later 1980s, local housing authorities were among the strongest supporters of the legislation. Even the Association of District Councils, which had shown the strongest opposition to the Act originally, eventually only wanted an option to offer non-secure tenancies which would become secure after twelve months (Association of District Councils, 1988). Second, the perception of council housing as a life-long tenure soon gave way under the onslaught of the Conservative government's right to buy measures and the increasing dominance of owner ocupation generally. Finally, from the late 1980s onwards, increasing interest in stimulating new forms of private renting led some local housing authorities to try to discharge their responsibilities towards the homeless by securing accommodation for them in the private rented sector (Campbell, 1993).

In this way, the factors behind the duty, new in 1977, to secure permanent housing for homeless people to some extent ceased to exist later on. Consequently, the position of the 1977 Housing (Homeless Persons) Act became increasingly precarious in spite of its initial stability which had rested on ideological consensus and all-party support.

## Homelessness policy 1977–94

A number of changes occurred after 1977 which cumulatively made it likely that the homelessness legislation would be reformed. These changes can be broadly summarized as processes of centralization, depoliticization and deregulation/marketization.

### Centralization

'Centralization' here refers to the growing breadth and depth of government control over local authority housing, which had begun long before the passing of the 1977 Housing (Homeless Persons) Act. The Act itself represented a centralization of one aspect of local authority allocation policy, as it required all housing authorities to follow the same rules in dealing with homelessness cases. After that, a number of further centralizing developments occurred, such as the institution of the Housing Investment Programme system in 1977, the conferring of Tenants' Charter rights in 1980, the launch of the Priority Estates Project (later decentralized) in 1979, the setting up of Estate Action in 1987 and the ring-fencing of Housing Revenue Accounts in 1989, to name but a few. Meanwhile, with the shift in emphasis from local authorities to housing associations, the centralizing power of the Housing Corporation, which is responsible, among other things, for funding and monitoring housing associations, grew apace. Taken together, all these developments made an extension of central government regulation of local authority allocation practice more likely.

*Depoliticization*

Over the years, a number of processes occurred which had the effect of reducing the salience of homelessness as a political issue. These processes can be summarized as bureaucratization, professionalization, and technical specialization. In addition, since 1988 in particular, a series of political attempts was made to narrow the official definition of homelessness and to represent specific homelessness crises as essentially temporary aberrations rather than recognize them as symptoms of more fundamental problems. Taken together, these changes made it easier for the government to achieve policy reforms, because they did not need to be so concerned about political opposition to their proposals and they made it likely that the trend of reform would be in the direction of the shrinking and the fragmentation of the sphere of homelessness policy.

First of all, the 1977 Housing (Homeless Persons) Act itself, by transferring homelessness duties from social services to housing, to some extent transformed the problem of homelessness from one of social welfare to a more technical one of housing administration (Somerville, 1990). In this way, the Act caused the problem of homelessness to be defined more narrowly and in more professionalized terms. Homelessness became a specialist area of work carried out by specially trained (housing) officers. A new specialism of homelessness law was created and the volume of court cases which followed was immense. Homelessness, in the narrow sense of rooflessness, was professionally set apart from its wider context of poverty and poor housing. As such, homelessness gradually became integrated as a need factor, or set of need factors, within mainstream local authority housing allocation policy and practice (Mullins, 1991). The political issue of solving the homelessness problem was replaced by a bureaucratic issue of how to secure a fair deal for those defined as in 'priority need' within the existing (unfair) system. Forms of homelessness which were not a priority under the Act, and homelessness in a wider sense than that recognized by the Act, tended to be ignored by most local authorities (see Chapter 8). As a result, such homelessness became a political issue only when it was highly visible and substantial, as in the case of street homelessness in London in the later 1980s (see below).

Partly as a result of these processes, the 'housing problem' generally slipped down the political agenda. It was, and continues to be, not so much a matter of housing policy being increasingly subordinated to economic policy or of housing being seen as somehow less important in relation to health, education, and so on, but a question of a narrowing of the scope of housing policy as such. When a large proportion of the population of Britain lived in slums and in overcrowded conditions, housing policies of slum clearance and substantial new building dominated the political scene. Such policies addressed the issue of homelessness in a wider sense, as meaning lack of secure, self-contained and minimally adequate accommodation, and some degree of success was achieved as has been noted above. This very success, however, led to less public concern, with the result that the continuing, pressing needs of a minority of households were increasingly ignored unless they actually became roofless – and even then, if they were not in priority need, they might be left to fend for themselves. The general problem of housing the bulk of the population tended to be reduced to a special problem of housing the homeless and other minority groups deemed to have 'special needs'. The identification of homelessness as a housing problem, which helped to make the 1977 Act possible in the first place, tended to obscure the reality of homelessness as a social problem.

More deliberate attempts to depoliticize homelessness occurred in response to the escalation in the numbers of both priority and non-priority homeless people in the 1980s. Most famously, in 1988, the Secretary of State for the Environment, Nicholas Ridley, implied that those with 'roofs over their heads' who were counted as homeless did not deserve to be helped (Shaps, 1988). In the years which followed, an assortment of housing ministers claimed that those found to be homeless by local authorities were not 'genuinely' or 'literally' homeless (for example, Sir George Young in *The Walden interview*, ITV, 17 January 1993). This view led directly to the anti-homeless assumptions and generalizations made in the 1994 consultation paper (see below).

Depoliticization also occurred in response to two specific crises of homelessness at the end of the 1980s – namely those of street homelessness and mortgage repossessions. In the first case, a huge rise in single homelessness created a highly visible problem in London and other major cities. Since the problem was substantial, in the public arena, and not a statutory responsibility of local authorities, the Department of the Environment felt under pressure to respond directly, and this led to the Rough Sleepers Initiative and other measures (Randall and Brown, 1993; Anderson, 1993). The general thrust of such initiatives, however, was to provide temporary solutions to what was seen by the government as an abnormal situation. The emphasis was, therefore, on securing short-term emergency accommodation such as hostels, and the long-term needs of single homeless people were not adequately addressed (Anderson *et al.*, 1993). Indeed, such needs were regarded as less legitimate than those of other types of household (Anderson and Morgan, 1996). However, the experience of such initiatives may have given the Department of the Environment new ideas about how to tackle the problem of homelessness more generally – through specific forms of short-term housing provision and support. The scene was therefore set for new forms of policy centralization and for the general tone and tenor of future policy reforms.

Repossession due to mortgage arrears had traditionally accounted for a very low proportion of homelessness cases, two per cent or less, but this escalated to a peak of 12 per cent in 1991 (see also Chapter 5). This increase was entirely due to the fall-out from the 'Lawson boom', but it represented a new factor in the housing market and one of particular concern to the government because of the priority which they had given to the expansion of owner-occupation. This unprecedented rise in homelessness for owner-occupiers called into question the practicability and desirability of the Conservative aim to achieve a 'nation of home owners' (Saunders, 1990). The politically sensitive nature of this development therefore prompted a policy response from the government in the shape of the housing market package in 1992 (Somerville, 1994). Again, as with the response to street homelessness, this was regarded by the Department of the Environment as a one-off measure to deal with a short-term emergency problem. The possibility that there existed long-term structural flaws in the owner-occupied housing market was simply not on the political agenda.

To sum up: from 1988 onwards, new homelessness policies of the Department of the Environment can be explained as specific and corresponding reactions to specific homelessness crises. The most important of these crises were the accelerating numbers of statutory homeless, the sharp rise in street homelessness and the unprecedented increase in mortgage repossessions. Each of these changes had the effect of pushing homelessness up the political agenda and in such a way as to provoke a response from government, though for different reasons in each case. Statutory homelessness could not be ignored politically because it was publicly recognized by the law of the land and was used by local authorities to argue for increased resources from central government. Street homelessness could not be ignored because of its highly visible character (see Chapter 4). And mortgage repossessions could not be ignored because they reflected badly on the government's political ideal of a property-owning democracy (see Chapter 5). In each case, however, the Department of the Environment's aim was primarily to depoliticize the situation, that is to seek measures which would have the effect of turning down the political heat and eventually removing the issue from the political arena altogether. Accordingly, their general approach was to dismiss the long-term structural causes of the problem and to concentrate on the symptoms in the short-term. In so far as they accepted that there was a real problem, their approach was to assume that it was inflated by the 1977 Act itself (the legal interpretation of homelessness being allegedly too generous) or that it arose from rigidities and inefficiencies in the public rented sector (as with the priority homeless) or that it was the fault of the homeless people themselves (as with mortgage arrears cases).

The Department of the Environment's responses to the new homelessness problems were plainly inadequate (see Somerville, 1994), but this inadequacy is easily explained. They simply wanted to exclude these problems from the political agenda as quickly as possible. Initiatives and packages therefore had to look good, but they could not be expected to strike at the root of these problems and they could not be allowed to endure over too long a period. It was, of course, primarily private sector failures – the unaffordability of private renting and the slump in the owner-occupied housing market – which led to the homelessness problems to which the Department of the Environment responded, but it was always extremely unlikely that the Department would be able to stomach this ideologically unpalatable fact. Where it could not entirely brush the problem aside with short-term palliatives, as was the case with statutory homelessness, it sought to play down the seriousness of the problem itself. Hence the attempts by Department of the Environment ministers since 1988 to redefine homelessness in as narrow terms as possible.

*Deregulation/marketization*

In the context of housing, deregulation has involved processes which run down local authority housing and liberalize private markets in owner-occupation and renting. Although the trend had existed for many years before, from 1989 onwards in particular, there were changes which involved reductions in tenants' rights, a greater reliance on less secure forms of accommodation as well as an increased emphasis on 'free markets' as the solution to housing problems. In future it was expected that the main providers of housing for low-income households would be 'independent' landlords such as housing associations rather than local authorities, as had been the case in the past.

Tory ideological unease with the statist approach embodied in the 1977 Housing (Homeless Persons) Act tended to grow after 1987. After the 1992 general election, in particular, this unease was reflected in prejudiced attacks on single parents and other alleged abusers of the legislative provisions, and these attacks grew in frequency and severity (Blake, 1993; Stearn, 1993; Wintour, 1993; Burns, 1994a). At local as well as national levels, the ideologies were concerned to 'blame the victim', seeking private sector solutions to housing problems and reduce the scope of the 'nanny state' in taking responsibility for meeting the needs of its subjects.

In the meantime, the running down of local authority housing made it less capable of coping with the numbers accepted as statutorily homeless. The search for alternative solutions in the private sector, therefore, became increasingly urgent for a wide range of local housing authorities (Campbell, 1993). Marketization became more and more a practical necessity as well as an ideological prescription. The nature of the safety net that local authorities could provide for the homeless gradually became more narrowly defined – for example the practice of securing an offer of private rented accommodation was pursued by an increasing number of authorities (Levison and White, 1993) and the tenancies involved were increasingly on a shorthold basis (Campbell, 1993). These changes in the practice of local authorities were generally endorsed by the courts (see below).

In harmony with government thinking, the judicial review of homelessness cases also tended to adopt a narrow interpretation of homelessness and of what qualifies as suitable accommodation for a homeless person to occupy. In 1985, for example, the House of Lords decided that the Puhlhofer family, consisting of two adults and three children living in one room in a bed and breakfast hotel, were not 'homeless'. In a series of cases in the 1980s, the courts developed a concept of 'settled' accommodation which contained echoes of the Poor Law meaning. In another series of cases, the meaning of settled accommodation was narrowed from its original interpretation as permanent accommodation to the extent that assured shorthold tenancies (for six months at a time) qualified as 'settled'. Finally, in the Awua case in 1985, the House of Lords held that, in fulfilling their duties towards the homeless, local authorities only had to secure 'suitable' accommodation, which was not necessarily permanent accommodation. Overall, therefore, the rights of homeless people, as originally understood, had become eroded in the light of market realities.

The events after the passing of the 1977 Housing (Homeless Persons) Act, which are particularly relevant to explaining more recent developments, can therefore be summarized as follows. First, there were centralization processes, involving increasing government control over housing management activities. The clear implication from these processes was that, eventually, the Department of the Environment would not confine itself only to homelessness in its attempts to regulate local authority housing allocation. Second, there were processes which had the effect of constructing homelessness as a technical or administrative problem rather than a social or political one – a problem of a small and 'different' minority rather than a major national issue. Third, there were specific political responses to certain crises of homelessness, such as the expansion of both priority and non-priority homelessness and the dramatic increase in mortgage repossessions. Fourth, there was a variety of factors prompting a shift towards what can be described as more 'free market' methods of dealing with homelessness problems – such as the deregulation of rented tenures, a more strident ruling class rhetoric of anti-statism and individualism or familism as well as a greater use of private renting by local authorities to accommodate homeless people and an erosion of the meaning of 'permanent' accommodation by the courts. Finally, as in the causation of the 1977 Act, it was the presence of widespread resistance from local authorities to any significant change in national policy on homelessness, as was revealed by the review of homelessness legislation (Department of the Environment, 1989), which persuaded the Department that legislation would be necessary if it was to achieve its political aims.

## The 1994 proposals – the Green Paper

In 1994 the Department of the Environment published a consultation paper (Green Paper) entitled *Access to Local Authority and Housing Association Tenancies*, which proposed that a number of changes should be made to existing legislation on homelessness. Arguably, three of these proposals were particularly important, namely that (author's italics):

1. The local authority duty towards those who are unintentionally homeless and in priority need should no longer be to secure *permanent* accommodation, but only accommodation for a limited period.
2. The duty should apply only if the applicant is literally roofless, and not if there is *suitable accommodation available to them*.
3. Local authorities should secure permanent housing *only* for applicants on their waiting list (the organization of which would in future be determined by Department of the Environment regulations).

The previous section provides the beginnings of an explanation of how the Department of the Environment arrived at these proposals. The processes discussed in that section help to explain why, in certain respects, the 1977 Act had become out-of-date by the early 1990s, even though it had received the seal of approval as recently as 1989. The original reasons for imposing a duty to rehouse on a permanent rather than temporary basis no longer applied to the same extent. Because of the sea change in local authority attitudes, the Department of the Environment could be confident that, by 1989, a duty to provide only temporary accommodation would not now be abused by the vast bulk of local authorities. Second, by 1980 it had become clear that council housing could no longer realistically be regarded as 'housing for life' and so the assumption that rehousing had to be on a strictly permanent basis was being called into question by a minority of authorities. Finally, although it was too early to speak of a revival of private renting following the deregulation of rents in the 1988 Housing Act, the historical iniquities of private landlordism seemed to have faded in the memories, not only of Conservative politicians but also of some academic commentators (Merrett, 1991; Crook, 1992). As a result, the Department of the Environment came to expect that the private rented sector would cope with the demands of homeless households (Department of the Environment, 1994), although research has indicated that such an expectation continues to be unrealistic (Bevan and Rhodes, 1996).

The 1994 paper reflected the changes discussed in the last section in the detail of its contents. For example, political prejudices against the homeless were voiced through an argument that homeless people had an unfair advantage over others in housing need because they were the only ones who had a right to permanent accommodation. Similarly, the Department of the Environment's prejudice against local authorities was expressed through the assumption that the rise in homelessness generally was due to a combination of municipal incompetence together with the manipulation of the system by homeless people themselves. To take a different example, the Department's experience of the Rough Sleepers Initiative paved the way for its conviction, in the 1994 paper, that the main requirement for homeless people – and now not just specific groups but all homeless people – was for temporary accommodation to deal with an unforeseen crisis or emergency. Its wilful ignorance of the underlying problem of unaffordable private rents, to which its own policies had contributed – through rent deregulation and the progressive removal of the social security safety net for young single people (Thornton, 1990) – appeared in the 1994 paper in the shape of the unsubstantiated assumption that it would cost less overall if a homeless household rented from the private sector rather than from a local authority (Department of the Environment, 1994, para. 27.1). Meanwhile, the issue of homelessness due to mortgage arrears was not even mentioned in the 1994 paper. It had already been consigned to political oblivion.

As with the changes generally since 1977, the 1994 proposals can be understood in terms of the same processes of centralization, depoliticization, and deregulation/marketization.

*Centralization*

As mentioned in the previous section, the 1977 Housing (Homeless Persons) Act represented but one step in a long-term process of increasingly detailed regulation of local authorities by central government. It was therefore to be expected that, sooner or later, the Department of the

Environment would seek to regulate housing allocation practice more generally. The 1994 proposals were designed specifically for this purpose, since they included, not only proposals to remove special rights for the homeless but also rules for the organization of waiting lists and for the eligibility of registration on those lists. A separate proposal in the paper – to encourage common housing registers between local authorities and housing associations operating in the same area – is another example of such creeping centralization, because of the control already exercised by the Housing Corporation in relation to housing associations.

*Depoliticization*

As discussed in the previous section, the 1977 Housing (Homeless Persons) Act effectively transformed homelessness into a technical problem of housing management, in spite of an exceptionally high number of cases of judicial review. In the 1980s, however, a number of changes thrust homelessness once more into the forefront of political concern. These developments prompted the Department of the Environment to respond by adopting measures which were intended to reduce the political problems once more to technical ones. The 1994 proposals can be understood in part as a continuation of this approach and indeed as a logical extension of processes of depoliticization which had developed over a long period of time. In the consultation paper, homelessness was still seen as a narrow housing problem, even though it was now explicitly linked with wider problems of housing allocation policy and practice. In addition, the proposals aimed to reduce the homelessness service to a mere fire-fighting service, involving the management of crisis situations by means of the provision of emergency accommodation only. Such political attempts at depoliticization, however, ran the risk of actually highlighting the problems of homelessness which they wanted to play down (see below).

*Deregulation/marketization*

As discussed in the last section, the changes in housing tenures over the years essentially undermined the capacity of local authorities to cope with homelessness demand and called into question the appropriateness of an offer of permanent council housing as the solution to a homelessness problem. Both of these effects were reflected in the Department of the Environment's 1994 proposals, since the latter involved a significant alleviation of local authorities' duties towards the homeless and affirmed that an offer of temporary private accommodation would be more reasonable. The practicability of such proposals, however, depended upon the adequacy of available tenancies in the private sector.

## From consultation to legislation 1994–6

*Responses to the Green Paper*

The 1994 proposals represented yet another example of how the Department of the Environment regularly seizes the initiative in housing policy and takes public sector housing organizations and pressure groups entirely by surprise. This does not mean, however, that the Department of the Environment is necessarily successful in its policy aims. On this occasion, the consultation paper attracted the largest negative response ever received for a set of housing policy proposals – nearly 10,000 written responses were received, the overwhelming majority of which were opposed to them (Stearn, 1994b). Only one representative organization, the London Boroughs Association, was in favour of them (Mason, 1994). Most of the objections focused on the alleged scapegoating of the homeless (York, 1994; *Housing*, 1994; Burns, 1994a) and on the abolition of the 'safety net' for the homeless (Stearn, 1994a; York, 1994; Campbell, 1994; Burns, 1994a; McKechnie, 1994). More wide-ranging and penetrating criticisms were made by *Housing Review* (1994a, 1994b), by the Chartered Institute of Housing (McGilp, 1994a), and by Shelter (Bradburn, 1994). The gist of these criticisms was: 'the whole farrago of proposals is unjust, unnecessary and unworkable' (*Housing Review*, 1994a). The proposals were felt to be *unnecessary* because current legislation was working well, *unjust* because they discriminated unfairly against the homeless – who unlike ordinary waiting list applicants would not be able to secure permanent accommodation – and *unworkable* because they depended upon homeless households finding private or housing association accommodation at the end of their period of stay in temporary accommodation (*Housing Review*, 1994b).

The government's response to these criticisms was one of disappointment, based on a feeling that their proposals had been misunderstood. The crux of their argument hinged on the expectation that: 'local authorities will be able to use the private rented sector to discharge their duty to people accepted as needing assistance with the provision of accommodation' (Young, 1994, p. 9). The Green Paper had appeared to suggest that local authorities would be forbidden from rehousing homeless people in permanent accommodation, but the government pointed out that a homeless household who found accommodation in the private rented sector 'could go on the waiting list, where its needs and priority for long-term accommodation will be compared with the claims of others on the list' (Young, 1994, p. 9). Similarly, the Green Paper had made no stipulation as to the nature of the temporary accommodation which local authorities would be obliged to secure for the homeless, but the government made it clear that this should be 'settled accommodation in a good quality environment' (Young, 1994, p. 9) or 'secure accommodation that provides a settled home'

(Stearn, 1994b). More sensitive drafting by civil servants could have avoided these 'misunderstandings'. As it was, they were interpreted by the government's opponents as *concessions*. There is an irony here, because it may have been the low political priority attached to the drafting of homelessness policy which, in the end, led to its high political profile due to the results of poor drafting.

In the consultation process as a whole, the above 'concessions', or corrections of misunderstandings, made by the Department of the Environment, look relatively minor (Burns, 1994b). The key proposals in relation to homelessness remained unchanged – namely the replacement of the 1977 duty to provide permanent accommodation with an undertaking to secure accommodation for a limited period (now proposed to last for twelve months, although nearly all commentators wanted much longer periods or unlimited periods) as well as the narrowing of the definition of homelessness to exclude anyone with access to 'suitable accommodation'. The Department of the Environment's opponents remained concerned that local authorities would cease to provide their own permanent accommodation for homeless people, who would consequently be shunted into a series of poor-quality short-term lets (Morris, 1994a).

In their post-mortems on the consultation process, the Chartered Institute of Housing and Shelter took the view that substantial lobbying work had achieved concessions on two other points – namely that the duty to provide accommodation while investigations are being carried out would remain and that forms of temporary housing such as refuges, hostels and bed and breakfast hotels should not count as 'suitable accommodation' (McGilp, 1994b; Burns, 1994b). There is some doubt, however, whether either of these actually represents a concession at all. As Burns (1994b) points out, the former was 'surely never a genuine starter' and, on the latter, it is not clear that the Department of the Environment had made up its mind about this at the time of drafting the consultation paper. It therefore suited the Department to present itself as making 'concessions' in order to demonstrate its responsiveness to public opinion when, in reality, it had no intention of yielding on any matter of substance whatever. Admittedly, however, this is a bitter pill for the housing lobby to swallow.

Historical explanations involve accounting for why potential events do *not* happen as well as why they do happen. The relevant non-event here is the absence of a Housing Bill in the Queen's Speech of Autumn 1994. Four factors would appear to have contributed to this. One is that social housing policy generally had a low political priority for the government, so there was no sense of urgency or political pressure to introduce new legislation. Second, this period saw the departure of the Housing Minister, Sir George Young, to the Treasury, which meant the loss of a high-profile campaigner for housing reform. His replacement was a politician who had relatively little housing knowledge or experience and therefore needed time to familiarize himself with his new brief. Third, the government probably felt that, after the storm of protest which greeted its proposals, a cooling-off period was required to allow the dust to settle. And finally, it is possible that the Treasury felt that the concerns about potential increases in the Housing Benefit bill, because of greater use of private rented accommodation, concerns which were expressed particularly by the London Housing Unit (Morris, 1994b), needed to be investigated before proceeding further with legislation. A possible fifth factor, which emerged later on, was that a postponement of legislation allowed time for senior civil servants to develop elements of a possible national policy on housing allocations (Morris, 1995). This would also be consistent with the Department of the Environment's continuing aim to seek more 'technical' solutions to pressing housing problems.

*The White Paper*

The next stage was the publication of the White Paper *Our Future Homes* in July 1995. In that paper, the Department of the Environment announced its intention to repeal the legislation giving homeless people priority in the allocation of life-long tenancies. Instead, the paper stated:

We are committed to maintaining an immediate safety net (temporary accommodation for up to twelve months), but this should be separate from a fair system of allocating long-term accommodation in a house or flat owned by a local authority or housing association. (Department of the Environment, 1995a)

This wording indicates that the Department of the Environment's position remained completely unchanged. Not surprisingly, therefore, the general response was the same as that which greeted the consultation paper – namely overwhelming opposition. Perhaps the only new point raised by objectors was that recent court cases had rendered the proposed changes in homelessness legislation unnecessary. This point related mainly to the House of Lords judgement in the Awua case in July 1995.

The Awua case (Healy, 1995) was of major importance in two respects. First, it made clear that those who live in temporary accommodation are not necessarily homeless according to the statutory definition, so long as it is reasonable for them to continue to occupy that accommodation. Second, with regard to the local authority's duty to secure accommodation for the homeless by means of an offer of suitable accommodation, the House of Lords held that, in certain cases, such suitable accommodation could be only temporary. This was a shock to everybody, because previously it had been assumed that a permanent rehousing duty could not be discharged by an offer of temporary accommodation (Coombes, 1995). Following the Awua case, however, commentators were quick to note that the judgment implied that it was not necessary to introduce new legislation in order to remove the duty to provide permanent accommodation (Campbell, 1995) and indeed, as Campbell pointed out, the Awua judgment went further than the White Paper proposals: 'A 12-month duty to house someone is going to be more generous than a mean local authority arranging a six-month shorthold' (Coombes, 1995). On the other hand, however, there was a weight of case law, relating to the meaning of 'suitable accommodation', which arguably provided protection for homeless people against unsuitable offers of short-term accommodation, and this protection would be lost if the homelessness legislation were repealed.

The Department of the Environment's response to the Awua judgment was given in a paper in October 1995 (Department of the Environment, 1995b). Essentially, its position was that its new proposals 'will remove any uncertainty' created by Awua, presumably because, under the proposals, homeless people could be assured of rehousing for twelve months rather than (at the very least) 28 days. The proposals did nothing, however, to clarify the meaning of 'suitable accommodation', and it is this which was the source of the greatest uncertainty (Holmes, 1995). Here, then, is another example of the Department of the Environment appearing to respond positively to new developments, in this case from the judiciary rather than the housing lobby, while in reality refusing to give an inch.

One unexpected benefit of the Awua judgment is that it highlighted a key point concerning the Department of the Environment's proposals. With the benefit of hindsight, it can be seen that it was the proposals, not the judgment, which involved removing the 'safety net' for the unintentional priority homeless. This is because, in the case of Awua, it was envisaged that the duty towards such homeless people would not be time-limited but would continue until such time as 'settled' accommodation was secured, provided only that they remained unintentionally homeless and in priority need. The Lords accepted that such people could not be required to leave the temporary accommodation secured for them unless they were provided with suitable alternative accommodation. In contrast, the Department of the Environment's proposals, both in the Green and White Papers, made it quite clear that the duty towards the homeless would be to secure accommodation for a limited period only (Department of the Environment, 1994, p. 7) – namely twelve months (Department of the Environment, 1995a).

*The Housing Bill*

The Housing Bill itself was finally published on 19 January 1996 (Department of the Environment, 1996a). The three key proposals of the Green and White papers survived intact in its legislative provisions, but had been qualified or clarified in a number of respects. For example (author's italics):

1. *The duty of local authorities towards the unintentionally homeless in priority need was still to be restricted to one of securing accommodation for a minimum of twelve months.* In addition, however, local authorities would have to review this duty before two years had passed and to cease providing the accommodation if the occupier no longer qualified for assistance. They would also be prohibited from offering council accommodation for more than two years continuously or for more than two years in a three-year period, irrespective of the number of applications made (except for hostels or leased accommodation).

2. *The duty of local authorities to secure accommodation for the unintentionally homeless in priority need was still to be abolished where the local authority was satisfied that other suitable accommodation was available in their district.*

3. *The requirement that local authorities offer secure tenancies only to people on their own register (which excludes homeless applicants) was still to be imposed.* Accompanying the Bill, a consultation paper was published (Department of the Environment, 1996b) in which the Department of the Environment set out its views concerning how such housing registers might be regulated.

The interesting point about the qualifications on the first duty above is that they harked back to the original scapegoating of the homeless in the 1994 Green Paper. The clear implication was that the homeless would be actively prevented from securing permanent accommodation. Not only was the national legal safety net to be abolished, but also local authorities were to be restricted in their efforts to substitute their own local safety nets in its place. The injustice of such an approach is precisely what was responsible for causing the outcry in the first place, so here we have yet another example of the Department of the Environment's intransigence. Understandably, therefore, the immediate response to the Bill was one of outrage (Dobson, 1996; Meikle, 1996a), followed soon afterwards by a mood of bitter resignation (Holmes, 1996). Within weeks, however, the Bill had been amended so that the duty to secure temporary accommodation was extended to a minimum of two years instead of one year (Morris, 1996). In addition, the Department of the Environment 'conceded' that local authorities would be allowed to allocate permanent accommodation to homeless households who had nearly enough points for this on their own waiting lists (*Inside Housing*, 1996a). This was, in fact, another example of a 'pretended' concession because there was nothing in the Bill's provisions which would prevent a local authority from treating such households as ordinary waiting list applicants, although of course they would not be *obliged* to do so, since local safety nets, of a restricted character, were to be entirely at the discretion of local authorities.

The success of the above amendment to the Bill is further evidence that backbench MPs can play an influential role in policy making once a Bill is going through the parliamentary process (Somerville, 1994). This was in fact the only significant change made to the homelessness provisions in the Bill and, from the Department of the Environment's point of view, it was not a major one because it still meant that a local authority's duty towards the homeless was restricted to the provision of temporary accommodation.

During the passage of the Bill, what appeared to change within the Department of the Environment was not so much the substance of the homelessness provisions as the attitude towards the homeless which under-lay those provisions, and which gave rise to them in the first place. The consultation paper on allocations (Department of the Environment, 1996b), for example, proposed that priority for rehousing should be given to, among others, people with an identified need for settled accommoda-tion and people with limited opportunities to secure settled accommodation for themselves – that is, people who are more likely to become homeless. This approach was quite at odds with the scapegoating of the homeless which was expressed in the 1994 consultation paper and was reiterated, to some extent, in the White Paper. This kind of ambivalence can be seen in relation to young single mothers, who had been demonized by Conservative politicians, including Sir George Young, but who now formed part of a category of 'families with children' deemed to be deserving of rehousing priority (Department of the Environment, 1996b). Commenta-tors were not slow in noticing these discrepancies (Meikle, 1996b). Although it is not clear whether they represented a genuine change of heart on the part of the Department of the Environment or not, credit for such a change was generally attributed to the Housing Minister, David Curry, who claimed that he 'always eschewed language about queue-jumping or moral-ity' (Meikle, 1996b).

The change in Housing Minister, from Young to Curry, certainly involved a shift in style, but it is not clear whether this meant a shift in substance. In the standing committee stage of the Housing Bill, for example, over a hundred amendments were considered in relation to those parts of the Bill dealing with homelessness and allocations, but most of these were relatively minor, and only two major ones actually succeeded – these were the extension to 24 months of the duty to secure accommodation and the inclusion of allocations criteria in the primary legislation instead of these being left to subsequent regulations (*Housing Review*, 1996). This does not suggest that the Housing Minister was prepared to yield on any of the Bill's provisions unless he was actually forced to do so. Similarly, at the report stage of the Bill, all the homelessness provisions survived unscathed (Coombes, 1996). How then, is it possible to explain the Minister's invita-tion to the Chartered Institute of Housing, the Law Society, the Association of Directors of Social Services and the British Medical Association, to make further suggestions on the Bill, once it was going through the House of Lords (*Inside Housing*, 1996b)? Again, this appears to be no more than a pretence of listening rather than a willingness to make concessions. Finally, in the House of Lords, the only major change accepted by the government was a provision for the Secretary of State for the Environment to allow a local authority, in certain circumstances and at its own request, to let homeless people stay in its own accommodation a further year after the minimum two years (West, 1996).

One interesting feature of this historical phase is the Chartered Institute of Housing's perception of its influence on the policy process. For example, the 'concession' mentioned above, allowing local authorities to rehouse homeless people into permanent accommodation if they had enough points, was presented by the Chartered Institute of Housing's chief executive, Christine Laird, as her own, significant achievement (Birch, 1996). In fact, of course, as commentators have noted (*Housing*, 1996), this so-called 'Laird protocol' would have little effect because responsible authorities would be exercising this discretion automatically and irresponsible ones would ignore it! Overall, the evidence does not suggest that professional groups such as the Chartered Institute of Housing had any more influence over the housing policy process in 1996 than they had in 1976 (Somerville, 1994). The system of agents or agencies illustrated in Figure 2.1 has changed hardly at all.

**Evaluation of the 1996 Housing Act homelessness provisions**

The importance of the 1977 Housing (Homeless Persons) Act lay in its decisive break from the Poor Law tradition of stigmatized welfare provided on a punitive basis. The basis of the Department of the Environment's 1994 proposals, however, signified a return to the Poor Law principle that homeless people should not be treated more favourably than others in housing need. In reality, of course, homeless people have not received preferential treatment, because they have tended to be offered poorer quality accommodation – not to mention the often appalling conditions of the temporary housing which they typically have had to endure beforehand. The 'fast track' for the homeless, which the consultation paper criticized, was typically only a fast track into inferior housing. If this fast track had been abolished, as the paper proposed, then homeless people would have been penalized simply for being homeless. Such a practice would have been manifestly unjust and morally reprehensible (Bayley, 1994). As it turned out, however, the treatment of the homeless in the 1996 Housing Act was not as severe as had been feared. But how exactly did the situation change over the two years, and what is the significance of the changes which took place?

One way of evaluating the changes is to go back to the original criticisms of the Department of the Environment's 1994 proposals, which were that they were unnecessary, unjust and unworkable. In defending the Housing Bill, Curry (1996) argued that the measures were necessary because:

The legal duty at present can be discharged by no more than 28 days' provision of accommodation. The Awua judgement, which laid down this interpretation, effectively leaves the idea of a legal safety net in complete tatters.

This was entirely untrue, because, as has been noted above, the Awua judgment did not remove local authorities' continuing responsibility towards the homeless. Another relevant point here is that, under the old legislation, there was no restriction placed on the period of time which homeless people could be left in (unsuitable) interim accommodation waiting for their 'permanent' home. Bad practice in this area could have been outlawed by a minor amendment of the old legislation, such as that of imposing time limits on the occupation by homeless people of accommodation which was not appropriate or reasonable for them to occupy as settled accommodation. The new legislation, however, did not do this, but instead specifically excluded accommodation such as hostels and bed and breakfast from the two-year rule. So, not only were the provisions of the new Act unnecessary for retaining a safety net for the homeless but they served to undermine that safety net (see below) and also failed to fill any of the holes in the safety net which had existed under the old legislation.

With regard to the alleged injustice of the changes, supporters of the 1996 Housing Act have claimed that it ensures a fairer system of housing allocation to groups of people who are themselves more likely to become homeless. By introducing a disincentive to become homeless for those who are not in the greatest housing need, they would assert that it helps to ensure that those who *are* in the greatest housing need receive the highest priority in rehousing. The problem with this argument is that it draws a rather artificial distinction between homeless and non-homeless. If, as the Act's supporters acknowledge, it is the same types of people who become homeless as who find themselves in the greatest housing need, what is the point of treating them differently in terms of access to secure accommodation? Even if it were 'just' to do so, in some moralistic or bureaucratic sense, it seems to introduce an unnecessary and cumbersome administrative complication.

Finally, the allegation of unworkability which was made against the original 1994 proposals now looks more difficult to substantiate. As long as it was assumed that the private rented sector would cater for the needs of homeless people, the new proposals looked completely unrealistic. Private rents continue to be unaffordable for low-income households, who include the vast majority of homeless people, and it is not reasonable to expect the Department of Social Security to subsidize such households increasingly through housing benefit. The only alternative, therefore, appeared to be to allow local authorities to use their own accommodation for homeless people. As mentioned earlier, this means secure tenancies for those homeless households at the top of the waiting list, although it had to involve non-secure tenancies for the rest. Such a situation, however, appeared remarkably similar to the practice which existed prior to the Act, where most homeless people were routinely placed in non-secure accommodation for varying periods, while a few gained immediate access to secure tenancies (see Chapter 7).

There are three main differences between the situation now and the previous one. First, the period of stay in non-secure local authority accommodation is limited to two continuous years (or two years out of any three). Second, entry to secure local authority accommodation can be gained only through the single housing register. Third, under the new legislation, local authorities do not have a time-unlimited duty to secure accommodation for homeless households. If a homeless household reaches the end of its two-year stay in non-secure accommodation without obtaining a secure, or assured, tenancy, then the local authority *may* review its case. Moreover, on the basis of the review, the local authority *may* secure accommodation for it for a further two years, but there is no obligation to do so. There is a sense therefore in which, beyond the two-year period, the legal safety net for the homeless has been lost. At the end of the day, however, if the homeless in question are in the greatest housing need, then any reasonable local authority, by this time, is going to be offering them secure accommodation. It appears, therefore, that the legislation has been changed simply in order to condone the practice of a small minority of unreasonable local authorities.

It can be concluded, then, that the 1996 Housing Act's homelessness provisions were *necessary* only in order to remove the long-term safety net for the homeless, which the Awua judgement did not do. They were *justified* only by reference to a contrived distinction between homeless and non-homeless people, and *unfair* in terms of their discrimination against most people unfortunate enough to become homeless. They turned out to be *workable*, however, because, unlike the 1994 proposals, the 1996 Housing Act assumed that, to a greater or lesser extent, local authorities would be using their own housing stock, rather than the private rented sector, to accommodate the homeless.

## Conclusions

The themes of state centralization, depoliticization and deregulation/ marketization, examined in earlier sections, had a common source – namely in the power enjoyed by the Department of the Environment.

Centralization occured as a means of strengthening this power. Depoliticization helped to defend this power against actual and potential opposition. And the drive towards greater privatization was a strategy by which the Department of the Environment in particular, and the Conservative government more generally, sought to maintain its rule. This paper has shown that the power of the Department of the Environment was crucial in the events leading to the 1977 Housing (Homeless Persons) Act, remained crucial throughout the period following the Act, and was again crucial in the events leading to the 1996 Housing Act. Because of its power, the Department of the Environment was always able to seize and retain the initiative in housing policy and, in contrast, the housing lobby was generally reactive because it was relatively powerless. The Department of the Environment prefered to have the co-operation of local authorities in implementing its policies, but it did not have to rely on such good will. It was quite capable of proceeding with policies to which the vast majority of local authorities and other housing organizations were implacably opposed.

Returning to Figure 2.1, it can be seen that the system of agents involved in homelessness policy in Britain has altered very little since the passing of the 1977 Housing (Homeless Persons) Act. As stated above, the overwhelming dominance of the Department of the Environment persisted and its perceptions of local authority practice continued to play a major part in influencing its proposals for legislative change. The influence of backbench MPs possibly declined, to some extent, but the impact of electoral opinion, expressed largely through the media, could occasionally be of some importance, as in the case of highly visible or ideologically sensitive problems (see Chapter 4). Structural factors became more complex, but there was a high degree of regularity and stability in their development, and this made it possible to detect with reasonable accuracy the nature and extent of their influence on the Department of the Environment in particular. Finally, the influence of pressure groups probably declined, to some extent, although this conclusion would undoubtedly be disputed by bodies such as the local authority associations and the Chartered Institute of Housing. Overall, therefore, the dominance of the Department of the Environment may actually have increased to some extent since 1977.

The most striking change which has taken place in the system of actors is not in the relative degrees of power which they hold, but in the policy positions which they have taken, and this is particularly the case with the Department of the Environment and local authorities. Whereas in the mid-1970s it was the Department of the Environment forcing through new rights for homeless people in the face of local authority resistance, in the 1990s it was local authorities defending those same rights against the Department of the Environment's attacks. In 1976, it was primarily non-co-operation from the local authorities which prompted the decision to legislate. Similarly, in 1995, it was the Department of the Environment's belief that a centralized system of housing allocation would not be achievable on the basis of local authority consent which motivated them towards new legislation. Throughout the whole period, the Department of the Environment's lack of understanding of, and indeed contempt for, local authorities (with one or two notable exceptions) persisted undiminished.

One final point is that the depoliticization sought by the Department of the Environment has largely succeeded. A distinction has to be drawn here between the perceptions of the electorate, who have consistently attached a high priority to homelessness problems and policy (Jowel *et al.*, 1994; Gallup, 1996), and the attention of the media to the passage of homelessness legislation in the 1990s, which was negligible (Grender, 1996; Summerskill, 1996). It can be concluded from this that it is certainly not the electorate which sets the political agenda and this is an uncomfortable conclusion to make in what is regarded by many people as a democratic society. Government has to respond to the electorate to some degree, but it can also manipulate the political agenda, to some extent, to suit its own interests and ideology, which may be far removed from those of most of the electorate. The basic and enduring ideological emphasis is on the responsibility of individual people and their families to cope with homelessness, and this is associated with a view of the state as having only to provide advice and assistance in times of crisis, and also to prevent such crises. Hence what is to count as 'suitable' accommodation, for example, must remain essentially vague, because each case is unique, and must be dealt with on its own merits.

## Acknowledgements

I am grateful to *Policy and Politics* for their permission to reproduce extracts from my 1994 article.

## References

Anderson, I. (1993) 'Housing policy and street homelessness in Britain', *Housing Studies*, vol. 1, no. 8, pp. 17–28.

Anderson, I., Kemp, P. and Quilgars, D. (1993) *Single Homeless People*, London: HMSO.

Anderson, I. and Morgan, J. (1996) *Single people's housing needs: A question of legitimacy?*, paper presented to Housing Studies Association Conference on Housing and Social Exclusion at the University of Birmingham, 16–17 September 1996.

Association of District Councils (1988) *Homelessness: A Review of the Legislation*, London: Association of District Councils.

Bayley, R. (1994) 'A tried and tested path to failure', *Inside Housing*, 11 March 1994.

Bevan, M. and Rhodes, D. (1996) *Housing Homeless People in the Private Rented Sector*, York: Joseph Rowntree Foundation.

Birch, J. (1996) 'Leading from the front', *Roof* (July/August), pp. 30–31.

Blake, J. (1993) 'The right to act?', *Roof* (September/October), p. 27.

Bradburn, H. (1994) *Home Truths: Access to Local Authority and Housing Association Tenancies: Responses to the Consultation Paper*, London: Shelter.

Burns, L. (1994a) 'Time to separate myth from reality', *Roof* (March/April), p. 9.

Burns, L. (1994b) 'Back of the queue', *Roof* (September/October), p. 8.

Campbell, R. (1993) 'Beyond the fringe', *Roof* (November/December), p. 13.

Campbell, R. (1994) 'Cathy comes back', *Roof* (March/April), p. 14.

Campbell, R. (1995) 'Back to no future', *Roof* (September/October), p. 17.

Coombes, R. (1995) 'Bomb blast leaves only temporary shelter', *Inside Housing*, 1 September 1995, pp. 12–13.

Coombes, R. (1996) 'Homelessness law intact as Bill heads for Lords', *Inside Housing*, 3 May 1996, p. 1.

Crook, T. (1992) 'Private rented housing and the impact of deregulation', in J. Birchall (ed.) *Housing Policy in the 1990s*, London: Routledge, pp. 91–112.

Curry, D. (1996) 'Need before morality', *Roof* (March/April), p. 9.

Department of the Environment (1989) *Review of the Homelessness Legislation*, London: HMSO.

Department of the Environment (1994) *Access to Local Authority and Housing Association Tenancies*, Consultation Paper, London: HMSO.

Department of the Environment (1995a) *Our Future Homes: Opportunity, Choice, Responsibility*, London: HMSO.

Department of the Environment (1995b) *Response to Awua*, London: HMSO.

Department of the Environment (1996a) *Housing Bill 1996*, London: HMSO.

Department of the Environment (1996b) *Allocation of Housing Accommodation by Local Authorities: Consultation Paper Linked to the Housing Bill*, London: Department of the Environment.

Dobson, J. (1996) 'Heat on Curry as homeless lose rights', *Inside Housing*, 26 January 1996, p. 4.

Gallup (1996) 'Poll reveals housing is neglected', *Housing* (July/August), p. 26.

Grender, O. (1996) 'The media and the massage', *Roof* (May/June), p. 11.

Greve, J., Page, D. and Greve, S. (1971) *Homelessness in London*, Edinburgh: Scottish Academic Press.

Hoath, D. (1983) *Homelessness*, London: Sweet & Maxwell.

Holmes, C. (1995) 'Removing uncertainty for who?', *Roof* (November/December), p. 11.

Holmes, C. (1996) 'Desperately seeking cohesion', *Inside Housing*, 9 February 1996, pp. 14–15.

*Housing* (1994) 'Unite against this misguided law', editorial, *Housing* (March), p. 9.

*Housing* (1996) ' "Humpty Dumpty bill", a nightmare for homeless', *Housing* (July/August), p. 21.

*Housing Review* (1994a) 'Pushing the weakest to the wall', *Housing Review*, vol. 43, no. 2, p. 19.

*Housing Review* (1994b) 'Response to the Department of the Environment Consultation Paper on Access to Local Authority and Housing Association Tenancies', *Housing Review*, vol. 42, no. 3, pp. 108–9.

*Housing Review* (1996) 'Housing Act update', *Housing Review*, vol. 45, no. 4, pp. 65–7.

*Inside Housing* (1996a) 'Department of the Environment offers councils greater discretion on homeless', *Inside Housing*, 8 March 1996, p. 1.

*Inside Housing* (1996b) 'Curry offers lobbyists hope of last minute change to homeless law', *Inside Housing*, 24 May 1996, p. 2.

Jowel, R., Curtice, J., Brook, L., Ahrendt, D and Park, A. (eds) (1994) *British Social Attitudes, 11th Report*, Aldershot: Dartmouth Publishing Company.

Levison, D. and White, J. (1993) 'Let them go private', *Roof* (September/October), pp. 28–29.

McGilp, J. (1994a) 'No access to our support', *Inside Housing* 18 March 1994, pp. 12–13.

McGilp, J. (1994b) 'The true battle has only just started', Housing (October), p. 8.

McKechnie, S. (1994) 'Taking a step back in time', *The Guardian*, 11 March 1994, p. 23.

Mason, P. (1994) 'Overwhelming majority slam government review', *Inside Housing*, 25 March 1994, p. 2.

Meikle, J. (1996a) 'Homeless to lose priority on council waiting lists', *The Guardian*, 23 January 1996, p. 12.

Meikle, J. (1996b) 'Building a fine reputation', *The Guardian*, 20 March 1996, p. 9.

Merrett, S. (1991) *Quality and Choice in Housing*, London: Institute of Public Policy Research.

Morris, H. (1994a) 'Wave of anger as the rights of homeless families are slashed', *Inside Housing*, 22 July 1994, p. 1.

Morris, H. (1994b) 'George's not so fond farewell', *Inside Housing*, 29 July 1994, pp. 12–13.

Morris, H. (1995) 'Officials prepare way for new curbs on homeless', *Inside Housing*, 13 January 1995, p. 1.

Morris, H. (1996) 'Homeless families gain new concession in bill', *Inside Housing*, 15 March 1996, p. 1.

Mullins, D. (1991) *Housing Services for Homeless People*, London: Institute of Housing.

Randall, G. and Brown, S. (1993) *The Rough Sleepers Initiative: An Evaluation*, London: HMSO.

Raynsford, N. (1986) 'The 1977 Housing (Homeless Persons) Act', in N. Deakin (ed.) *Policy Change in Government*, London: Royal Institute of Public Administration, pp. 33–62.

Saunders, P. (1990) *A Nation of Home Owners*, London: Unwin Hyman.

Shaps, M. (1988) 'Rubbishing the act', *Roof* (November/December), pp. 14–16.

Somerville, P. (1990) 'A roof over one's head', *Housing Review*, vol. 39, no. 6, pp. 147–8.

Somerville, P. (1994) 'Homelessness policy in Britain', *Policy and Politics*, vol. 22, no. 3, pp. 163–78.

Stearn, J. (1993) 'Singled out for unfair treatment', *Inside Housing*, 15 October 1993.

Stearn, J. (1994a) 'Plans to scrap legislation will leave homeless out in the cold', *Inside Housing*, 28 January 1994, p. 1.

Stearn, J. (1994b) 'Minister backtracks on central aspect of homelessness plans', *Inside Housing*, 15 April 1994, p. 1.

Summerskill, B. (1996) 'Subtext', *Roof* (July/August), p. 17.

Thornton, R. (1990) *The New Homeless*, London: SHAC.

West, T. (1996) 'New powers turn heat up on nuisance tenants', *Inside Housing*, 26 July 1996, p. 2.

Widdowson, B. (1988) 'Turning back the clock', *Housing* (September), pp. 13–15.

Wintour, P. (1993) 'Housing right "abuse" to end', *The Guardian*, 8 October 1993, p. 7.

York, J. (1994) 'Back to the bad old days', *Inside Housing*, 28 January 1994, pp. 10–11.

Young, G. (1994) 'The government's housing proposals need to be analysed as a whole', *Inside Housing*, 11 February 1994, p. 9.

# 3 The problem of homelessness: a European perspective

*Brian Harvey*

**Summary**

This chapter starts by a brief examination of what is known about homelessness in the European Union, its nature, extent and characteristics, using the most up-to-date information from the European observatory on homelessness, which has gathered in and synthesized information from national correspondents in each of the member states since 1991. The chapter examines the different perceptions of and approaches to homelessness within the member states. There is an examination of whether a policy community now exists for the development of policies to respond to homelessness at the European level. Finally, there is a discussion of how the European experience of homelessness may be applied to Britain.

## The current state of knowledge about homelessness in Europe

Our knowledge of homelessness in Europe comes from two principal sources. In the first instance, it comes from research carried out in individual member states by academics, non-governmental organizations (NGOs) and, to a very limited extent, by national, regional or local governments and their various research instruments. Until the 1990s, such information was limited and patchy. In the second instance, our knowledge and interpretation of homelessness come from the European Observatory on Homelessness, established in 1991 by the European Federation of National Organisations Working with the Homeless, FEANTSA. The purpose of the observatory was to remedy, in a systematic way, the serious gaps that existed in the knowledge, understanding and analysis of homelessness in the

Union. The European Observatory works through a network of national correspondents in each of the member states, whose reports are prepared on a standardized basis each year. These reports concentrate on the collection of general information on trends in homelessness in each member state and, each year, select a theme for more detailed examination. This information and these thematic reports are then summarized each year, an annual report then being produced and published (Daly, 1992, 1993, 1994; Avramov, 1995, 1996). The collection of information on trends and the thematic approach are designed to build on the knowledge of homelessness across Europe year by year. The funding of the observatory by the European Commission has made possible a substantial growth in the quantity and quality of information on homelessness in Europe over the past six years.

The principal outcomes of this research are reviewed in this chapter. The findings are drawn substantially from the reports of Daly and Avramov and are, except in specific cases, not individually referenced hereafter. Subsequent interpretation is that of this writer.

Before doing so, the problematic nature of statistics and information on homelessness should be emphasized. Few national or local governments keep any usable or consistent statistics on the national level of homelessness (Britain is an exception, though even there the figures are contested). Statistical information is essentially dependent on the numbers of homeless people presenting for services. Furthermore, those compiling information must make important distinctions between the numbers using services at any one time (stock) and the numbers using services over the course of time and statistics for the duration of time used (flow). Some services are ill-equipped or uninterested to participate in information-gathering exercises.

In the light of these difficulties and in the knowledge that any outcome figure is likely to be scientifically imperfect (though not necessarily valueless), it would be tempting to abandon the attempt to present macrodata on homelessness and concentrate on more manageable tasks. However, FEANTSA took the view that it was essential to construct some picture of the scale, size and scope of the problem of homelessness. Such an overall picture was an important prerequisite to the defining of appropriate policy responses to homelessness and the type of resources which must be deployed. It attempted to overcome the statistical problems inherent in the exercise by the use of a standard definition of homelessness,[1] by the common training of national correspondents, by asking correspondents to assess and synthesize the respective governmental and non-governmental data and by insisting that in presenting figures they take a cautious and conservative approach.

As a result of this exercise, it was possible for the observatory to provide numerical data on the scale of homelessness and some of its key trends.

The basic numerical data on European homelessness are as follows:

- 15m badly housed people live in severely substandard and overcrowded dwellings;
- 1.6m people are subject to eviction procedures each year and are at risk of homelessness;
- 400,000 people are evicted in Europe each year;
- 1.8m people are dependent on public and voluntary services for homeless people; and
- a further 2.7m homeless people rotate between friends and relatives, furnished rooms rented on a short-term basis and other services for homeless people. A table illustrating the level of homelessness in each member state is provided in the appendix.

The highest numbers are found in Germany, France and the UK. The numbers involved are significant, together adding up to $1\frac{1}{2}$ million people, nearly 1 per cent of the total populations concerned. The second group of countries includes Belgium, Italy, Luxembourg, the Netherlands and Ireland. These states have lower recorded homelessness of between one and two homeless persons per 1,000. Finally, at the lower end of the scale are Denmark, Portugal and Spain.

Homelessness is not a static phenomenon, but a dynamic one, one with links and relationships to the changing social and economic processes of late 20th-century Europe. The numbers of homeless people reported in Europe have been rising. In 1993–4, for example, the growth in reported homelessness over 1993 was 5 per cent in Flanders, 8 per cent in the Netherlands, 16 per cent in Luxembourg and 20 per cent in the UK, just to give four examples. If one were to extrapolate present trends, the number of people homeless in the then 12 Union countries may rise to 6.6m by 2001.

The age of homeless people is falling. The principal age range is now 30 to 39 years, with the young homeless teenager an identifiable subset. This age group accounts for 55 per cent of the homeless population, compared to only 30.5 per cent of the Union population as a whole. Street children have become more and more noticed in Spain and Portugal. The numbers of homeless people over 60 years are very small, though this may reflect high death rates among homeless people.

The number of women in the homeless population is rising. A long-term trend has been precisely measured in Denmark, where the number of women seeking shelter rose from 6 per cent of the sheltered population in 1976 to 20 per cent in 1989. Women constitute, on average, between a fifth and a third of the homeless in most countries. Most of these women have children with them when they are homeless. The average age of homeless women is, in general, lower than the average age of homeless men. A significant number of homeless women are lone parents; a significant number (40 per cent in one country) flee from physical or sexual abuse.

There are distinct links between marital breakdown and homelessness. In looking at shelter populations in Belgium, Germany, Spain, Italy and Luxembourg, the proportion divorced and separated lies in a band of 29 per cent to 35 per cent. Solitude is an important aspect of homelessness. The observatory records that typically 90 per cent of homeless men and 60 per cent of homeless women have no current partner. Whereas men tend to be found in traditional-type shelters, women and younger people are more likely to be found in poor housing, squats and other non-institutional provision. This may reflect the lack of availability of suitable shelter accommodation for women or for women with children. This in turn makes homeless women less countable, less visible; but their homelessness is nonetheless real.

Migrants and refugees constitute a small but important element of the homeless population, between 10 and 20 per cent. This is especially true for three countries: Germany, which received the bulk of migrants moving west from the former Soviet Union and its satellite states; Greece, which received a wave of migration from Asia minor during the Balkan conflict; and Italy, the point of entry to Europe for many migrants moving northwards from the southern Mediterranean basin.

Deinstitutionalization is an important element in homelessness. While poor health – either physical or mental – is an inevitable consequence of homelessness, FEANTSA received abundant evidence that poor health preceded homelessness, suggesting that both caring and penal institutions failed to provide an appropriate or safe level of protection or aftercare. In England and Wales between 30 and 50 per cent of those sleeping rough had a background of mental illness; looking at the issue from another perspective, in Westminster, one in eight of former residents of mental hospitals is now homeless. In Belgium, 15 per cent of the men and 5 per cent of the women had spent time in a psychiatric institution and 21 per cent of the men and 2 per cent of the women had spent time in prison. 75 per cent of Ireland's homeless and 42 per cent of Italy's homeless had been institutionalized at some stage of their lives. But it is important to be quite rigorous in interpreting these figures, because it is equally clear that for the majority of homeless people, problems of stress, substance abuse (principally alcohol) and mental illness followed rather than preceded homelessness.

Homeless people have poor employment records. Low-paid work with frequent interruptions is the norm for many homeless people. Many have worked in the shadow economy, marginal work which confers few if any state entitlements. In Europe, regular, well-paid employment exists side-by-side with the growth in temporary, insecure work which confers few or no social benefits.

About two-thirds of all services for the homeless in Europe are provided by non-governmental, voluntary organizations. Most typically, voluntary providers emerged from and were left to fill the vacuum created by inadequate or absent statutory responses. There is a heavy reliance on the religious sector to provide services for the homeless. Often emerging from a charitable motivation, these services tend to be of an emergency character. Services are very selective. Some organizations restrict their services to a particular client group while others deal with all the homeless without distinction. A number of differentiating criteria exists: sex/gender, age, family status, citizen status. The application of these criteria varies from member state to member state.

Meeting basic needs is the principal service priority: an average of 80 per cent of the providers surveyed offer such services. Over 60 per cent of the organizations provide an information service, usually in association with other activities. The third priority of service provision in the domain of homelessness concerns re-integrative aims, that is, to support and enable the homeless person's re-integration into the labour market and/or a settled way of life. About half of the organizations across the Union direct their activities in a major way towards the long-term integration of the homeless person. The final set of services could be labelled 'political' in that they are directed to improving public consciousness and information and to increasing resources available to services working for the homeless. Such activities are the least widespread, accounting for only about a fifth of the activities of the organizations surveyed.

The right to housing exists only in a minority of European states: Portugal (from 1976), Spain (from 1978), the Netherlands (from 1982), France (from 1990) and Belgium (from 1994). In several other countries, access to public services is guaranteed through the social welfare code. In some countries, legal protection for homeless people is minimal.

**The understanding and interpretation of homelessness in Europe**

An understanding of the nature of homelessness is essential if appropriate services are to be provided by non-governmental organizations and if appropriate policies are to be put in place by governments. Lack of agreement and understanding between the three key actors in this area – NGOs, governments and the academic community – has been an impediment to the development of more successful policies to combat homelessness.

The understanding of homelessness has varied according to the locus of the research. NGOs, concentrating on the important task of meeting day-to-day needs, have tended to emphasize the underfunding of services for the homeless and lack of demonstrable government concern, and have echoed their clients' complaints of low levels of social security provision. Governments, for their part, have tended to explain homelessness in terms of complex social phenomena to which they endeavour to provide a variety of appropriate responses or in terms of bureaucratic failure (normally, the shortcoming of a lower tier of government). Academic reports tend to explain homelessness in a variety of ways – social, psychological, personal and structural. Issues of personal and social responsibility may often be found at the heart of the debate, with dividing lines between those who favour structural explanations of homelessness and others who place greater emphasis on personal, individual factors. These divisions and differences of emphasis are crucial, for they shape popular and governmental attitudes as to where responsibility for addressing homelessness lies: with the individual, or society; with families, or the community as a whole; with non-governmental organizations; or with government at large. In examining the reports of the European observatory's national correspondents, Fitzpatrick made a critical and valid comment when she asked whether their different positions 'simply reflect different political positions and/or scientific approaches, or are the result of genuine differences in the nature of the phenomenon in different countries' (Fitzpatrick, 1995, p. 10).

*An emerging understanding*

Until the 1980s, homelessness was generally explained pathologically, as the admittedly sad but unavoidable problem that emerges when inadequate personalities prove unable to adjust to changes in rapidly industrializing societies, what is popularly called the 'mad, sad, bad' explanation. The persistence and indeed growth of homelessness at a time of unparalleled economic prosperity, combined with the presence in night shelters of individuals and families whose fate could not be attributed solely to personal dysfunction, forced a rethink of this paradigm, at first within the academic community and then wider afield.

The European observatory on homelessness has attempted to provide a synthesis of the many factors which contribute to homelessness, giving its own indications of the relative weight which should be apportioned to each. The reports of the observatory have explained the perseverance of homelessness as associated with rising levels of poverty which have escalated since the 1970s. Homelessness is connected with changing social conditions in the member states. Principal of these are: unemployment, currently running at over 17 million in the European Union; the steady disinvestment for over 15 years now by national governments in housing provision for people on low incomes; the deinstitutionalization of psychiatric units without adequate attention being given to comprehensive community care facilities in their place; the discharge of ill homeless people on the streets; and the lack of either income support systems, or their insufficiently low level. Processes of family fragmentation have played an important role, such as the general decrease of marriage; increase of divorce rate; decrease of remarriage rate; increase in consensual unions; increase of one-parent families; and changing home-leaving patterns for young adults. A key accomplishment of the observatory has been to link homelessness to the way in which government influences the housing market (Daly, 1993; Avramov, 1996); the nature of non-governmental provision (Daly, 1992) and the legislative framework for the homeless (Daly, 1994; Avramov, 1995). Questions of income support also emerged as key issues. These insights and contributions to the understanding of homelessness are explored in more detail below.

This contemporary current synthesis explaining homelessness glosses over years of struggle by the observatory with issues of the definition and language of homelessness. The term 'homeless', though having clear connotations in English, does not translate easily into other European languages. Equivalent terms have come increasingly into the academic, governmental and popular discourse, such as *sans abri* ('without shelter') in French and *wohnungslos* ('dwellingless') in German. Conversely, continental European terminology about the 'reinsertion' (French *réinsertion*) and 'reintegration' of the homeless 'into society' are deemed to be excessively prescriptive to English-speaking ears, who prefer such terms as 'resettlement'. In practice, services for the homeless throughout Europe are much less different than these semantic overtones might lead one to believe.

Leaving aside the issue of semantics, the framework in which homelessness is perceived, understood and met in Britain is probably unrepresentative of Europe as a whole. These are some examples. Although relationships between the non-governmental sector which works with the homeless in Britain and its government agencies have been problematic, the volume of information on homelessness in the UK – whether emanating from government, voluntary organizations or the academic community – has been much richer than most other parts of the European Union. Especially in the southern countries (e.g. Greece), the level of research, information and data on homelessness is still very low. In Britain, the provision of services for the homeless is closely tied to a legal definition. In other countries, the role of the law is different – stating aspirations in some countries (e.g. Portugal), providing a planning framework in others (e.g. France). The level of welfare provision in Britain, despite restrictions in the 1980s and 1990s, covers a range of situations, problems and categories of people who do not have social protection in, for example, Greece, Italy, Portugal, Spain and France. The national response to homelessness by both the government and voluntary sector in Britain contrasts with the way in which policies concerning housing and homelessness are determined at the regional level in many other countries (e.g. Spain, Italy). The voluntary sector is different too: large national campaigning organizations like Shelter in Britain can be contrasted with exclusively small-scale, localized, city-

and town-based initiatives in Italy, regional bodies (e.g. Belgium) and federal coalitions of regional organizations (e.g. Germany). Turning to public administration, the long tradition of local authority planning which developed in Britain after the war (and which has enabled some good practices of assisting homeless people to develop) has yet to become embedded in countries like Spain and Portugal which established democratic structures only after 1974–5 and regional structures some time later. Likewise, voluntary organizations there were permitted a very circumscribed role under Salazar and Franco and cannot be expected to have attained the same level of organizational maturity as British organizations running social services for fifty years.

Likewise, social conditions vary across the European continent, in turn shaping different responses to homelessness. Refugees are a minor part of the homeless problem in Britain, but returnees from colonies are a major concern in Portugal; accommodation for Germans from the east has been a preoccupation of the German authorities; and returning migrants a concern of the Greek authorities. Portugal and Spain report problems of many thousands of people living in primitive and basic shanty accommodation at the outskirts of cities, a problem which does not exist in Britain. These are specific examples, but there are broader issues. Compared to Britain, household formation takes place at a much later age in some southern European countries. Families are expected to play a much more important role in supporting an extensive range of members through unemployment and the other misfortunes which can precipitate homelessness in northern countries. The approach of governments to the housing market is quite different, rented accommodation being more prominent, owner occupation less so.

Despite these differences, which underline the importance and benefits of examining homelessness from a number of perspectives, it would be wrong to conclude that homelessness in Europe lacks common features or a core of measures which cannot be applied across the member states. The following section identifies some of the common trends.

*Common trends*

The European observatory has placed considerably emphasis on the way in which governments determine, influence and manipulate housing policy and the housing market. A range of policies and patterns of financial investment affect housing supply and demand: taxation, housing or construction targets, financial incentives, policies for rental, home ownership or social housing. For homeless people, perhaps the most significant element is the degree to which the housing market offers access to people with very low incomes, whether that be access to the public, municipal sector, the social housing sector, or the private sector (Daly, 1994; Avramov, 1995, 1996).

A key observation of trends in European housing policy is that private ownership is on the increase, with the implicit and in some cases explicit support of government. About 60 per cent of housing stock in the Union is now in private hands and a noticeable element of national policies in some countries is the encouragement of this form of ownership. Second, the extent of public housing, municipal or social of some kind, compares quite unfavourably with that of private ownership, averaging about 12 per cent of European housing stock. The 1980s and 1990s saw disinvestment in public housing in most parts of the Union and an expressed preference for market-led housing policies.

The European population rose 2.8 per cent over the period 1981 to 1991, whereas the housing stock rose 9.5 per cent during the same period. However the crucial figure in this is the rise in household formation during this period, which was 17.0 per cent, showing that the supply of housing is increasing at only half the rate of households. This invariably means more pressure on housing markets and that is before one takes into account the crucial questions of equity and distribution.

There is a serious problem of poor housing in the Union which touches on the homelessness problem in a number of respects. Just over 20 million people in the Union do not have access to an inside WC. Just over 30 million do not have an inside bathroom or shower room. Aggregating Eurostat data, it seems that over 71 million Union citizens are now living in dwellings which do not accord with national criteria of good quality. Such data must be interpreted cautiously, for many people live in low-quality but secure dwellings (especially in the southern countries); nevertheless the border-line between on-the-street homelessness and poor-quality insecure accommodation may be tenuous. It is clear that at the time of a major surge in housing demand, European governments opted for decreasing social housing, deregulating the market and reducing the cheap housing supply. This will inevitably produce tensions at the lower end of the housing market for years to come and there will be most acute competition between the poorly housed, the insecure, the unemployed and the homeless.

Turning from housing policy to income support, the inadequate nature of many income support mechanisms is very apparent. Such mechanisms are all the more important since very few homeless people have work and since most do not have complete social insurance records. Despite this, not all countries provide homeless people or other indigent citizens with an income, either because of the nature of entitlement criteria or because the administrative system is insufficiently flexible to respond to the needs of homeless people. For example, 20 per cent of shelter residents in Belgium, a northern European State with a comparatively well-developed welfare system, do not receive income support and are dependent on begging or theft to survive. In Luxembourg, where proof-of-origin and documentation requirements are high, only 23 per cent of homeless people receive any social assistance. In Italy, which does not have a national system of income support, of those homeless people for whom data are available, only 34 per cent receive state (or regional) income support, the rest being dependent on assistance from a private agency (15 per cent) and theft or begging (51 per cent). A key lesson arising from this analysis is the importance of basic minimum income and that it be organized in such a way as to ensure homeless people and night shelter residents are able to avail themselves of its provisions.

The importance of a legislative framework for homeless people has been emphasized by the observatory. Laws form an important role in laying down the proper relationship between citizens and the State; in underlining the role of social solidarity in society; and in exhorting higher standards of public administration than discretionary systems alone would achieve. The observatory made a detailed analysis of how existing legal obligations towards the homeless had fallen short of their potential and how such laws had been poorly put into practice, through such imperfections as the inadequate application of the law, the provision of insufficient resources to underpin the law, the exclusion of certain groups from its provision and the multiplication of administrative and juridical procedures.

### The policy community around homelessness in Europe

A key question is to examine whether a policy community exists in Europe to address homelessness; and if so, its nature, strength and possibilities. At European level, a policy community may be said to exist in the non-governmental sector, within some of the institutions of the European Union and among its citizenry. In one crucial area, however, the intergovernmental, it is fractured.

The non-governmental community is mobilized through FEANTSA, which has over fifty members in the countries of the European Union and, indeed, further afield in eastern and central Europe, Russia and the United States. The work and activities of FEANTSA are flanked by a number of European networks which bring together national and regional organizations which are indirectly concerned with homelessness. Most may reasonably be presumed to share the general outlook of FEANTSA. The principal such networks and European movements are: Caritas; Emmaus; Salvation Army; Society of St Vincent de Paul; European Anti-Poverty Network; CECODHAS, the European movement for social housing; EUROPIL, the European association of organizations concerned with resettlement; and

OEIL, the European association of groups involved in the finding of work and employment for young people.

Several of these networks have combined to form what is termed the Charter group, a Paris-based coalition designed to ensure that the needs of the homeless are presented in a unified way at European level and even further afield. Such presentations have been made to the European Union and the United Nations. They have emphasized the centrality of housing policy in an understanding of homelessness, the importance of adequate resourcing of non-governmental organizations and, recently, the need to amend the European treaties to ensure the Union may develop effective instruments to confront homelessness. Submissions to the United Nations have stressed that homelessness is an acute problem in developed as well as developing countries.

The idea of European action against homelessness has won strong support from the European Parliament, which has passed two resolutions on the housing of homeless people, in 1987 and 1996. The European Commission, as part of its activities in combating poverty throughout Europe, has supported non-governmental action against homelessness and has provided financial support for the European networks. The point at which this policy community has broken down is at intergovernmental level.

Most, though not all, European national housing authorities take the view that homelessness is exclusively a national responsibility. (An exception is Italy, which takes the view that housing policy and homelessness are regional concerns. There is no national housing minister.) Although the European housing ministers have met once a year since 1992, their post-conference communiqués start (and indeed end) with ringing assertions that housing and the issues associated with it are national matters and that they meet only for the exchange of information and goodwill. Not until their 1996 meeting did the European housing ministers even discuss homelessness: the British government minister attending went to some efforts to make it clear that he regarded action against homelessness at European level to be both unnecessary and undesirable.

In their submissions to the European green paper *European Social Policy: A Way Forward for the Union*, several member States (Belgium, Denmark and Ireland, with implied support from others) argued that housing, and by implication homelessness, should become European competences. However, these submissions were written for the most part by national departments of social or labour affairs and probably did not seek or obtain agreement from their colleagues in housing departments.

Second, a particular initiative by non-governmental organizations has contributed to the development of a European policy community around homelessness. This is the growth and development of street newspapers. Virtually unknown till the 1990s, such papers have now become an important force in mobilizing public opinion around homelessness and appropriate action to respond to the problem. Examples of the street papers are *Big Issue* (Britain and Ireland), *Das Magafon* (Austria), *NEMO* (Belgium), *Hinz and Kunz* (Germany), *Piazza Grande* (Italy), *Straatniews* (Netherlands), *Na Dne* (Russia), *La rue* (France) and *Asfalto* (Spain). These papers have attracted wide public support, some papers winning circulations of over 120,000. Up to seventy such papers are now reckoned to be in publication. Reader research has found that they attract professional readers, the decision-making age groups in their 30s and 40s, and have a notable female readership. Many papers plough their profits back into social housing and related projects. While some criticize them for capitalizing on public sentiments against welfare by their 'hand-up, not a hand-out' image, they have nevertheless brought homelessness to a much wider citizenry and made them part of the European policy community on homelessness.

*How an understanding of homelessness in Europe can contribute to more effective policies in Britain*

FEANTSA and other European advocacy organizations concerned with homelessness have argued for a European policy response to homelessness. They do so for several reasons. First, because homelessness is a phenomenon which transcends national borders and has a relationship with international changes in the labour market and social protection, it could benefit from international measures, internationally applied. Second, advocates take the view that measures and responses to homelessness deployed in some countries could usefully be adapted to other countries. This can only be done by the sharing of information, experience, news and analysis at international, European level. Third, at a practical level, a European competence in housing would permit European Union financial instruments to be available to projects, activities and programmes concerned with the homeless. It would permit housing-based projects concerned with the homeless to be eligible for funding under such structural fund instruments as the European Social Fund, the European Regional Fund and the Community Initiative Programmes. Extending this argument further into the legal domain, a right to housing as an aspiration within the European treaties could do much to spur governmental and popular action against homelessness at all levels.

It is fair to record that this framework is not universally shared. The European housing ministers have collectively made it clear that housing policy is exclusively a national or sub-national concern. By contrast, those who have favoured a European Union competence in housing, and related homelessness policies, argue that their purpose is to add a European dimension, a European tier to the struggle against homelessness and poor housing, but not to replace decision-making in these areas at national and regional level. They acknowledge that housing policy will continue to be decided, and resources allocated, in the main by national and local governments. So far, their quest for such a European tier has made little headway and was not incorporated into the Treaty of Amsterdam, 1997.

Turning to national policies, the lessons which may be learned from the examples of other member states at first sight appear limited. The number of member states which appear to have policies which minimize or address homelessness are small in number. Only two states seem to have developed comprehensive policies against homelessness: Denmark, where a range of services may be acquired through the passport of the social security system; and France, with its co-ordinated, integrated and diversified programme of measures for the homeless. The *Loi Besson* (1990) combines, at least in theory, a number of key elements in the struggle against homelessness. These are the principle of the citizen's right to housing; a commitment to enhance the support and availability of diversified forms of accommodation through financial incentives; the principle of partnership of national government, local government, owners, tenants and local associations; the linking of housing provision to measures to help the rehoused to enter the labour force; requirements that local authorities submit plans as to how all this will be done; and the earmarking of special funds to support the operation of the law ( *fonds de solidarité logement*). To this list one might add another example: Germany's Federal Public Assistance Law (#72) lists advice and personal care services, employment and training as help which should be provided along with basic income assistance. This is the kind of approach which, if applied elsewhere, could make a difference to services for the homeless.

Such a government-led approach is unusual, but it does mean that one should not despair of the concept of government-led responses to the homeless. They do exist, although they are few and far between. Elsewhere, the inadequacies of official policies are more evident, but they point the way towards how official policies may be improved in those and other countries. First, there are inadequacies within specific policies – such as the failure to invest sufficiently in the public or social housing sector or to make specific social provision available for homeless persons. Secondly, there is a failure to co-ordinate policies across different spheres – such as housing, family support services, education and training, social security. A key reason for policy inadequacy is the failure to consult the voluntary sector sufficiently, where there rests a huge store of knowledge and experience about the nature of homelessness and how it can best be combated (Daly, 1992).

Negatively and positively, the European experience can indeed point the way towards the key ingredients of national policies on homelessness. This experience emphasizes the need for a clear national policy on homelessness, with resources and authority for its implementation delegated to the regional and local levels as appropriate. It indicates that integrated

responses are needed – responses that transcend conventional policy fron-
tiers and provide for the housing, economic, employment, social and
familial needs of all sectors of the population. They indicate the importance
of settlement services and the provision of housing, rather than temporary
shelter, for the homeless (Harvey, 1998). Strong governmental leadership
requires significant commitments of resources to services and towards
homeless people themselves in the form of income maintenance.

Like governments, NGOs have much to learn from each other from their
counterparts in other European countries. Some examples already exist.
The development of the *foyer* movement is one, for it follows ideas, practices
and experience developed in France. Although some people in Britain
disagree with the *foyer* movement and its approach, it represents a concrete
example of the application of one non-governmental approach, suitably
modified to take account of national differences, to another country.
FEANTSA's research of services for the homeless in Europe in 1991 found
a concentration on the meeting of immediate needs and inadequate
resources devoted to networking, campaigning, advocacy and the development of long-term policy perspectives. In some countries, some NGOs
provide an integrated range of services (shelter, information, reintegration,
documentation and lobbying). These provide a model for others, and there
is an argument which suggests that both governments and the voluntary
sector should favour and argue for NGOs which provide integrated services
rather than those which provide single elements in isolation. Related to
that, governments (and the voluntary sector) should support the development of those elements in NGO provision which are still weak and
underdeveloped, such as reintegrative services and those in the areas of
documentation and lobbying. NGOs which meet basic needs but which do
not confront the long-term consequences of homelessness may, ultimately,
exacerbate the very problems which they claim to meet. The high level of
homelessness in Europe may, at least in part, be a reflection of the failure of
NGOs to devote a higher level of their time, work and resources to lobbying,
information and documentation work.

*Conclusion*

From this overview of European homelessness, one reaches the following
conclusions. Homelessness is a severe problem within the European Union,
one associated with and linked to much larger issues of social exclusion,
poverty, unemployment and the appropriate role of the state in the late
20th century. A synthesis of views on the nature of homelessness has now
developed, albeit one based on imperfect information on homelessness and
considerable difficulties in standardizing such information. A policy community around homelessness now exists among the European networks and

in some key European institutions (e.g. the Parliament, the Commission), though intergovernmental approaches to homelessness have become frustrated by the myopic approach of national housing departments to the international, frontier-transcending nature of homelessness. Despite this difficult picture, there are many ways in which lessons learned from the European experience of homelessness may be fruitfully applied to individual national situations like Britain, both to improve the policies of governments towards the homeless and the role and record of non-governmental organizations.

## Note

1.  Homelessness is defined as 'the absence of a personal, permanent, adequate dwelling. Homeless people are those who are unable to access a personal, permanent, adequate dwelling or to maintain such a dwelling due to financial constraints and other social barriers and those people who are unable to access and maintain such a dwelling because they are unable to lead a fully independent life and need care and support but not institutionalisation' (Avramov, 1996, p. 71).

*Acknowledgments*

I wish to acknowledge, with thanks, comments on this draft received from Dr Dragana Avramov, Director of Research in FEANTSA (European Federation of National Organisations Working with the Homeless); from Professor David Clapham of the Centre for Housing Management and Development, Department of City and Regional Planning, University of Wales, Cardiff; and the guidance of Dr Susan Hutson of the School of Humanities and Social Sciences, University of Glamorgan. Their assistance is very much appreciated.

*References*

Avramov, D. (1995) *Homelessness in the European Union: Social and Legal Context of Housing Exclusion in the 1990s*, Brussels, FEANTSA.
Avramov, D. (1996) *The Invisible Hand of the Housing Market: A Study of the Effects of Changes in the Housing Market and Homelessness in the European Union*, Brussels, FEANTSA.
Daly, M. (1992) *European Homelessness: The Rising Tide*, Brussels, FEANTSA.
Daly, M. (1993) *Abandoned: A Profile of Europe's Homeless People*, Brussels, FEANTSA.
Daly, M. (1994) *The Right to a Home, the Right to a Future*, Brussels, FEANTSA.

Fitzpatrick, S. (1995) *Homelessness in the European Union,* paper presented to the European Network for Housing Research Working Group on European Integration and National Housing Policies held in Schloß Laudon, Vienna, 13–15 September 1995.

Harvey, B. (1998) *Settlement Services for the Homeless in Europe,* Dublin, Homeless Initiative.

*Appendix*

The most recent national figures for European homelessness are as follows

| Country | Numbers homeless on an average day | Numbers homeless in the course of a year |
|---|---|---|
| Austria | 6,100 | 8,400 |
| Belgium | 4,000 | 5,500 |
| Denmark | 2,947 | 4,000 |
| Finland | 4,000 | 5,500 |
| France | 250,000 | 346,000 |
| Germany | 490,700 | 876,450 |
| Greece | 5,500 | 7,700 |
| Ireland | 2,667 | 3,700 |
| Italy | 56,000 | 78,000 |
| Luxembourg | 194 | 200 |
| Netherlands | 7,000 | 12,000 |
| Portugal | 3,000 | 4,000 |
| Spain | 8,000 | 11,000 |
| Sweden | 9,903 | 14,000 |
| UK | 283,000 | 460,000 |
| | 1,133,011 | 1,836,450 |

*Source*: Based on Avramov, 1996, p. 77.

# 4 Homelessness: the media, public attitudes and policy making

*Mark Liddiard*

## Introduction

Homelessness has a long and distinguished media pedigree. Throughout the 19th century, for instance, vagrancy was a theme of regular media interest in both the UK and the USA (Hoch, 1987; Jones, 1982). More recently, the drama documentaries *Cathy Come Home* (1966), about a family becoming homeless and spending time in temporary accommodation, and *Johnny Go Home* (1975), about the risks facing a young man coming to London with nowhere to stay, provoked widespread public outrage and anger. Indeed, it has been claimed that *Johnny Go Home* was instrumental in the setting-up of a government Working Group (Beacock, 1979, p. 131), while Nick Raynsford, Labour's shadow housing minister, suggested that *Cathy Come Home* had a quite profound impact on public opinion, which in turn contributed to the passing of the 1977 Housing (Homeless Persons) Act (Raynsford, 1986, p. 44). In short, a number of commentators have been quite explicit in citing media coverage of homelessness as making an important contribution to raising its public profile and so promoting favourable policy responses.

Homelessness is certainly a topic of very considerable media interest and attention. For a number of reasons which I have highlighted elsewhere (Hutson and Liddiard, 1994, pp. 73–98), homelessness is a particularly media-friendly topic, offering – or more often than not being induced to offer – lurid tales of sex, drugs and violence which are the common currency of the press. In addition to the perennial media interest every Christmas, homelessness agencies and campaigning groups such as Shelter and CHAR have shown themselves to be particularly adept at attracting media coverage for many aspects of homelessness. Increasingly, agencies, pressure groups and even academics have attached much importance to securing favourable media treatment, often with a substantial degree of success and certainly with more success than has been gained in many other areas of social concern:

Increased awareness of the central importance of media coverage has convinced many pressure groups that they need to seek the aid of the media in order to achieve their aims. ... The belief that one ought to capture the media as a prerequisite to shaping perceptions and definitions of problems so as to win an argument has now filtered down from politicians to trade unionists to pressure and lobby groups. (Negrine, 1994, p. 139)

Yet this raises something of a paradox. Despite these largely successful moves to excite media interest and coverage, the scale of homelessness increased dramatically throughout the 1980s and housing was one of the areas to experience the full wrath of Thatcherite welfare restructuring and the diminution of state responsibility for welfare. This raises two questions. First, despite the growing importance that agencies attach to media coverage, what impact – if any – does this have on public attitudes towards homelessness? Second, what kind of influence – if any – does this media coverage have on policy making? In order to address these questions, the chapter is divided into three sections. The first seeks to examine the nature of the media and how homelessness agencies and campaigning groups perceive their roles. The second part examines the impact of media coverage on public attitudes towards homelessness. The final section then seeks to consider the various influences that media attention may, or may not have, on policy making.

## Homelessness agencies and the media

In the UK, single homelessness is generally dealt with by the voluntary sector, and voluntary agencies working with the homeless perceive themselves as fulfilling a number of roles. For many, their priority is the provision and supply of direct services for the homeless, which may take the form of accommodation and related support services, information and advice. Yet, as Saunders (1986) points out, many voluntary organizations are also faced with something of a dilemma between, on the one hand, providing the services for homeless people for which they were originally set up and, on the other, campaigning for the homeless in an effort to change, or at least modify, opinion. This is a quandary which some homelessness agencies are happier with than others, because adopting an explicit campaigning role can incur the wrath of politicians and lead to potential funding difficulties. This is a problem endemic to parts of the voluntary sector (O'Mahony,

1988). Nonetheless, many homelessness agencies, such as CHAR and Shelter, view their campaigning role as an increasingly important part of their work. In turn, they perceive the media as having an important, even crucial, role to play for a variety of different reasons:

The media are crucial to the agencies for the part their publicity can play in legitimising them and their version of the problem, gaining them resources and ensuring their survival. (Beresford, 1979, p. 152)

Moreover, there is often an explicit acknowledgement that the importance which homeless agencies and campaigning groups attach to cultivating the media and securing favourable media coverage is time and effort well spent:

The consciousness-raising and information activity of voluntary organisations has played an effective part, as it still does, in altering representations and attitudes among both politicians and the public. There tends to be a better grasp of the scope and social character of the problem. (Study Group on Homelessness, 1993, p. 105)

This is a bold statement, but although the Study Group on Homelessness present some very interesting cross-national evidence of the kinds of information campaigns being run by voluntary organizations in the UK and in the rest of Europe they present no evidence whatsoever about the impact which these information campaigns have had on public opinion or policy. One simply cannot assume that, because a myriad of voluntary agencies are engaged in promoting a more balanced view of homelessness, this has any impact whatsoever on either public opinion or policy. As Negrine (1994, pp. 142–3) notes, the assumption of a clear link between media content and the policies and decisions emanating from the policy process is a pervasive but nonetheless highly questionable one. Similarly, the Study Group on Homelessness (1993, p. 106) suggests that 'information and awareness-raising campaigns stemming from international initiatives have an even greater impact on public and governmental attitudes', citing the 1987 International Year of Shelter for the Homeless. The argument that these campaigns help to familiarize the public with the problem of homelessness and sustain political interest is certainly an interesting one. Again, however, the effect that these media and information campaigns actually have on public attitudes and the government remains inherently unclear. The first need is to understand more about the nature of these campaigns and the media themselves.

Of course, it is first important to recognize and acknowledge that the media are far from homogeneous. I have noted elsewhere (Hutson and Liddiard, 1994, pp. 73–89) that the content and style of presentation can vary dramatically between the press and television. Moreover, even if one is solely considering the role of the press, it is important to acknowledge that they, too, are far from homogeneous. On the simplest level, for instance, there is an obvious distinction between the tabloids and the broadsheets. In terms of the press influence on public opinion and policy making, this may be an important distinction (Negrine, 1994, p. 143), as the tabloids are more generally concerned with sport and scandal than pressing political issues, while policy makers themselves are more likely to be readers of the broadsheets which contain more detailed political coverage and comment. Of course, it is quite conceivable that the broadsheets only reflect a restricted and somewhat elite set of opinions and thoughts which in terms of reader numbers are likely to have less influence than that of the mass circulation papers. However, in light of the policy making process, the broadsheets may conceivably have a disproportionate impact.

What of television? Interestingly, it has been suggested by the Glasgow University Media Group that there is some real substance to the finding from opinion poll data that 70 per cent of people see the TV news as their most important channel of communication, although Dunleavy (1987, p. 87) has attached some reservations to this finding. However, it is difficult to say much with certainty about the role of television in the context of a social problem. Certainly, television can be seen to be important in terms of influencing the manner in which debates are conducted and I have already looked at the manner in which television deals with a social problem such as homelessness (Hutson and Liddiard, 1994, pp. 87–9). It is important to recognize, however, that political and social issues are often treated by television as if they were a form of public entertainment. This can certainly be useful and helpful for encouraging public interest in a topic such as homelessness, but it can nonetheless leave misconceptions and stereotypes as well as trivializing serious issues. Moreover, it may ultimately have little or no impact on opinions and attitudes, as we shall see. It is also important to acknowledge that the oft lauded neutrality of television coverage is somewhat mythical. Far from being some kind of objective and neutral presentation of the facts, television coverage is the consequence of a variety of subjective decisions. The style and content of television are ultimately set by the agendas of television journalists, although of course these journalists would argue that they are simply reflecting the views and value-systems of the society to which they are broadcasting. Nonetheless, there has been a long and on-going debate about the political objectivity of television in the UK (Eldridge, 1993, p. 5). The implication is an obvious one, because it means that only the ideas, notions and concepts which are consistent with pre-existing media agendas will be accepted and promoted. In this sense, although agencies may rightly or wrongly view the media as being in a position of enviable power to influence public opinion and policy making, these agencies must first subscribe to media agendas, in order to attract media interest, and may even need to modify or even prostitute their messages and concerns to do so. We shall see, for instance, that many journalists employ stereotypical images of the homeless because they make good copy. Importantly, homelessness agencies will often collude with such images in their enthusiasm to attain media coverage of the problem:

Much of the energy of the voluntary agencies is directed towards campaigning and fund-raising. They compete with other social causes and even among themselves for influence and resources. To command attention, they often present an alarmist picture of the extent and dangers of homelessness. The problem is packaged in black-and-white terms to ensure easy public assimilation and to provoke unambivalent feelings of anxiety, pathos and guilt. (Brandon *et al.*, 1980, p. 26)

As Waters (1982) notes, these efforts will often produce much needed finance, and donations will rise, particularly over the Christmas period, but the perpetuation of such stereotypical images may inadvertently serve to alienate the homeless further, and confirm the misapprehensions that people may already adhere to.

It is important to recognize that the media can provide a powerful source of communication, enabling issues to be conveyed to millions of people who may not otherwise have been involved or even particularly interested. Despite the criticisms that I have levelled at television, for trivializing important social problems and issues, the ability to reach and sensitize so many people to concerns such as homelessness is not to be minimized. The fact remains that homelessness agencies and researchers are often surprisingly successful in terms of securing extensive media coverage. Over the Christmas period, in particular, it is common to find a plethora of press articles about homelessness, as the press increasingly recognizes the newsworthiness of the topic. Moreover, extensive press coverage in turn increases the likelihood that television will run similar stories:

If three or four national papers run a major story it won't be ignored by TV news. . . . TV journalists operate completely within an overall climate of professional news values which is quite largely constituted by print journalists and newspaper output. (Dunleavy, 1987, pp. 86–7)

In this sense, therefore, if homelessness agencies and pressure groups are successful in attracting extensive press coverage, they can generally expect coverage by TV, with the extended audience and perceived neutrality that this media attention brings. This is obviously important because the myriad of media coverage with which policy makers are faced implies that a story in just one newspaper is unlikely to have any significant impact. In short, therefore, homelessness agencies and pressure groups are often remarkably successful in seeking and obtaining maximum publicity value from the media, certainly in comparison with other social problems. However, the relative success with which homelessness is able to attract the media's attention makes the relative inaction of policy makers all the more perplexing.

## The media and public attitudes towards homelessness

Before we look in more detail at the media impact on policy making, it will first be fruitful to consider the role of this coverage on public attitudes and opinion, because there is an evident relationship between the two:

The link between opinion or representations and policies or policy approaches is mutual. On the one hand, opinion is shaped by current policies. On the other hand, it shapes prospective policies. Consequently, representations, attitudes and policies can be interactively consolidated, so that the influence of the voluntary sector on public opinion and policies is highly important. (Study Group on Homelessness, 1993, p. 105)

Public attitudes towards the homeless is a notoriously nebulous area to delimit. Public opinion is profoundly heterogeneous – levels of knowledge and interest in social issues such as homelessness vary enormously. Nonetheless, a number of key points can and should be made, not least the importance of stereotypes. For many members of the public, homelessness is simplistically equated with 'rooflessness', which of course excludes many of the very groups that homeless agencies and campaigning groups are working with, such as the 'hidden homeless', people staying with friends temporarily for instance, squatters and those living in temporary accommodation such as bed and breakfast. Of course, there are a number of reasons for the promotion and maintenance of these stereotypes, not least the very profound difficulties with any agreed definition of homelessness (Greve et al., 1971; Watson, 1984; Bramley, 1988; Hutson and Liddiard, 1994). However, the visibility and conspicuousness of the roofless are also an element in the maintenance of these stereotypes and one which the media are frequently keen to exploit, for it contains so many of the elements of a good story. I have argued elsewhere that journalists often exaggerate those aspects of a social problem that are deemed to be the most newsworthy, such as sex and drugs, and that this is particularly pronounced in the field of homelessness (Hutson and Liddiard, 1994, pp. 81–3). The equation of the roofless with the homeless is easily understood by the public and, in a practical sense, the street homeless are relatively easy to find and to interview. As the manager of one homelessness advice centre explained to me:

It's when they become roofless ... that they become an image that can be understood by most people, because the image of a young person living in a squalid bedsit would be difficult to film ... but with these young people [the street homeless], you just send the cameras down.

The active promotion and endorsement of these stereotypes, however, is much more than simply an academic issue. On the contrary, simplistic images of homelessness are important in terms of their influence on public attitudes and policy making. Namely, they may minimize the scale of the homelessness problem that we are faced with and, importantly, they may simplify the complexity of the homelessness problem. This may lead to ill-informed and simplistic solutions and proposals, as well as stigmatizing the homeless as being somehow distinct from the rest of the population. This may arguably make it more difficult for the public to identify with the homeless (Study Group on Homelessness, 1993, p. 102). Certainly, one could convincingly argue that these stereotypes pervade discussions about the causes of and solutions to homelessness, which too often individualize the problem and are couched in simplistic terms of personal fecklessness and shirked responsibility. Undoubtedly, the manner in which issues such as homelessness are personalized by the media may serve effectively to depoliticize homelessness as a social problem. Indeed, these notions do permeate into the homelessness legislation, where a clear distinction is made between voluntary and involuntary homelessness and applications are consequently processed according to these notions of deservingness and undeservingness. Certainly, O'Mahony (1988, p. 2) feels strongly that the manner in which the media employ crude stereotypes in discussions about homelessness does have a detrimental impact on public attitudes towards homelessness, which are too often crude and misguided:

Some of this ignorance has to do with the way in which the young are portrayed. Newspapers, especially, latch on to a particular stereotype that is both visible and easy to define.

Of course, in any discussion of public attitudes, it is crucial to acknowledge that the media are just one of many varied influences on public opinion regarding homelessness, which may be mediated by personal experience, by that of friends and family, by education or by a myriad of other stimuli. In the words of C. Wright Mills (cited in Negrine, 1994, p. 3)

... men and women live in second-hand worlds. .... The quality of their lives is determined by meanings they have received from others. Everyone lives in a world of such meanings.

However, few would disagree that, with the advent of television, the public are exposed to the media more than ever before, such that the mass media have become fundamental to the way in which we understand the outside world. What is far more contentious, however, is the precise manner in which cultural audiences interpret and receive the myriad of messages and images that they receive.

This is an issue which has long concerned academic commentators, although there have been marked shifts in how they have approached the issue (Barrat, 1986, pp. 16–18; Curran and Seaton, 1991, pp. 249–76). One view – the so called 'hypodermic syringe' model – perceives the media as having a direct and inherently straightforward impact on the viewing audience. This view claims that media images are adopted in a straightforward and wholesale manner by the public. Certainly, this direct-effect model has had some impact on studies of the media, such as the effect of media violence, particularly on young audiences (Belson, 1978) and the effect of media images of women and sexuality (Ferguson, 1983; Tuchman, 1981). However, this model is now largely discredited because of the way in which it simplistically assumes that the audience passively and uniformly absorbs whatever media messages are presented to them.

Researchers have instead shown that the impact of the media on the public is more complex than the simple hypodermic syringe model assumes and is actually mediated by a number of factors. For example, the influence of neighbours and particularly 'opinion leaders' has been shown to be important in determining how media messages should be interpreted (Katz and Lazarsfeld, 1956). Similarly, Trenaman and McQuail (1961) showed that the public select and interpret the media according to their existing viewpoints. In other words, the public, far from being *passive* recipients of media messages, are actually highly *active* in their interpretation of the media messages and images with which they are presented. Morley (1980), for instance, showed that only those media messages which reinforced what individuals already believed were selected by the audience. Negrine (1994) speaks of the press *resonating with* rather than *affecting* the public. In this way, the same media item can be interpreted differently by different categories of people. Cumberbatch *et al.* (1986, p. 5), for example, found that after wide media coverage of the 1984–5 miners' strike in Britain, audience views as to what the strike was about varied considerably. The authors conclude that: 'While the public may have all watched the same news, they didn't all see it in the same way.' In terms of media coverage, this may mean that: 'The public audience is perfectly able to hear, but not really prepared to listen' (Forman, 1985, p. 113). The result is a mass public which is largely ill-informed of key social issues, and whose knowledge is only modified or mediated by media coverage on the basis of their own pre-existing agendas and misapprehensions. In short, the role of media coverage on public attitudes towards homelessness is far from encouraging. But what impact does media interest in homelessness have on policy making?

## The media and policy making

Does media coverage of homelessness and other social problems have a significant influence on policy makers, in promoting the importance of some issues over others? This is a difficult issue to address, for as Negrine (1994, p. 151) acknowledges, we know surprisingly little about the impact of the mass media on the decision-making process:

Publicity is a valuable asset but the issue of its 'effectiveness' still remains. Until we can find out more about how 'policy makers' view the media and what they do with information culled from the media, our knowledge will be based on circumstantial evidence and informed guesswork.

Nonetheless, one can begin to unravel the role of the mass media by considering the various influences on policy making and the role of the media within this. In terms of the initial stages of policy-germination, for instance, the key role of agencies operating as pressure groups, such as Shelter, is to identify issues and social problems and, crucially, place these issues onto the political agenda. Indeed, it is interesting to consider that, on occasions, these pressure groups have been actively encouraged to take part in the process of policy-formulation. A number of homelessness agencies, for example, found themselves involved in the genesis of the Rough Sleepers Initiative. However, *involvement* in the policy process is very different from *influence* and it was certainly the case that some of those consulted by the government felt that their involvement amounted to little more than a legitimation exercise – highlighted perhaps by the Director of Centrepoint's criticism of the Rough Sleepers Initiative shortly after he was invited to evaluate it (Randall and Brown, 1993). However, the potential importance of the media in being able to play a role in this process is clearly identified by a number of authors:

In playing their part at this early stage of the policy- and decision-making process, pressure groups depend very heavily on their ability to excite the interest of the media. Without such media assistance many of their campaigns would never get off the ground at all. (Forman, 1985, p. 86)

We have just seen that the impact of the media on public opinion is far from straightforward. However, even if we assume (and it is a large assumption) that the media coverage of an issue such as homelessness does have a widespread influence on public attitudes, this still leads us to consider the influence of public opinion on policy making. In a sense, of course, it is not surprising that politicians are often very sensitive to public opinion. After all, without public support, politicians would not be in office, and the importance of the electorate is paramount. However, we must acknowledge that this is a somewhat simplistic approach. Government can, and regularly does, ignore public opinion. For example, public opinion has been shown to be consistently opposed to rail privatization, and yet this has not proved to be a particular obstacle to the implementation of this policy. In part, this may be a consequence of the political system in the UK, where the government can be in a strong position of power even without the support of the majority of the voting electorate. Nonetheless, it would be erroneous to discount completely the role of public opinion and attitude in influencing policy. The Poll Tax fiasco was certainly one example where public opinion did, eventually, play a decisive role in modifying policy (Butler *et al.*, 1994).

The impact of public opinion on policy making is thus far from clear. Of course, there are instances and examples, such as the genesis of the Rough Sleepers Initiative, where media coverage and in turn public opinion may have had a decisive impact on policy formulation (Hutson and Liddiard, 1994, pp. 93–8). However, I would suggest that the key issue here was a forthcoming election and the perceived impact that detrimental media coverage of homelessness was having on public opinion, and in turn electoral behaviour. It is certainly very difficult to pinpoint accurately the effects of media coverage on legislative change. Even in relation to the two well-known drama documentaries, *Cathy Come Home* and *Johnny Go Home*, which undoubtedly did provoke public anger and concern, it is difficult to identify any concrete effect which they had on subsequent policy. Moreover, it is important to remember that media attention does not have a *consistent* impact on either public opinion or policy making. Rather, the influence of media coverage is, in some ways, mediated by the wider social context in which this coverage is taking place, a point outlined at length by Somerville (1994; see also Chapter 2). For example, Raynsford (1986) acknowledges that the significant impact of *Cathy Come Home* on public opinion was only as pronounced as it was because of what was happening to the housing market more generally – in particular, a growing acknowledgement that the slum clearance programmes of the 1960s were actually contributing to the rise in homelessness by displacing people whom the local authorities were then failing to rehouse. This may be an important point, because it is clear that the main perceived causes of homelessness at that time, namely the impact of slum clearance programmes and eviction by private landlords, were evidently not the responsibility of the homeless themselves. Of course, the same can be said in the 1990s – when the main causes of homelessness are clearly connected to dramatic changes in the housing market and the labour market – but the issue is one of public perception. Throughout the 1980s, for instance, discussions of homelessness frequently took place within the agenda set by the Conservative government, which was explicit in seeking to place the responsibility for the homeless directly onto the homeless themselves. As Margaret Thatcher herself said in Parliament, in response to evidence of increasing homelessness in London:

There is a number of young people who choose voluntarily to leave home; I do not think that we can be expected, no matter how many there are, to provide units for them. (*Hansard*, 7 June 1988, vol. 134, p. 713)

The impact which these approaches have had on public opinion is evidently open to discussion but it is nonetheless clear that these agendas and notions of individual culpability largely informed much media coverage and debate. In this sense, it is crucial to remember that the link between the media and policy making operates in both directions, with policy makers and politicians often playing a crucial role in terms of informing, even manipulating, the media (Broadbent, 1993; Miller, 1993). Certainly, it is clear that the needs of the homeless in general, and the single homeless in particular, are a low priority for the government, and this is highlighted by the 1996 Housing Act and the proposals contained within it (Williams, 1996; see also Chapter 8). When the public are overwhelmingly encouraged to view homelessness as a consequence of individual failure, and this is reflected by consequent media coverage, then we should not be unduly surprised if the media do not act as a vehicle for changes in public attitudes and the implementation of favourable policy responses.

It has been suggested elsewhere that the stereotypical representations of homelessness, paraded by the press, have had an important impact on policy. For instance, such coverage may play a role in informing policy responses when the homeless are seen as simply

... a blemish to be removed, a nuisance detrimental to the community's own self-image. This accounts for the administrative and police measures aimed at segregating the homeless and preventing their congregation, measures which as reported in Denmark have gone to the extreme of removing the benches from the public parks. (Study Group on Homelessness, 1993, pp. 103–4)

The parallels between this and the clearing of the Bullring in Waterloo, London in 1990 and the subsequent attempts to prevent homeless people from entering Lincoln's Inn Fields are striking. Moreover, it is evident that the homeless are increasingly being criminalized, as the 1994 Criminal Justice and Public Order Act have made the homeless a particular target for the Criminal Justice system. Yet this is despite the fact that homelessness is a social problem rather than a law and order issue. The way in which notions of personal fecklessness have permeated into homelessness policy is evident by the way in which homeless people are increasingly being dealt with by the Criminal Justice system, at considerable cost and to the obvious detriment of the homeless, while simultaneously the 1996 Housing Act seeks to restrict the priority given to homeless people (Williams, 1996). In short, policy responses to social problems such as homelessness may have less to do with media coverage and public opinion, and much more to do with wider political ideologies and agendas. In the words of Somerville (1994, p. 165): 'Media attention and public sympathy are not by themselves sufficient to produce policy change.' This is an important, even crucial, point because we have so far assumed that policy makers are rational social actors, unquestioningly accepting mass media accounts and willing to react to social problems as they are made aware of them. Yet this is evidently simplistic, and we must acknowledge that some policy makers may be unwilling to react to some social problems for ideological reasons, however much media attention is devoted to them. This is certainly the view of Ropers (1988, p. 189) in relation to the homelessness problem in the USA:

By the mid-1980s, the problem of homelessness was recognised as one of America's leading social problems. Despite this recognition, no coherent national response has been made by the federal government or most local governments. Instead, the issue of homelessness, while increasingly acknowledged, has become increasingly politicised. Because competing political and economic philosophies and policies understand the origin of the current homeless problem in conflicting terms ... there has been little consensus or concerted action to help the homeless.

For these reasons alone, it is probably fair to suggest that the media have only a limited impact on public opinion and policy making. After all, it is important to remember that policies are made in response to a variety of diverse pressures, of which agenda setting by the media is only one. This must surely limit the impact of even protracted and highly favourable media coverage. Nonetheless, it does seem clear that the media have an important role to play in terms of actually setting the parameters for policy debates about homelessness and, at least, playing a small part in framing policy discussions. In the words of Golding and Middleton (1979, p. 19), the mass media may:

... shape the political climate ... so that ultimately legislation and the overall allocation of resources are influenced by mass-mediated versions of priorities and necessities [and] they influence the cultural context ... by setting the tone for public discussion and providing the imagery and rhetoric ... [for] administrators.

The stereotypical portrayal of the homeless, often unquestioningly adopted by the media and in turn the public, undoubtedly plays an important role in terms of framing policy approaches to the problem. When discussions are couched in terms of the homeless being somehow different from main-stream society, the policy response invariably becomes one of distinctive and segregated assistance, with the homeless representing a particular burden on welfare and the economy which should be reduced.

This chapter has so far made somewhat depressing reading for those of us who are interested in the plight of the homeless and who would like to see homelessness move up the policy agenda. However, I want to end on a more positive and optimistic note. Namely, there is certainly some limited evidence to suggest that in some European countries, such as the Netherlands, voluntary organizations have been successful in encouraging a more rounded perception of homelessness as opposed to simply rooflessness (Study Group on Homelessness, 1993, p. 107). Similarly, in Britain, it is encouraging that the Housing Corporation is now acknowledging the need for a comprehensive special needs housing strategy for young people (Williams, 1996), while the Treasury has provided some £50 million for the Rough Sleepers Initiative, although the political motives for this attempt to minimize the highly visible problem of rooflessness are clearly questionable. Moreover, I noted earlier that the experience of *Cathy Come Home* suggests that media coverage, which is successful in terms of affecting changes in opinion or policy, is usually dependent on a favourable socio-economic context. I would suggest that such a favourable socio-economic context may be identifiable at the moment (see Chapter 5). In the UK, for instance, the rise and fall of the home ownership dream of the 1980s has left many feeling particularly insecure, compounded by the fact that approximately 1000 homes continue to be repossessed every week (Lowe, 1992; Forrest and Murie, 1994). Coupled with a widespread feeling of job insecurity, this situation could encourage more people to appreciate, empathize and identify with the problems of socio-economic exclusion and impoverishment, of which homelessness is an integral part. It may be, therefore, that the socio-economic context is ripe for homelessness agencies and campaigning groups to begin finally to shape a more rounded image and appreciation of homelessness in the minds of the public which can, in turn, influence policy. Ultimately, it is perhaps too easy to over-emphasize the potential impact of the media on public attitudes and policy making. The very real importance of the media may simply be in terms of modifying public perceptions of the homeless, and raising public consciousness of the problem which we face.

## References

Barrat, D. (1986) *Media Sociology*, London: Tavistock.

Beacock, N. (1979) 'Campaigning for the homeless and the rootless', in T.Cook (ed.) *Vagrancy: Some New Perspectives*, London: Academic Press.

Belson, W. (1978) *Television Violence and the Adolescent Boy*, Farnborough: Saxon House.

Beresford, P. (1979) 'The public presentation of vagrancy', in T. Cook (ed.) *Vagrancy: Some New Perspectives*, London: Academic Press.

Bramley, G. (1988) 'The definition and measurement of homelessness', in G. Bramley *et al.* (eds) *Homelessness and the London Housing Market*. Occasional Paper No. 32, School for Advanced Urban Studies, Bristol: University of Bristol.

Brandon, D., Wells, K., Francis, C. and Ramsay, E. (1980) *The Survivors: A Study of Homeless Young Newcomers to London and the Responses Made to Them*, London: Routledge.

Broadbent, L. (1993) 'Backyard on the front page: the case of Nicaragua', in J. Eldridge (ed.) *Getting the Message: News, Truth and Power*, London: Routledge.

Butler, D., Adonis, A. and Traders, T. (1994) *Failure in British Government: The Politics of the Poll Tax*, Oxford: Oxford University Press.

Cumberbatch, G., McGregor, R. and Brown, J. (1986) *Television and the Miners' Strike*, London: Broadcasting Research Unit.

Curran, J. and Seaton, J. (1991) *Power Without Responsibility: The Press and Broadcasting In Britain*, 4th edn, London: Routledge.

Dunleavy, P. (1987) 'The influence of the press', in M. Burch and M. Moran (eds) *British Politics: A Reader*, Manchester: Manchester University Press.

Eldridge, J. (1993) 'News, truth and power', in J. Eldridge (ed.) *Getting the Message: News, Truth and Power*, London: Routledge.

Ferguson, M. (1983) *Forever Feminine: Women's Magazines and the Cult of Femininity*, London: Heinemann.

Forman, F. (1985) *Mastering British Politics*, London: Macmillan.

Forrest, R. and Murie, A. (1994) 'Home ownership in recession', in *Housing Studies*, vol. 9, no. 1, pp. 55–74.

Golding, P. and Middleton, S. (1979) 'Making claims: news media and the welfare state', *Media, Culture and Society*, 1, pp. 5–21.

Greve, J., Page, D. and Greve, S. (1971) *Homelessness in London*, Edinburgh: Scottish Academic Press.

Hoch, C. (1987) 'A brief history of the homeless problem in the United States', in R. Bingham *et al.* (eds) *The Homeless in Contemporary Society*, Newbury Park, CA.: Sage.

Hutson, S. and Liddiard, M. (1994) *Youth Homelessness: The Construction of a Social Issue*, London: Macmillan.

Jones, D. J. V. (1982) *Crime, Protest, Community and Police in Nineteenth Century Britain*, London: Routledge.

Katz, E. and Lazarsfeld, P. (1956) *Personal Influence: The Part Played by People in the Flow of Mass Communications*, New York: Free Press.

Lowe, S. (1992) 'The social and economic consequences of home ownership' in J. Birchall (ed.) *Housing Policy in the 1990s*, London: Routledge.

Miller, D. (1993) 'The Northern Ireland Information Service and the media', in J. Eldridge (ed.) *Getting the Message: News, Truth and Power*, London: Routledge.

Morley, D. (1980) *The 'Nationwide' Audience*, London: British Film Institute.

Negrine, R. (1994) *Politics and the Mass Media in Britain*, 2nd edn, London: Routledge.

O'Mahony, B. (1988) *A Capital Offence: The Plight of the Young Single Homeless in London*, London: Routledge.

Randall, G. and Brown, S. (1993) *The Rough Sleepers Initiative: An Evaluation*, London: HMSO.

Raynsford, N. (1986) 'The 1977 Housing (Homeless Persons) Act', in N. Deakin (ed.) *Policy Change in Government*, London: Royal Institute of Public Administration.

Ropers, R. (1988) *The Invisible Homeless: A New Urban Ecology*, New York: Human Sciences Press.

Saunders, B. (1986) *Homeless Young People in Britain: The Contribution of the Voluntary Sector*, London: Bedford Square Press.

Somerville, P. (1994) 'Homelessness policy in Britain', *Policy and Politics*, vol. 22, no. 3, pp. 163–8.

Study Group on Homelessness (1993) *Homelessness*, Strasbourg: Council of Europe.

Trenaman, J. and McQuail, D. (1961) *Television and the Political Image: A Study of the Impact of Television on the 1959 General Election*, London: Methuen.

Tuchman, G. (1981) 'The symbolic annihilation of women by the mass media', in S. Cohen and J. Young (eds) *The Manufacture of News: Social Problems, Deviance and the Mass Media*, 2nd edn, London: Constable.

Waters, J. (1982) *The Nature of Single Homelessness*, Norwich: University of East Anglia.

Watson, S. (1984) 'Definitions of homelessness: a feminist perspective', *Critical Social Policy*, 11, pp. 60–73.

Williams, G. (1996) *Homelessness and the Law: A New Rights Agenda*, St Catherine's Conference Report 52, Windsor: King George VI and Queen Elizabeth Foundation of St Catherine's.

# 5 Home ownership, mortgage possession[1] and homelessness: public policies and private troubles?

*Janet Ford*

## Introduction

Throughout the 1980s and 1990s, successive governments have consistently presented home ownership as a success story. While this may be true for many households, what such statements do is to sweep to one side some uncomfortable issues. For example, since 1984, more than 510,000 households have lost their homes through the possession process and, moreover, mortgage arrears, while cyclical, have had a broadly upward trend in that, following each increase, they have not fallen back to their previously low level. The most recent, and highest ever, peak for possessions was in 1991, when 75,450 households lost their property. In 1996, the figure was 42,560.

When required to confront these issues, government spokespersons tend to present them as a 'one-off' crisis, the product of unlikely-to-be-repeated circumstances and 'under control'. The suggestion, presented in this chapter, is that the roots of these problems are more long-established, more entrenched and more persisting than such statements allow and that homelessness among owner occupiers is the albeit unplanned outcome of the interaction, over some time, of a number of public policies – housing policy, aspects of economic policy, labour market policies and policy towards social security provision. As will be indicated below, the precise interaction between this cocktail of policies is itself variable over time. Both the environment and the different policies shift, amplifying or containing the fundamental contradictions and tensions that result in mortgage default and potential possession, but not resolving them.

This chapter will consider two main issues. First, it will explore the emergence of mortgage arrears and possessions over the 1980s as influenced by a number of policy developments. Second, the limited public policy response to the growth of mortgage arrears and possession will be considered briefly. This will be contrasted with the extent to which, and the ways in which, the issues remain located in the market and, at the same time, operate as a private pre-occupation for the households concerned. Finally, by way of conclusion, some brief consideration will be given to the prospects for mortgage arrears and possessions.

## Mortgage default and possession: a policy 'own goal'?

It has been argued that social and economic policy in the 1980s was more ideological than had been the case for some time, concerned to promote self-reliance, to roll back the involvement of the state but also to control local government more effectively. Policy has aimed to develop and lubricate market processes through the mechanisms of privatization and de-regulation and, at the same time, to target and de-politicize welfare. These and other concerns shaped a wide range of policies, several of which impacted on home ownership and home owners.

## Housing policy

The expansion of owner occupation has been a policy objective of all post-war governments in Britain, but the election of a Conservative government in 1979 brought renewed vigour to this objective. In 1980, 53 per cent of households were home owners. In 1996, the figure was 67 per cent. This expansion coincided with a rise in the percentage of households who would 'most like to be living (in owner occupation) in two years' time' – from 69 per cent in 1975 to 81 per cent in 1995. The percentages who 'hoped to be living in (owner occupation)' in ten years' time rose from 62 to 85 per cent (BMRB, 1977–95) and so the expansion in home ownership is clearly meeting expectations with respect to tenure choice. Rising average incomes were one factor underpinning these preferences, but so too were notions of status and access to wealth (Saunders, 1990), alongside which there was both a growing restriction of, and growing disenchantment with, public rented housing (Cole and Furbey, 1994).

The expansion of owner occupation was assisted by the 1980 Housing Act which promoted further the (already existing) right of council tenants to buy their homes by ensuring substantial discounts and a right to a mortgage. Between 1980 and 1995, 1.4 million local authority homes were bought. Typically, it was the better properties, in good locations and with gardens which were bought by better-off tenants who were often middle-aged and in work (Forrest and Murie, 1990). This process, along with restrictions on local authority replacement building, reinforced the social and economic homogeneity of the sector that was increasingly seen as 'residualized' (Cole and Furbey, 1994).

## Financial deregulation

For most households, access to owner occupation has always been dependent on mortgage finance. Until the mid-1980s, there were considerable constraints on access to credit and mortgage rationing (hence the significance of the guarantee of a mortgage given to right-to-buy purchasers). Credit access was eased, however, by the Financial Services Act 1985 and the Building Societies Act 1986, which deregulated the credit market(s). This brought additional players into the market, increased competition and led to a substantial relaxation in lending, as borrowers were now sought rather than rejected. The number of advances to first-time mortgage borrowers rose rapidly from 318,000 in 1981, increasing each year until 1986, when 619,000 such advances were made.

Easier credit, pent-up demand and a reduced stock of local authority housing acted together to fuel house price inflation. This in turn acted as a pressure on those who were considering home ownership to buy before prices rose further and, given the inelastic nature of housing supply, additional entrants reinforced the price rises.

One further policy was also significant. During the 1980s, mortgagors were eligible for tax relief on the interest on the first £25,000 (subsequently increased to £30,000) of their mortgage (MIRAS). Where two 'unrelated' people bought together, they were eligible for double MIRAS. One effect of this policy was to bring owner occupation within the reach of some additional people, but there was also a debate as to the extent to which MIRAS encouraged buyers to buy to the interest limit, as well as concern in some quarters that MIRAS was both a substantial and indiscriminate subsidy to owner occupiers. Clearly, housing policy was not neutral with respect to tenure (Kemeny, 1981) and MIRAS created a further incentive to own. However, the debate around MIRAS, and mounting evidence of a runaway housing market, led Nigel Lawson, in April 1988, to announce that double MIRAS would be scrapped – but in three months' time. This merely led to yet another scramble to get into the housing market and further upward pressure on house prices.

One of the major consequences of the changes outlined above was to draw into owner occupation households with lower incomes and/or less secure employment. For example, between 1979 and 1991, the proportion of mortgagors in the bottom income decile increased from 11 per cent to 27 per cent (before housing costs were taken into account). By 1991, 59 per cent of skilled manual workers had a mortgage, compared to 32 per cent in

1979. Among semi-skilled and unskilled workers the growth was from 9 per cent to 42 and 25 per cent respectively.

On average, for first-time buyers, and comparing 1981 and 1991, the average advance as a percentage of house prices rose from 79.1 to 82.7 per cent; the average advance to average income increased from 1.74 to 2.21 and average repayments, as a percentage of average income, rose from 15.8 to 24.7 per cent. Thus, households entering owner occupation in the late 1980s were particularly stretched, and increasingly so, the lower down the income scale they were, given that it was this group which had the highest average percentage of income committed to mortgage costs of all mortgagors.

### Safety net provision for mortgagors

Owner occupiers have always had a lower risk of unemployment than tenants, in part because, until the late 1970s, home ownership was primarily a white collar tenure but also because of the traditional entry criteria adopted by lenders – a deposit and limited income multiples on loans. Even into the 1980s, the extent to which a female working partner's income was taken into account ranged from not at all to a little. However, as a result of the policies implemented in the 1980s and noted above (primarily financial deregulation and right to buy), a higher proportion of mortgagors were *potentially* 'at risk' of any downturn in the economy.

The potential risk was, to some extent, mitigated by the state safety net provided to those eligible to claim income support (previously supplementary benefit), which was first introduced in 1948 and which met the claimant's mortgage interest payments (ISMI). However, there has never been any in-work, means-tested support for home owners who suffer a reduction in income (as opposed to a complete cessation) such as can occur as a result of a reduction in hours of work, changes to incentive or commission payments or who face an increase in housing costs as a result of an interest rate rise. In this respect, there is no benefit for in-work mortgagors comparable to housing benefit available to tenants.

The safety net for mortgagors has twice been restricted since 1987, although it was always limited in the situations it addressed. First, in 1987, the payment of mortgage interest from the start of an eligible income support claim was limited to 50 per cent for the first 16 weeks with payment in full thereafter. The second occasion was in October 1995 when more draconian restrictions were imposed. The principal changes were, for existing borrowers, a qualifying period of two months, followed by four months of 50 per cent interest payments before full interest might be met. Other changes capped the size of eligible loan to £100,000 and introduced a standardized rate of interest. For borrowers entering owner occupation after October 1995, no help was available for the first nine months of an income support claim. As will be seen below, these changes were a response to both financial and ideological concerns.

## The turning of a boom

For much of the 1980s, the expansion of owner occupation looked not only unproblematic but appeared to be a major social, economic and political success. The rise in house prices made people feel better-off and many used the increase in the value of their properties to fund other activities – leisure and consumption goods, home improvements and business expansion – by withdrawing equity. However, the processes outlined above, rising demand, expanding credit and house price inflation all contributed to the rising level of inflation and the intervention of the government in 1988 to curb the economy, in general, by increasing interest rates. This intervention coincided with the point at which personal indebtedness peaked, either as a result of households having to borrow substantially to gain housing, particularly towards the end of the 1980s, or due to households withdrawing equity.

Between 1988 and 1990, already heavily committed households faced mortgage interest rate rises from 9.5 per cent (May 1988) to 15.4 per cent (February 1990). Over the same period, average weekly mortgage costs in the UK rose from £37.83 to £60.39. In addition, rising interest rates slowed the economy and contributed to the ensuing recession which impacted on the labour market in the form of rising unemployment, but also contributed to the collapse in the housing market. The phrase 'from boom to bust' was used to capture the housing market experience.

## A recessionary labour market

Unemployment began to rise in 1989, first in the south east of the country, then spreading out. Unlike most previous recessions it affected both white and blue collar workers. Unemployment among mortgagors increased to five per cent in 1993 although manual worker mortgagors were still twice as likely as white collar mortgagors to be unemployed. Cyclical factors were clearly important in the growth of unemployment, but so too were more long-standing structural changes in the labour market that were becoming clearer (Beatson, 1995; Gregg and Wadsworth, 1995) and which were resulting in the growth of part-time work, temporary working and self-employment, much of which was lower paid, less secure and so resulting in higher employment turnover.

These developments, and particularly the increasing rate of unemployment, as well as small business failure and reductions in income from commission-based jobs, added to the difficulties in many households. As is discussed in more detail below, one in five mortgagors reported that they experienced financial difficulties during this recessionary period. The later they had entered the market in the 1980s, the more stretched were their finances and so the more vulnerable they were to recessionary forces.

## A depressed housing market

The housing market was badly affected by interest rate policies and the ensuing recession (see Forrest and Murie, 1994 for a developed discussion). Average house prices fell nationally, with the process starting in the south east, where the largest falls were experienced, but few regions escaped the phenomenon of negative equity. At the height of the crisis, estimates of the number of households owing more than their property was worth ranged from over a million to almost two million. The number of transactions fell dramatically. The absence of buyers trapped those who were free to sell while growing numbers could not contemplate selling because of their level of indebtedness (Forrest and Kennet, 1996).

## Mortgage arrears and possession

The outcome of the policies of expanding owner occupation and de-regulating the financial markets, introduced in the early 1980s, alongside the policy interventions in the late 1980s which raised interest rates and restricted the safety net for mortgagors, resulted in a rapid increase in the number of households who could not meet their monthly mortgage payments. In addition, a substantial percentage of mortgagors reported that they had 'problems' in meeting their payments.

A national survey of mortgagors showed that, between 1991 and 1994, around one in five of all mortgagors had experienced some difficulties with their mortgage payments. Table 5.1 shows the nature of these experiences.

On a year-by-year basis, the changes in the number of borrowers reported by lenders to be owing two or more months' payments can be seen from Table 5.2. While not shown on the table, the incidence of arrears peaked in 1992, when approaching a million mortgagors were in arrears.

The fall in house prices and the low number of housing transactions blocked one means of adjustment traditionally used by borrowers with actual or potential financial difficulties – namely selling and moving to a smaller property or out of owner occupation and into the rental sector.

Table 5.1 Payment difficulties and arrears

| Reason | % |
|---|---|
| No arrears but current payment problems | 9 |
| Arrears previously and no current problems paying | 3 |
| Arrears previously and currently facing problems paying | 3 |
| Arrears previously and again in arrears | 1 |
| In arrears for the whole of the past three years | 1 |
| Fallen into arrears for the first time in the previous three years | 3 |

*Source*: Ford, Kempson and Wilson (1995).

Table 5.2 Mortgage arrears and possessions 1980–96

| Year | 1980 | 1985 | 1987 | 1989 | 1991 | 1993 | 1995 | 1996 |
|---|---|---|---|---|---|---|---|---|
| Number of mortgages at year end (000) | 6,210 | 7,717 | 8,283 | 9,125 | 9,185 | 10,137 | 10,510 | 10,510 |
| Possessions during year | 3,480 | 19,300 | 26,390 | 15,810 | 75,540 | 58,540 | 49,410 | 42,560 |
| Cases in mortgage arrears | | | | | | | | |
| 12+ month arrears | – | 13,120 | 14,960 | 13,840 | 91,740 | 151,810 | 85,200 | 67,020 |
| 6–12 month arrears | 15,530 | 57,110 | 55,490 | 66,800 | 183,610 | 164,620 | 126,670 | 100,960 |
| 3–5 month arrears | – | 97,000 | 121,000 | 122,000 | 305,500 | 242,050 | 179,050 | 152,710 |
| 2 month arrears | – | 140,000 | 164,400 | 153,900 | 269,800 | 198,400 | 119,751 | 148,350 |

*Sources*: Housing Finance, Council of Mortgage Lenders and J. Ford, *Roof* (figures for 2 and 3–5 month arrears). Author's analysis.

*Notes*: Properties taken into possession include those voluntarily surren-dered. 6–12 and 12+ months arrears are for the end of the year. 2 and 3–5 months arrears figures are for the March of the year. Changes in the mortgage rate have the effect of changing monthly repayments and hence the number of months in arrears which a given amount represents.

Evidence indicates that, towards the end of the 1980s, around nine per cent of movers had moved for this reason (Dodd and Hunter, 1990). The restrictions to the social security safety net also exacerbated the difficulties, even of those who were eligible to enter a claim. Thus, while the numbers claiming rose substantially to peak at 550,000 in 1993, among those able to claim ISMI only three out of ten received the full amount of their mortgage interest (Ford *et al.*, 1995).

Table 5.2 indicates that, for many households, arrears were not just a limited, short-term experience but that the incidence of longer-term arrears was substantial. Several factors contributed to this situation, including the delayed response of many lenders to the emergence of arrears. Thus, while the problem was growing in the late 1980s, many lenders did not review their polices, practices and commitment towards arrears management until 1991 or 1992. By this time, a growing proportion of borrowers had sizeable arrears.

Traditionally, the response to long-term arrears, on the part of borrowers and lenders, had been a mixture of either an attempt to sell the property or the return of the property to the lender through the possession process. Many borrowers, made homeless by this process, could apply to the local authority to be rehoused on the grounds of homelessness. As noted above, selling became increasingly difficult while allowing possessions to rise was also problematic. If the pre-1991 approach, whereby cases of 12 or more months arrears were typically 'solved' by taking possession, had continued to be used, possessions in 1992 would have run at over 200,000. The repercussions of this for the lenders, local authorities, central government and the already depressed housing market were deemed unacceptable and, during 1991, lenders began to hold back from entering possession proceedings (Lord Chancellor's Department, 1992). As it was, a predicted figure for 1991 of approaching 80,000 possessions resulted in emergency talks between the lenders and the government and agreement about a raft of initiatives. These included the payment of ISMI direct from the DSS to the lender, protection for borrowers in receipt of ISMI, the implementation of maximum forbearance as well as the development of 'mortgage rescue' schemes which would facilitate 'tenure transfer' whereby mortgagors could become tenants without moving home. In addition, the government launched a Housing Market Package whereby housing associations could take blocks of possessed properties on short leases and bring them into the rental sector, thereby precluding any further detriment to the housing market and providing housing for homeless households.

Details of the proposals, noted above, are outlined further in Foster, 1992; Ford and Wilcox, 1992; and Wilcox and Williams, 1996. These, and other reports (Ford *et al.*, 1995), have also provided some evaluation of the impact of the initiatives. But two points are worth noting at this juncture. First, there must be doubt as to the extent to which the response can be deemed a 'public policy' response and, second, with possessions still remaining at around 42,500, it is difficult to accept the validity of the official claims made for the initiatives such as the then Prime Minister's comments in late 1991 that, following the agreements with lenders, 'the repossessions crisis has been solved'. Table 5. 2 indicates that this assessment was both flawed and complacent. Since that time (1992), a further 275,000 households have lost their properties.

## A public policy response?

Faced with the difficulties in the housing market, particularly possessions, and also surrounded by hostile comment on this issue from both the press and a wide range of agencies, the government's response was limited. There were no immediate changes to policy with respect to assistance to homeless households, no funding was available to pump prime or sustain mortgage rescue, and the Housing Market Package, which was designed to help organizations to acquire and rent out houses in possession, was both time and cash limited. All this suggests a tactical rather than strategic intervention. The introduction of the payment of ISMI direct from DSS to lenders was an administrative change, but it did not represent a substantive change of policy. In practice, responsibility for responding imaginatively to the situation was left with lenders, borrowers and the courts where district judges sometimes exercised their discretion in ingenious ways to assist borrowers (Ford et al., 1995). For a contrary view on the role of judges see Nixon and Hunter (1996). This was still the case in 1996. Despite having courted the home owner, the government, in line with its market orientation, has left any resolution of the problem to the market, and this can be seen not only with respect to arrears and possessions, but also for other housing market developments such as the emergence of negative equity.

The evaluations of the initiatives indicate their varying impact. By December 1993, only eight per cent of lenders had instituted mortgage rescue schemes (although some had already withdrawn from this activity by December 1993) and, while 700 borrowers had been enabled to remain in their homes as tenants, possessions and serious arrears remained high. Much of the potential of mortgage rescue faltered in the face of financial, legal and managerial constraints (Ford et al., 1995). In addition, a substantial proportion of borrowers, who might have been assisted, were less than enthusiastic about becoming tenants, or rather, tenants in homes they had previously 'owned'. Most lenders have now withdrawn from mortgage rescue, although by 1995, approaching 2,000 households had been rehoused (Wilcox and Williams, 1996). ISMI payment 'direct' is now established practice, but the assumption behind its introduction – that the absence of direct payment resulted in a substantial percentage of recipients withholding the money from their lenders, thus creating or worsening arrears – proved to have little, if any, substance (Ford and Wilcox, 1992; Ford *et al.*, 1995). Rather, the structure of the safety net itself is the issue (Ford and Griffith, 1994). Various schemes, including the Housing Market Package, appear to have made almost 11,000 possessed dwellings available for rent between 1991 and 1994 (Wilcox and Williams, 1996). But by far and away the greatest impact on stemming possessions has come from lenders' restructuring of forbearance, although the consequence of this has been the substantial and persistent level of long-term arrears.

Finally, the evidence on the rehousing of households which are homeless as a result of mortgage arrears and possession shows that, over the period 1991 to 1995, the percentage of such households being rehoused by the local authorities under the legislation has been falling (Ford, 1997). This finding is, in part, accounted for not only by the characteristics of those giving possession and the not unrelated balance between voluntary and compulsory possession, but also by the unwillingness of those offered rehousing to accept bed and breakfast or hostel accommodation. Frequently, anxieties are expressed about the impact of such accommodation upon children and/or adult relationships and these anxieties have been sharpened by the reduction in the local authority stock consequent on right to buy and the constraints on building new stock. So, for a variety of reasons, an increasing percentage of households losing their property through mortgage possession are taking responsibility for their own rehousing.

Thus, the advent of mortgage arrears and possession has not resulted in any significant constructive adjustment to either housing policy or social security policy. Indeed, it could be argued that public policy changes have worsened the outlook for households in financial difficulties. Changes introduced to social security policy, with respect to ISMI in October 1995, potentially worsened the position of mortgagors who lose all income (Birch, 1995; Burchardt and Hills, 1997; Ford *et al.*, 1997). Recent budgets have cut heavily into social housing provision (Roof, 1996), potentially reducing the availability of both temporary and permanent re-housing for homeless households. The implementation of the 1997 Housing Act, with respect to its homelessness provisions, represents yet further detriment. The area of public policy development, with regard to the court process, where changes more supportive of indebted households are potentially likely, is discussed in the Woolfe Report (Woolfe, 1996).

**Mortgage arrears and possessions: a personal trouble?**

Early research on arrears and possessions, typically spanning the period of the late 1970s to the mid-1980s, often highlighted the extent to which societal attitudes to debt embodied the individualistic assumption that debtors were in that position because they were, at best, poor managers and, at worst, feckless. Individuals and households were therefore viewed as personally responsible for a large part of their situation (Rock, 1973). Further, the evidence indicated that those in default, including mortgagors, typically internalized these views. Although they recognized that structural factors had played a part in determining their current circumstances (particularly unemployment), they also believed that, as a result of their own actions, they were culpable. This situation, and its consequences, were noted by Adler and Wozniack (1981, p. 232) as follows:

... the only surprising feature of the default debtor's perceptions is the extraordinary extent to which they had internalised the prevailing view that default is associated with incompetence. This must be quite a psychologically damaging position to hold ... only partially offset by the belief that default can be attributed to bad luck ... default debtors ... attribute [their] circumstances to bad luck rather than any structural aspect of society.

More recent studies suggest that there may have been some change in attitudes to default. First, with respect to the views of those in mortgage default, Davis and Dhooge (1993) for example, contrast the earlier individualistic emphasis with a growing belief, among those with arrears, that they are 'victims' of government policy and thus not personally culpable. More generally, Maclennan (1994) notes the extent to which mortgagors now know someone else who is experiencing default. This, alongside the evidence that one in five households experienced some problems in meeting their mortgage payments between 1991 and 1994, also adds to the likelihood that the appreciation of default, particularly its likely causes and locus of responsibility, might also have changed. However, there is still no major sample survey available against which to test these indications from more qualitative research.

Whatever the extent of the change in societal attitudes to default, which potentially might reduce the extent to which the issue is seen as having an individual 'cause', recent studies of households with mortgage arrears, or giving up possession, also indicate the continuing salience of other processes. In particular, they indicate that the experience of arrears and possessions is one that continues both to stigmatize and exclude socially. These two factors contribute to the continuing reality of arrears as a personal trouble. Further, recent studies also explore some of the consequences of the limited public policy response by examining the ways in which individuals and households themselves develop and experience 'solutions' to their housing difficulties, in the context of the complex interplay of the housing system, including the actions of lenders, courts and the local authorities. The remainder of this chapter takes up these themes and considers the extent to which, and ways in which, arrears and possessions are still experienced as isolating, stigmatizing, private and personal matters. The evidence discussed comes from a series of studies of borrowers in arrears, and giving up possession, published in the 1990s (for example, Jenkinson, 1992; Davis and Dhooge, 1993; Ford, 1993; 1994; Ford *et al.*, 1995), as well as from studies of over-indebtedness in non-mortgage areas (for example, Parker, 1987; Bradshaw and Holmes, 1989; Berthoud and Kempson, 1992). These studies are either directly quoted or contain material supportive of the arguments put forward here.

## Stigmatizing?

Many households in default report that they feel discredited and embarrassed by their arrears and the potential loss of their home. Many believe that others will view things this way too and these beliefs constitute pressures to restrict any knowledge of arrears and the potential loss of the property to the household concerned. This stance could be thought questionable in the light of the suggestion above that attitudes to default may now be less individualistically oriented, although, as already noted, the extent and nature of attitude change are as yet poorly researched.

Clearly, there is likely to be a relationship between the nature of wider societal attitudes to debt and the extent to which debt stigmatizes, although in the long run there is an expectation that the two will be relatively well aligned. However, attitudes to debt may differ between different groups and, even if they are gradually changing in the same direction, they may do so at different rates. Equally, it may be important to distinguish between a recognition that default is essentially a product of structural, macro-economic processes and a recognition that the *processes* surrounding the management of arrears and possession, and the consequences of default, are ones that still discredit or embarrass in some way. There is, for instance, a debate about the extent to which owner occupation remains a valued 'positional' good, given the rapid growth in home ownership. Notwithstanding the expansion of owner occupation, which may have altered the status of home ownership, many mortgagors would regard movement into the rental sector as downward mobility and evidence of some failure to maintain a socially valued status. Despite everything that has happened in the housing market in the 1990s, as noted towards the beginning of this chapter, over four-fifths of households still aspire to owner occupation within two years. Equally, negotiations with lenders, the court process and the process of having to apply for rehousing on the grounds of homelessness might well, of themselves, be seen as personally discrediting – merely through having to make public the tangle of one's circumstances, which risks a judgement. Norms relating to the discussion of personal financial matters still stress the impropriety of doing so, although less so when related to 'success' than 'failure'.

Evidence from qualitative research indicates several ways in which households feel their debts discredit or embarrass them – either signified through the response of others and/or felt keenly by themselves:

If I knew our family knew the extent of our debts, and his family, I wouldn't be able to handle it. All the time I know they're ignorant of our situation I'm OK. But I couldn't . . . I'd be so embarrassed. That's half the reason we don't tell them. (Davis and Dhooge, 1993, p. 69)

I didn't want to admit I couldn't afford it . . . it would have been humiliating. (Davis and Dhooge, 1993, p. 69)

Other individuals highlighted the ways in which, once they had managed to set up repayment arrangements with lenders, their ability to maintain them was often fragile. Survey data, drawn from borrowers and lenders, indicates that, among borrowers in default who make a repayment agreement (around three-quarters), about a third do not maintain the agreement (Ford *et al.*, 1995). Thus a substantial minority of borrowers often have to provide explanations as to why they have 'failed' to make the payments which they have agreed and promised to meet. Others felt they had to 'grovel' to gain agreement from lenders:

You make one payment, then you fall back again. You can't pay it. And I know they say whatever happens you still keep in touch with them. But it gets more of an embarrassment in the end. (Davis and Dhooge, 1993, p. 21)

I had to . . . say [agree with the lender] a little bit more than we could afford. And on each occasion we'd pay a few payments . . . and then we'd get behind again. . . . Then I'd be back on the phone . . . grovelling for another arrangement. (Davis and Dhooge, 1993, p. 78)

Mortgage possession (but not arrears) may also stigmatize borrowers in other ways, not least because those possessed through the courts are listed as in receipt of a County Court Judgment. There is also a possession register operated by the Council of Mortgage Lenders which covers households in both compulsory and voluntary possession. The former register is publicly available. Both registers could have damaging implications for households – their entry to the private rented sector could be jeopardized (depending on landlords' attitudes), their access to personal credit will be restricted and, in some circumstances, their employment prospects constrained (Ford and Wilson, 1994). Access to a number of key resources is therefore circumscribed because the existence of debt is perceived as both discrediting and as raising questions about the individual's reliability.

## Socially excluding?

Borrowers in arrears, between 1991 and 1994, owed on average £2,500, although the range was wide and one in ten reported that they owed more than £5,000 (Ford *et al.*, 1995). In addition to attempting to repay these arrears, many borrowers were also expected to meet their routine monthly payments (after some time if not initially) which were, on average, higher than for non-arrears borrowers. Those with arrears and in possession also had lower average incomes (*Survey of English Housing, 1994/5*). The financial circumstances of those in arrears were therefore 'tighter' than non-arrears borrowers. A search for economies characterizes many of the accounts of those in arrears and the key economies identified relate to reductions in the kind and amount of food consumed, curtailment of leisure activities, holidays, the purchase of clothes and allowing insurance payments to lapse.

Many of these economies, in turn, led to a reduction in social contacts and exclusion from social activities:

We used to go out now and again because we were in a club, but we hardly ever do that now ... I wouldn't want to go out because I can't do it as I would like to. I can't mix with anyone. I can't afford to. (Ford, 1995, p. 29)

In another instance, a borrower, who lived in an isolated area, had had to give up her car in order to economize. She commented:

I rarely leave the house ... it's like being a prisoner in your own home. (Ford, 1995, p. 24)

But the distribution of exclusion varies within households, with children being protected from this process wherever possible. Thus expenditure on goods to ensure the children did not suffer vis-à-vis their peers at school (clothes, accessories and outings) or at Christmas was often maintained even if it had to be funded through credit-based catalogues (Oppenheim and McEvaddy, 1987; Daly and Walsh, 1988):

We used to buy shirts and shoes without thinking about it, but now you have to think of the kids and try and make sure if anyone gets anything it's them. (Ford, 1995)

I didn't mind having to cut back ... but I won't have the boys go without. I'd do anything rather than let them go without. (Davis and Dhooge, 1993, p. 66)

There is also some evidence that, in a minority of instances and under certain circumstances, men retain their ability to socialize and so are less socially excluded than women (Ford, 1988; Parker, 1987). Such cases as have been reported have been associated with households where there appears to be a differential commitment to owner occupation (with male partners less committed to owning in the first place and less committed to retaining the home) or where women manage the household's budget and are reluctant to reveal the situation to their partner. In the majority of instances, however, mortgage default results in a more restricted social life on both material grounds and through the processes of stigmatization. As one household expressed it:

We hardly see anyone now, you have to be very careful who you talk to, they think you're no good. (Ford, unpublished fieldnotes, 1995)

## Individualized outcomes

One consequence of the lack of any developed public policy response to arrears and possessions, and the emphasis on market responses is that market players, in the form of lenders, can and do treat borrowers in different ways, even when their circumstances and situations are broadly comparable. Recent research, which explored the perspectives and responses of both borrowers and lenders (Ford *et al.*, 1995), indicates the variety of responses among lenders, with respect to the nature of their arrears management. Lenders varied, for example, in the number of times they would re-negotiate repayment agreements with borrowers, the point at which they took the case to litigation and the level of arrears which triggered this response. Borrowers with different lenders faced different scales of charges for the same 'services' – such as a letter, re-negotiating an agreement, changing the locks on possessed property, legal fees for court-related work, etc. Lenders also varied as to whether or not they would pursue borrowers for any residual debt following a possession sale.

These variations in lenders' practice, which produce variations in outcomes for borrowers, are informed by a wide range of influences. These include the perceived attitude of the borrower, which leads to lenders differentiating between 'deserving' and 'undeserving' debtors (Ford *et al.*, 1995), the assessment of whether their circumstances provide a realistic chance that the arrears will be repaid, the extent of equity in the property as well as a set of business values and business objectives. Further, borrowers entering a financial agreement with a lender are unlikely to have any information about their lender's arrears management policy, even as it operates at that point in time (Whitehead, 1996). They therefore have no basis for identifying and selecting lenders who might adopt more, as opposed to less, supportive polices and practices from the borrowers' point of view. The consequences for individual borrowers are therefore potentially inequitable outcomes vis-à-vis some other borrowers.

Finally, brief mention can be made of the extent to which the rehousing process, following possession, remains an individual responsibility. As noted earlier, less than half of those losing their homes through the possession process are rehoused in the first instance following acceptance as 'officially' homeless, and hence the majority of households giving possession are officially 'unrecognized' as homeless (Ford, 1997). Research shows that such households are heavily reliant on the private rented sector, but that they experience considerable mobility, moving from place to place in response to both landlords' actions and their own, in the face of unsuitable accommodation (Ford *et al.*, 1995). The search process, along with securing the means of access (deposits and/or rent in advance), is typically undertaken without assistance. Two-thirds of the households close to or at the point of possession and seeking advice from local authorities (who now have a responsibility for providing such advice) reported that they were merely told what their position would be with regard to local authority rehousing, but not about the wider range of housing available.

## Conclusions and discussion

This chapter has sought to indicate the ways in which the substantial growth in mortgage arrears and possessions, and the homelessness associated with these developments, is largely rooted in public policy developments. In particular, aspects of housing policy, policies to de-regulate the financial markets, social security and labour market policy, along with fiscal interventions, have all contributed to the increasing unsustainability of owner occupation for a growing number of households. The response to these developments, however, shows little by way of a public policy dimension. Rather, the policy is to leave the response to the market and its individual players.

It is uncertain whether, and to what extent, societal attitudes to debt (and so to mortgage default) are changing and, perhaps moving away from notions of individual culpability. But households with such debts continue to report their situation as one which they perceive as stigmatizing and, where the lack of state assistance for most defaulters requires them to put in place stringent economic regimes of mounting social isolation. Borrowers bear the experience and the costs of default individually, as a personal trouble, even in those cases where they themselves reject the idea of personal culpability. In this sense, more recent research continues the themes of earlier studies.

Faced with persistent problematic ownership, and a reliance on the market to resolve the difficulties, this chapter concludes with a brief consideration of the nature and impact of market responses and the likely continuation of arrears and possessions. Providing protection from arrears and possessions is seen as one area where the private insurance market can play an important role, and the restrictions on ISMI, introduced in October 1995 by the government, were explicitly linked to this expectation. However, although mortgage payment protection policies have been widely available since the early 1980s, take up is still only around 15 per cent of all mortgagors, although closer to 30 per cent among new borrowers (Ford and Kempson, 1997). Such policies are unnecessarily costly (Burchardt and Hills, 1997) and cover only a limited number of specified events (unemployment, accidents or sickness). Currently, between 20 and 25 per cent of claims are also rejected, and there is a significant cancellation rate among policy holders (Ford and Kempson, 1997). Thus this particular market solution will alleviate only some of the potential increase of arrears and possessions.

But there are also other pressures likely to continue to place some borrowers at risk of arrears, possession and homelessness. In particular, there are growing risks to borrowers – from an increasingly flexible labour market (Ford and Wilcox, 1994), from potentially volatile costs associated with the globalization of credit markets, from a low inflation economy which reduces the opportunity for debts to erode rapidly and from the continuing reliance of owner occupation on two earners (Hogarth et al., 1996) in a context where household dissolution is marked. Few of these eventualities have an associated safety net – public or private.

## Note

1.  The term mortgage 'possession' refers to a situation where households lose or give up their property to the lender. The term 'repossession' can also be used to describe this process.

## References

Adler, M. and Wozniak, E. (1981) *The Origins and Consequences of Default*, Research report for the Scottish Law Commission, no. 5, London: HMSO.

Beatson, M. (1995) *Labour Market Flexibility, Research Report*, London: Department of Employment.

Berthoud, R. and Kempson, E. (1992) *Credit and Debt: The PSI Report*, London: Policy Studies Institute.

Birch, J. (1995) 'There may be trouble ahead', *Roof*, March.

BMRB (1977–95) *Series of Home Buyer Surveys*, London: British Market Research Bureau.

Bradshaw, J. and Holmes, H. (1989) *Living on the Edge: A Study of the Living Standards of Families on Benefit in Tyne and Wear*, Tyneside: CPAG.

Burchardt, T. and Hills, J. (1997) *Pushing the Boundaries: Private Welfare Insurance and Social Security*, York: Joseph Rowntree Foundation.

Cole, I. and Furbey, R. (1994) *The Eclipse of Council Housing*, London: Routledge.

Daly, M. and Walsh, J. (1988) *Money Lending and Low Income Families*, Dublin: Combat Poverty Agency.

Davis, R. and Dhooge, Y. (1993) *Living with Mortgage Arrears*, London: HMSO.

Dodd, T. and Hunter, P. (1990) *Trading Down and Moves Out of Owner Occupation*, London: OPCS.

Ford, J. (1988) *The Indebted Society: Credit and Default in the 1980s*, London: Routledge.

Ford, J. (1993) 'Mortgage possession', *Housing Studies*, vol. 8, no. 4, pp. 227–40.

Ford, J. (1994) *Problematic Home Ownership*, Loughborough: Loughborough University.

Ford, J. (1995) *Which Way Out? Borrowers with Long-Term Mortgage Arrears*, London: Shelter.

Ford, J. (1997) 'Mortgage arrears, possession and homelessness', in R. Burrows, N. Pleace and D. Quilgars (eds) *Homelessness and Social Policy*, London: Routledge.

Ford, J. and Griffith, A. (1994) 'Preventing mortgage arrears: A shrinking safety net', *Benefits*, 10.

Ford, J. and Kempson, E. (1997) *Bridging the Gap? Safety Nets for Mortgage Borrowers*, York: Centre for Housing Policy.

Ford, J., Kempson, E. and Wilson, M. (1995) *Mortgage Arrears and Possessions: Perspectives from Borrowers, Lenders and the Courts*, London: HMSO.

Ford, J. and Wilcox, S. (1992) *Mortgage Arrears: An Evaluation of the Initiatives to Reduce Mortgage Arrears and Possessions*, York: Joseph Rowntree Foundation.

Ford, J. and Wilcox, S. (1994) *Affordable Housing, Low Incomes and the Flexible Labour Market*, London: National Federation of Housing Associations.

Ford, J. and Wilson, M. (1994) 'Employers, employees and debt', *Employee Relations*, January.

Forrest, R. and Kennet, P. (1996) 'Coping strategies, housing careers and households with negative equity', *Journal of Social Policy*, vol. 25, no. 3, pp. 369–94.

Forrest, R. and Murie, A. (1990) *Selling the Welfare State*, London: Macmillan.

Forrest, R. and Murie, A. (1994) 'Home ownership in recession', *Housing Studies*, vol. 9, no. 1.

Foster, S. (1992) *Mortgage Rescue: What Does it Add Up To?*, London: Shelter.

Gregg, P. and Wadsworth, J. (1995) 'A short history of labour turnover, job tenure and job security 1975–93', *Oxford Review of Economic Policy*, vol. 11, no. 1.

Hogarth, T., Elias, P. and Ford, J. (1996) *Mortgages, Families and Jobs*, Warwick: Warwick University, Institute for Employment Research.

Jenkinson, S. (1992) *Repossessed*, Catholic Housing Aid Society and National Debtline.

Kemeny, J. (1981) *The Myth of Home Ownership*, London: Routledge.

Lord Chancellor's Department (1992), Mortgage Possession Statistics.

Maclennan, D. (1994) *A Competitive UK Economy*, York: Joseph Rowntree Foundation.

Nixon, J. and Hunter, C. (1996) *Better a Tenant Than a Borrower Be*, paper presented at the Housing Studies Association Conference, September.

Oppenheim, C. and McEvaddy, S. (1987) *Christmas on the Breadline*, London: CPAG Ltd.

Parker, G. (1987) 'Making ends meet: Women, credit and debt', in C. Glendinning and J. Millar (eds) *Women and Poverty in Britain*, London: Wheatsheaf.

Rock, P. (1973) *Making People Pay*, London: Routledge.

*Roof* (1996) *Briefing*, no. 19, November.

Saunders, P. (1990) *A Nation of Home Owners*, London: Unwin Hyman.

*Survey of English Housing 1994/5*, London: Office of National Statistics.

Whitehead, L. (1996) *The Legal Process of Repossession: Does it Help or Hinder the Mortgagor?*, paper presented to the Housing Studies Association Conference, September 1996, University of Birmingham.

Wilcox, S. and Williams, P. (1996) *Coping with Mortgage Default: Lessons from the Recession*, London: Council of Mortgage Lenders.

Woolfe, Lord Justice (1996) *Access to Justice*, London: HMSO.

# 6  Gender and homelessness
## Joan M. Smith

This chapter is about both the particular problem of homelessness faced by many women and their special need for low-cost permanent social housing. It considers evidence of the particular ways that women present as homeless and explains why some government initiatives, such as the Rough Sleepers Initiative, do not meet the needs of most young homeless single women.[1] It also compares the different accounts of household friction given by young homeless women and men before they leave home and considers their quite different patterns of domestic responsibilities which require an enhanced provision of low-cost social housing for young women. It argues that the undermining of social housing provision, which has taken place over the past twenty years, has been partly justified by a reversal of the family ethic which once underwrote government's support of lone mothers and which recognized their special requirement for housing.

### Welfare and the family ethic

The importance of the 1966 television film *Cathy Come Home* was that it exposed family homelessness at a time of house building and followed the publication of the first studies delimiting the continuing existence of poverty within welfare-state Britain (Abel-Smith and Townsend, 1965). The subsequent growth of charities working against poverty among the elderly and families with children, together with the work of the housing charity Shelter, helped shape the political climate over the following ten years which showed widespread concern over the welfare state's failure to protect the most vulnerable.

Public acknowledgement of poverty and homelessness among the elderly and the low paid was accompanied by a rediscovery that families could be quite deadly places in which to live and grow up. Kemp and Kemp (1969) drew attention to the continuing existence of child abuse in post-war Britain and this report led to the reorganization of social services, with a greater emphasis on child protection. This was quickly followed by the growth of the National Women's Aid Federation (Wilson, 1976) and Pizzey's highly publicized writings on 'battered wives' (Pizzey, 1974). The Select Committee on Domestic Violence (1975) stressed the importance of housing provision as a safety net for women and children. Housing provision for single-parent families also become an issue following divorce reform in 1971. An increasing number of divorced and separated wives became dependent on social housing and this was acknowledged in the Finer Report (Department of Health and Social Security, 1974).

One of the most long-lasting outcomes of this wave of social concern over poverty, single-parent families, the elderly, and the abuse of children was the passing of the Housing (Homeless Persons) Act in 1977. This Act has been an important pillar of social protection, over the last twenty years, for homeless families with dependent children and homeless elderly (over the age of 60) – giving them the statutory right to apply to the local authority housing departments for rehousing in permanent, local authority-owned or accessed accommodation. The selection of these two groups – families and the elderly – for protection under the Act was a reflection of the two principles which had sanctioned the use of state resources for welfare provision in the past – the family ethic and the work ethic. These principles underwrote the use of collectively owned housing resources as additional support for those caring for dependent children or for those who were too old to work. Two conditions were applied – that the applicant should not have made themselves intentionally homeless and, also, that they should be a local resident or have connections with the local area (Audit Commission, 1989).

Children were among the chief beneficiaries of the homeless persons legislation as, by 1990, four out of every five homeless acceptances were households with children or where a woman was pregnant and so the 400,000 persons accepted as homeless included approximately 200,000 children (Greve and Currie, 1990, p. 10). As the primary care-givers to children, women had a statutory right to apply for housing when homeless, whether the primary cause of their homelessness was that of domestic violence or because they were lone mothers on benefits or because their waged income was too low to sustain them in the private housing market.[2] Through homeless persons legislation, women could access shelter where they had a permanent right to live and to care for themselves and their children. Therefore, households headed by women were more likely to live in local authority-owned or housing association-owned social housing. In

1991 nearly a half (45 per cent) of divorced or separated female heads of households occupied social housing compared with 28 per cent of divorced or separated men. In the same year 31 per cent of single female heads of households occupied social housing compared with 18 per cent of men (Woods, 1996, p. 69).

Whatever the failings in the supply and quality of social housing, many women have relied on this provision. This does not, however, mean that such women are not discriminating consumers – wanting houses in respectable areas which offered a future for themselves and, particularly, their children.[3] However, they have an overriding need for shelter they can afford and which they have a right to occupy permanently.

### Threats to women's routes into social housing

Three developments pose a threat to the provision of social housing for women in the UK. Firstly, there is a growing shortage of good quality social housing, as council houses have been sold and local authority new-build has disappeared (Bramley, 1994; Balchin, 1995). Although, in some areas, there is still a supply of social housing stock, albeit often in isolating and excluding estates, this is not the case in London and the South East, where social housing has always made up a lower proportion of the housing stock or in rural areas, where a high proportion of council houses have been sold. In such areas families have waited many months in bed and breakfast or hostel accommodation (Balchin, 1995).[4]

Secondly, encouraged by Conservative governments' stated policy that the provision of housing should be withdrawn from the duties of local authorities, some local authorities disposed of their entire housing stock. Wandsworth Borough Council was brought to court for its failure to fulfil the statutory duty of providing social housing for homeless families and it was this local authority which encouraged the Department of the Environment's first effort to repeal the statutory duty of local authorities to provide housing to homeless families. The Consultation Document (Department of the Environment, 1994) was overwhelmingly rejected by nine thousand housing providers and experts. Nevertheless many of its proposals surfaced in the 1996 Housing Act, which provided for homeless applicants to be placed in temporary accommodation for two years in the first instance, during which time they were to be assessed for the housing waiting list (see Chapter 2). Many of the justifying arguments rehearsed in the original White Paper, which also surfaced in public debate on radio and in newspapers, centred on the argument that the 1977 Act had given lone mothers the right to 'jump the queue' through being rehoused under the homeless persons legislation, and so gained priority over two-parent couples on the housing waiting list.[5] It was argued that welfare support for families should be prioritized towards 'traditional' two-parent families rather than single-parent mothers as part of a wider political agenda aimed at the re-moralization of society.

Although the sections of the 1996 Housing Act, which repealed the right of homeless families to permanent social housing, have been reversed through new legislation by the Labour government, the situation which gave rise to the 1996 Act remains unresolved. It is not apparent that the Labour government will fully reinstate the role of local authorities as housing providers despite a commitment to release capital receipts from the previous sale of local authority housing to enable some social housing new-build. In many areas, these capital receipts have already been used or earmarked for debt-reduction or repairs and maintenance to existing stock rather than for new-build. In addition, the punitive attitudes towards lone mothers, which surfaced in the 1994 Consultation Document, have partially resurfaced in the guise of 'from welfare to work' policies from New Labour. It is apparent that the once universally accepted family ethic, which under-wrote welfare and housing support of families with dependent children (including lone mothers), is under pressure.

A third development, which has threatened the provision of social hous-ing for women, has been the shift of public attention away from the less visible problem of family homelessness to the very visible problem of street homelessness among young single people. The growth in family home-lessness during the 1980s is well documented and demonstrated by the trebling of applications under the homeless persons legislation from 53,000 in 1978 to nearly 149,000 in 1991 (Balchin, 1995; Bramley, 1994) and by the growth in numbers of households discovered 'doubling up' in the 1991 census, which showed 198,000 households sharing housekeeping at the same address as well as some 95,000 households living in non-permanent accommodation such as caravans. Both 'doubling up' and caravan dwelling showed a 17 per cent rise over the 1981 census figures (*Roof*, 1994). Despite this picture of increasing housing stress and concealed homelessness among families, public attention has shifted away from this form of home-lessness, which affects predominantly women and children, to those sleeping rough, who are predominantly young men. The growth in family homelessness has been overshadowed by the extraordinary rise in home-lessness among young single people.

The outcry against family homelessness has been muted for several reasons – social housing and homeless persons legislation is still seen to be a safety net which works for families, the right to social housing has been portrayed by many politicians as being abused by single-parent mothers and public concern over homelessness has shifted to a concern over the increas-ing and visible homelessness of young single people. However, the separation of family and single homelessness into separate problems is artificial.

**Single and family homelessness: differential access to housing**

Since the 1977 Housing (Homeless Persons) Act, homelessness has been divided into two quite separate problem areas – statutory homelessness and non-statutory homelessness, which is primarily single homelessness. Studies of those who qualify as homeless under the Act have been concerned with the following areas – the criteria of 'priority need' and how they are applied by different local authorities, the proportion of applicants accepted and the reasons for applicants' rejection, the length of waiting time and the type of emergency accommodation offered to accepted applicants as well as the quality of the social housing which is offered and whether or not single-parent mothers are being directed towards 'sink' estates (Thomas and Niner, 1989; Hills, 1993; Power and Tunstall, 1995; Burrows, 1997).

Studies of the single homeless and of the roofless have been concerned with quite different issues relating to the process by which the young person becomes homeless – the numbers of young people becoming homeless, the problems of 'runaways' and rough sleepers, unemployment and youth homelessness, mental health, drug and alcohol abuse issues associated with homelessness as well as criminality and criminalization among and of young homeless people (Anderson *et al.*, 1993; Hutson and Liddiard, 1994; Carlen, 1996; Evans, 1996). What is lost sight of, in separating statutory and non-statutory homelessness or family and single homelessness, is that the heads of households accepted as family homeless are often in the same age-cohort as the single homeless. Homelessness among young people aged 16–25 years includes young single mothers, young couple parents as well as those who are young and single. Moreover, many single-parent mothers who are homeless will have once been homeless single young women.

**The rise in single homelessness**

In the 1980s, a marked rise in the numbers of young single homeless people became evident. The 1977 Housing (Homeless Persons) Act did not treat homelessness among single person households as a priority issue. Prior to the 1980s, single homelessness appeared to be an issue affecting mainly older men, in their 40s and 50s, and without families, who were largely accommodated in traditional hostels, as well as a very few older women. However, from the end of the 1970s, increasing numbers of young single people were found to be arriving at traditional shelters which had previously been designed to provide basic accommodation for older men. One of the earliest studies of single homelessness provided evidence of growing home-lessness among young single people (Drake, 1981). Interestingly, this study found that a third of the single homeless included in the survey were women, and among those under 29 years the proportion was 40 per cent.

By the mid-1980s, the number of homeless young single people had grown sufficiently large for churches and voluntary agencies to begin providing, first, additional night shelters, and then, residential accommodation specifically for young people (Garside et al., 1990). The YMCA, for example, allocated an increasing proportion of their beds to homeless young people. As board and lodgings allowances and income support payments were withdrawn from 16–18 year olds, in 1985 and 1988, rising numbers of young single homeless meant that many were forced to live on the street, particularly in London (Evans, 1996). Policy issues raised by the increase in single homelessness among young people included: the additional provision of emergency and hostel accommodation for young single people; the provision of specialized care and support, including specialized accommodation for those under 16; provision for those with mental health or drink/drug problems; as well as the provision of employment, training and move-on accommodation.

It was noticeable that, as homelessness among young people became ever more visible, media attention turned from investigations of family homelessness and life in bed and breakfast hostels to in-depth reports of the life of young street-dwellers or runaways (see Chapter 11). Homelessness became seen as a problem affecting young single people rather than families. Public attention was shifted from the policy issue of providing social housing for homeless families to the problem of emergency accommodation and youth residential projects such as *foyers* for young people. This shift in public awareness has a major gender implication as it involved a transfer of attention from the housing problems of women and children to the housing and training problems of young homeless men.

All the studies of single homelessness published since the late 1980s have found a high preponderance of young men, generally 70 per cent (Anderson et al., 1993; Stockley et al., 1993; Hutson and Liddiard, 1994). By default, the image of single homeless young people which was presented came predominantly from the experience of young single homeless men, often at the bottom of the 'downward spiral of homelessness' and living in marginalized situations. Policy solutions to single homelessness, such as emergency accommodation through the Rough Sleepers Initiative and accommodation with training through foyers, more closely fit the picture of homeless young men. However, is single homelessness less of a problem for young women?

Both surveys of single homelessness and qualitative studies, using in-depth interviews, involved tracing and interviewing young people living in hostels, squats, sleeping rough or attending soup-runs. However, fewer single homeless women are found in these situations; they are more likely to use youth residential hostels or live in shared housing. Young homeless women, even single homeless women, are more likely to report as homeless to local authority housing departments or housing associations, and these agencies are not generally used as sample sites to contact homeless young single people. Therefore, the picture derived from studies of single home-lessness has been highly gendered.

Official figures from the local authorities also underestimate home-lessness among young single women. Because young single women are often more likely to report as homeless from living with friends or relatives, rather than from sleeping rough or from emergency accommodation, they are more likely to be classified as 'not homeless' by these agencies. There is also evidence that the 'downward spiral of homelessness' described by Hutson and Liddiard (1994) takes different forms for young men and young women. By the age of 19 years, many young women are not single homeless but single-parent homeless (see Table 6.2, below).

A common explanation of why women were being under-represented in surveys was that it must be these women, who are sleeping on friends' floors and not approaching agencies, who make up the category identified as the 'hidden homeless' (Greve and Currie, 1990). However, homeless women would never have been hidden if information from local authority housing departments and housing associations had been included in the surveys of young single people or if surveys had been conducted across all homeless people in a particular age group regardless of their household structure. For this reason, the recent survey of homelessness in seven cities and four London boroughs, undertaken by the author and colleagues on behalf of the National Inquiry into Youth Homelessness and the YMCA England, included all clients approaching all housing and homeless agencies, what-ever their domestic responsibilities, over a three-month period.[6]

**Seven Cities and Four London Boroughs Survey: making women visible**

A recent agency survey of over 15,000 young clients of housing and home-less agencies by the author and colleagues (Smith *et al.*, 1996) found, as expected, that approximately half of the young homeless in any city were women. The reason for the different gender pattern found in this survey, compared with other surveys of youth homelessness, is first that all young housing clients of any domestic or parenting status were included and second that information was collected from all types of housing and homeless agencies – including housing departments and housing associa-tions.[7]. In this way, information was collected on an entire cohort of homeless young people aged between 16 and 25 years, including single homeless, single-parent homeless, couple and couple-parent homeless.

The information (see Table 6.1) was collected over a three-month period in seven cities spread across Britain, each of which had a population of over a quarter of a million, and in four Inner London Boroughs. Young housing clients were classified by the agencies they went to as being 'homeless' or 'in housing need'. From the three-month figure of those recorded by agencies as homeless, and with double counting eliminated, it was estimated that one in twenty of the 16- to 25-year-olds living in these cities, or between five and seven per cent, would present as homeless annually. To gain this estimate, the contact rate within the three-month period was multiplied by four to get an annual rate, and 10 per cent was added to adjust for young people not included in the survey (in each city one or some agencies – social services departments, probation services and housing associations – could not provide data). This figure was compared with the same-age cohort registered by the Office of National Statistics (ONS) in their mid-year estimates.

Of the 10,906 individual cases of young people approaching housing and homeless agencies in seven cities, 6,879 cases were recorded as homeless and the rest as being in housing need. This count provides a more accurate figure of youth homelessness than previous estimates and supports the argument that there are at least 120,000 young homeless people seeking help in any one year in our cities.[8]

Despite popular perceptions of youth homelessness being predominantly a problem affecting young single males, in five cities the majority of young homeless people were women. Only in Manchester and Glasgow were more men recorded. Table 6.2 shows that, although the most common domestic status for homeless women was 'single', a high proportion (between 25 and 44 per cent in any city) fell into the 'single-parent' category. The main difference between homeless young men and homeless young women (see Figures 6.1 and 6.2) was that most homeless young men remain without domestic ties while up to half of the women are mothers without a permanent domestic partner. This pattern echoes the findings of Wilson's

Table 6.1 Homeless young people in seven cities, April–June 1996

| City | Young people 16–25 years ONS 1995 | Homeless young people 16–25 years | Estimate for year multiplied by 4 plus 10% | Percentage of homeless young people |
|---|---|---|---|---|
| Birmingham | 145,739 | 1,487 | 6,543 | 4.5 |
| Leeds | 104,347 | 1,201 | 5,284 | 5.0 |
| Liverpool | 71,587 | 539 | 2,372 | 3.3 |
| Manchester | 75,386 | 1,024 | 4,506 | 6.0 |
| Bristol | 59,821 | 677 | 2,979 | 5.0 |
| Cardiff | 43,260 | 668 | 2,939 | 6.8 |
| Glasgow | 91,527 | 1,283 | 5,645 | 6.2 |
| All cities | 591,667 | 6,879 | 30,268 | 5.0 |

Source: Smith et al. (1996).

research into the USA 'underclass' (1987) where he puts forward the thesis of a declining 'marriageable pool' of bread-winning males, due to unemployment and the increasing involvement of young men in marginalized activities including crime. This leaves women to raise their children as single mothers.

Although the reasons why more young women have become single mothers and also homeless are not as easily explained as Wilson's thesis would suggest, it was notable that very few young single homeless men were in employment or training. From the third of the sample for which data were available, only eight per cent of young single men were in full- or part-time work and five per cent were in training or education. Young single women had higher rates than this – 15 per cent were in full or part-time work and 12 per cent were in education or training. Although these figures should be treated with extreme caution, the same trend was found at an earlier date in Birmingham (Smith and Gilford, 1993) and in North Staffordshire (Smith and Gilford, 1991), even controlling for age. Arguments about the need to push young people into the world of work and off

Table 6.2 Domestic and parenting status among young homeless people by gender (%)

|  | Leeds | Liverpool | Manchester | Birmingham | Bristol | Cardiff | Glasgow |
|---|---|---|---|---|---|---|---|
| Female status (%) | | | | | | | |
| Single | 45 | 52 | 60 | 42 | 50 | 42 | 60 |
| Single parent | 44 | 35 | 30 | 41 | 33 | 37 | 25 |
| Couple | 3 | 7 | 3 | 7 | 8 | 9 | 4 |
| Couple parent | 9 | 6 | 7 | 10 | 9 | 12 | 11 |
| N = | 624 | 258 | 476 | 819 | 270 | 330 | 484 |
| % of all city homeless | 54 | 53 | 48 | 56 | 45 | 57 | 44 |
| Males status (%) | | | | | | | |
| Single | 87 | 90 | 93 | 79 | 84 | 78 | 89 |
| Single parent | 3 | 2 | 2 | 3 | 3 | 2 | 2 |
| Couple | 5 | 6 | 2 | 8 | 9 | 10 | 3 |
| Couple parent | 4 | 2 | 3 | 10 | 4 | 10 | 6 |
| N = | 528 | 227 | 522 | 603 | 311 | 226 | 570 |
| % of all city homeless | 46 | 47 | 52 | 44 | 55 | 43 | 56 |
| Total N = | 1,152 | 485 | 998 | 1,422 | 581 | 556 | 1,054 |

Valid cases = 6,248
Missing cases = 626
Source: National Inquiry/YMCA Survey; see also Smith et al. (1996).

welfare have often misunderstood that the orientation to the world of work is gendered in so far as more young single homeless women are already engaged in work, training or study. Their rates of employment and training only drop to the same rates as men when they are single parents. Then, the problems they face are the age-old problems of finding affordable safe shelter with sufficiently well-paid employment or training and child-care.

Percentages for Inner London are not included in Tables 6.1 and 6.2 because the numbers of homeless young people in the Inner London Boroughs (Camden, Westminster, Southwark and Lambeth) were esti-mated differently. In all, 4,254 cases of youth homelessness were identified over this three-month period and an estimate of 5 per cent of the Boroughs' young population as homeless in one year was produced, which does not differ significantly from the seven cities. Of the 4,254 homeless cases identified in the four boroughs, 56 per cent were young men and 44 per cent were young women. Inner London showed the highest preponderance of single homelessness among young women – 85 per cent. This reflects the

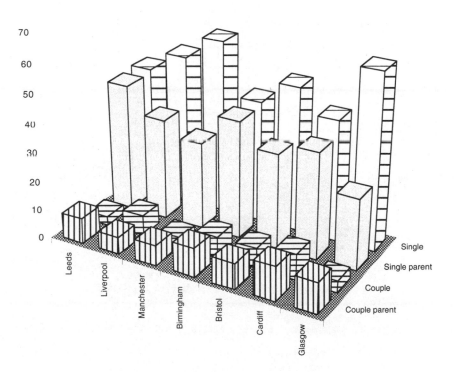

Figure 6.1 Females only: domestic and parenting status in seven cities (%)

predominance of youth residential hostels in the area and the absence of data from housing associations – almost all of which had closed their waiting lists at the time of the study and which would have given higher proportions of single mothers. Again, young women were more likely to be in full- or part-time work (9 per cent for single women; 4 per cent for men) or training/studying (27 per cent of women; 14 per cent of young men). In all, two-thirds of young single homeless women in London, for whom there was an employment record, were unemployed, compared with over three-quarters of young single homeless men.

**Women are not jumping the queue**

Although the Consultation Document (Department of the Environment, 1994) argued that women jump the housing queue, this survey shows that many young single mothers are, in fact, rejected by local authorities. In both

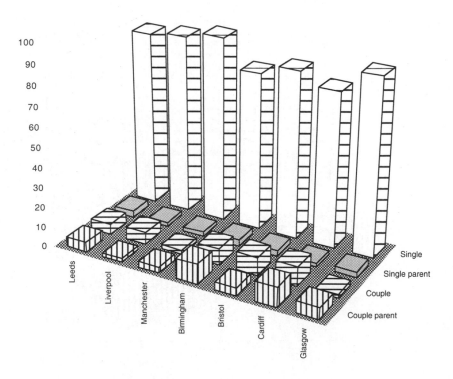

Figure 6.2 Males only: domestic and parenting status in seven cities (%)

the cities and the Inner London boroughs, housing departments rejected 35 per cent of single-parent mothers' applications as priority need homeless and classified them as being housing need, while housing associations rejected 55 per cent. Overall, homeless and housing agencies were more likely to classify young men as homeless compared with young women. Sixty-one per cent of all women applicants were classified as homeless compared with 71 per cent of men applicants. The reasons for this pattern are associated with the different routes which young women take into home-lessness. Even those young women who are classified as homeless are more likely to present from friends and relatives or their own homes whereas young men are more likely to present from rough sleeping, emergency accommodation and institutions.

Almost all London agencies keep records on where young people sleep the night before they come to the agency, and this information was available for over three-quarters of all young homeless people in the Inner London survey. The greatest difference between young men and young women was whether they had slept rough the previous night – 23 per cent of young men had slept rough compared with only 11 per cent of young women. Seven per cent of all young homeless people (6 per cent young men and 8 per cent young women) came to agencies from their parental homes. One in four came from a friend's home or from the family home (22 per cent young men and 29 per cent young women). Only three per cent of young men and women came from their own homes.

This difference in previous-night's accommodation is not just due to the fact that some women had responsibilities for children and therefore avoided being on the streets. Figure 6.3 shows the night-prior experience of *single* young men and young women in London and the proportion of young women with no fixed abode is still significantly lower (11 per cent of single women and 29 per cent of single men). Young single women were more likely to present from friends or families (38 per cent compared with 28 per cent of young single men). Single-parent mothers were less likely to present from friends and families than single women (33 per cent) and more likely to present from emergency shelters than single young women. Considering the survey as a whole, as would be expected, only eight per cent of young single mothers/pregnant women presented from no fixed abode or rough sleeping situations.

Outside London, most agencies kept records of night-prior circum-stances, the rates of rough sleeping or no fixed abode were lower than in London (3 to 8 per cent). In five cities, where records were comparable, between 9 and 18 per cent of young homeless people came to agencies directly from their parental home. Considering relatives, parents, friends and partners' homes as one category, it is possible to say that, in each of the seven cities, between 47 and 67 per cent of all young homeless people presented from friends and relatives and, in each city, proportionately more young women than young men came from here. Between 8 and 14 per cent came to agencies directly from their own home, with proportionately more young women coming from here. Large numbers of young people presented to agencies from other institutional situations – 9 to 27 per cent from hostels or emergency accommodation and between 1 and 10 per cent from institutions such as probation hostels, social service hostels and hospitals.

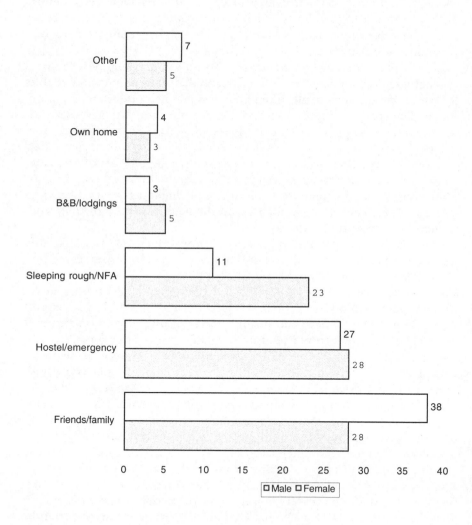

Figure 6.3  Night-prior accommodation of young single homeless men and women London only (%)

Although the pattern of where they had slept the night before was different for young men and young women, these differences were not as marked as in London because of the lower proportion of all young people who were sleeping rough when they approached agencies – although 8 per cent of young men reported sleeping rough compared with 3 per cent of young women. In only three cities outside London was there information from voluntary agencies on whether their clients had ever slept rough. Among their clients, the proportion who had *ever* slept rough was high – in Leeds it was 43 per cent, in Cardiff 48 per cent and in Birmingham 38 per cent. Again, young single homeless women were much less likely to sleep rough than young men. Because of the Rough Sleepers Initiative, a majority of agencies in London also keep information as to whether their clients have *ever* slept rough. This information was available for half of the recorded cases in London. These also demonstrate the differences in patterns of rough sleeping among young homeless men and women – with 59 per cent of men and 33 per cent of women having slept rough.

These gender differences existed across all ethnic groups but were notably greater among young women of British African-Caribbean and African origin. In Inner London three-quarters of single young men of white European origin[9] had slept rough in the past compared with half of single young women of white European origin. But while less than half of young men of Black British (42 per cent) or African (35 per cent) ethnic origin had slept rough, only one in five of young Black British and African women had (18 per cent) (Smith *et al.*, 1996).

Part of the reason why women are less likely to be classified as homeless may be due to a changing definition of homelessness. While the 1977 Housing (Homeless Persons) Act never included rough-sleeping as part of its definition of homelessness, the establishment of the Rough Sleepers Initiative in London in 1990, and its extension to other cities in 1996, has equated homelessness with rough-sleeping. An initial study (Douglas and Gilroy, 1994, p. 134) found that only one quarter of those helped by the programme were young women. The Housing Corporation responded by suggesting that women might be by-passing the Initiative and gaining accommodation through being deemed vulnerable. However, our study suggests that, on the contrary, women's different night-prior history leads to both young single women and even young single mothers in some areas being *less* often classified as homeless the night before and shows that a lower proportion of women in the study had been classified as homeless.

Rough sleeping presents particular difficulties for all women, not only because of the increased danger of sexual harassment and abuse, but also because of the importance of cleanliness for women. Golden (1992) has argued that this is not only because of the problems of remaining clean during menstruation but also that remaining clean and respectably dressed is a method of self-protection for women. Young single women make extreme efforts to stay off the streets even if they have been homeless for a long time whereas, for most homeless young men, periods of street sleeping are common when they reach the bottom of the 'downward spiral' of homelessness (Hutson and Liddiard, 1994). The shift in provision for single homeless young people, which has been brought about by the Rough Sleepers Initiative, has encouraged homelessness to be equated with roof-lessness. This move threatens provision for young single women and young men of ethnic origins other than white.

Clearly there are differences between the routes which young women and young men take into homelessness and differences between their night-prior experiences. This still leaves the question of how different are the ways in which young men and young women leave their parental home and questions as to why so many young women are single-parent homeless. A study of the family conflict which commonly precedes youth homelessness by the author and colleagues (Smith, Gilford and O'Sullivan, 1997) indicates further the way in which gender mediates the way in which homelessness is experienced and described.[10]

## Experience and discourses in family conflict and homelessness

This study of the family background of young homeless people suggested that there were significant gender differences in the way young people left home from different types of households. In 'non-disrupted' households – where a young person had lived with the same parents (including step-parents) from an early age – gender differences were particularly noticeable. Although the numbers of such households involved in the study were not large, there were some striking similarities in the reasons given for leaving home, both by the young people and their parents. Nearly all the young women reported that they had left because of friction over their relationships with young men who were involved in crime and drugs and who, in some cases, were often significantly older than themselves. An 18-year-old woman describes the situation:

Then I started going with a boy and he was black, and they weren't much for that. Then he was sent to prison, so they definitely weren't much for that! Then, you know, they were seeing me getting in cars with him that he'd nicked and things, and just arguments blew up from that, and I mean it was all my fault, I must admit.

In another case a long-term stepfather reported:

But knocking about with that lad were the worst thing her did you know ... We didn't like it at all, I had to stop it 'cause he was on drugs and everything bloody else ...

Many parents said that they had hoped that their daughters would 'make something' of themselves or at least 'find a decent bloke' to leave home with. In fact, many young women were eventually asked to leave, or left, in an atmosphere of escalating conflict.

Conflict between young men and their parents, from stable families, was explained rather differently. It often began with trouble at school, through drug-taking and/or stealing as well as trouble with the police. More often, it was a case of young person 'back-chatting' their parents. This could result in 'slapping' which could escalate into violence. Eviction from the family home was often triggered by the young man stealing money or valuables from his parents. The mother of a 19-year-old boy, who has now returned home, remembers the time when he left:

I think even to this day, it's torn me apart and his Dad. I mean there's stuff, some of my jewellery I found that'd gone and he took his Dad's things that he'd saved . . . . some of my Wedgwood , , , jewellery. . . . Most of them we found in a second-hand shop. . . . You can imagine . . . a young child stealing from you . . . all you know, your possessions. . . . That was the last thing really, the last straw.

In these households, parents often used threats of eviction in an attempt to control the behaviour of both young women and young men but young people would often retaliate by walking out. The gender difference lay in the involvement in crime by young men as against the involvement of women often with boyfriends, similarly involved in criminal or drug life-styles.

Other young people faced a quite different household situation. Rather than facing conflict within stable families, these young people from disrupted households had experienced changes in parenting, often involving a recent step-parent. These young people were made homeless because their parental families broke up or their parent(s) started a new life without them. In some cases the household dissolved around young people. For example, one young woman was made homeless when her mother was thrown out by her father. Her father then sold the house and, as a result, the girl was passed around between family members. A more common situation was when parents wished to make a new life for themselves and found teenage children getting in the way. The conflict was commonly triggered by a step-parent coming into what had been a lone parent family. The presence of the step-parent was openly resented for, as an 18-year-old woman said:

I think that children should come first because they're part of you aren't they?

In both these situations, where households dissolved or rejected children, there was less difference between young men and young women, in their explanation and their experiences. There were, however, some differences in the way in which they left. Young women were more likely to leave the parental home as soon as they were aged 16 years – often following a major argument. Young men were more likely to move out when actually pushed out by their parents. Some tried to force young men to move out to any employment with accommodation. Among the young men interviewed, three had been pushed into joining the army. A young man explains:

It was mostly me stepdad. ... He was saying: 'Join the army' and me Mum was backing him up, but it was mostly him telling me to join the army or he'd kick me out.

The least difference between young men and young women, in leaving home, came from those who left abusive households. They reported facing similar home situations. These mainly came from disrupted households, although a minority had been in and out of care homes. Around a third of the young people interviewed reported physical abuse or neglect from step-parents and natural parents, and two girls reported sexual abuse. For example, one young man reported being hit every day by his mother and a girl reported physical abuse from her stepmother in the following terms:

Well she [stepmother], she'd slap and slap, and she wouldn't stop slapping. And then one day she punched me sister in the face.

For all the homeless young women who were interviewed, whatever the situation behind them leaving home, there was a strong possibility that they would become lone mothers. Young women from stable homes often left home in order to retain a relationship with a boyfriend who was not approved of. Young women, from dissolving or rejecting homes, may have left for different reasons but were very likely to establish a new relationship as a substitute for their previous family. Overall, many young women who had left home at 16 were single-parent mothers or pregnant by the age of 18 or 19. Interestingly, pregnancy for some was seen as a passport back home rather than a passport into social housing. A young woman said:

I wanted to get pregnant so I could just move back home ... 'cause I missed me mum and dad that much that I just got pregnant on purpose. ... She's always wanted a grandkid.

While young women from stable families often had children in order to be re-integrated into their existing family, young women from dissolving or rejecting families expressed a desire for children because they wanted a family of their own. Most of the young men, however, saw children and a family as a possibility in the future rather than a present reality.

Overall, there were considerable commonalities given in the accounts of different young women leaving non-disrupted homes compared with those of young men from similar homes, and some commonalities between the accounts of both young men and young women of leaving disrupted homes and abusive homes. Many homeless young women expressed different reasons for becoming homeless single mothers, according to their parental background. Only one young woman we interviewed had even considered the possibility that having a child would help them become rehoused quicker. The view of young single mothers as being rational self-serving welfare dependants, which was put forward during the debates on homeless persons legislation between 1994 and 1996, is simply not true. Many young single-parent mothers who are homeless have been homeless young single women who, above all else, want a family of their own just like everyone else. Unfortunately they are living in a period when the needs of themselves and their children are at the centre of a public debate over a new welfare settlement.

## The re-moralizing of welfare and the provision of housing support

Over the past century, welfare provision in the UK has been constructed on two principles – the family ethic and the work ethic. The family ethic was built on the belief that families were composed of bread-winning males and financially dependent women and children, which meant that unsupported mothers with children needed support from the state. Women on welfare received support as 'mothers' rather than as individual citizens. This was most apparent in the welfare system which developed in the USA, where Mothers' Pensions and later Aid to Dependent Families preceded any welfare payment to two-parent families (Abramovitz, 1996; de Acosta, 1997). In the UK, both single men and women have been entitled to Income Support, and so support to lone mothers was less distinctive. However, from the 1970s, additional support was offered to lone mothers through the family allowance/child benefit system and the single parent benefit paid in addition to child benefit. As in other parts of Europe, mothers of young children were not expected to seek work but to be at home in order to raise their children.

These principles were embodied in the homeless legislation. However, those who drew up the 1977 Housing (Homeless Persons) Act could not have anticipated the transformation that was to occur in patterns of family formation over the next decades. The passing of the Act coincided with a fundamental shift in attitudes towards marriage and cohabitation. By the end of the 1970s, cohabitation had become a strong alternative choice for young couples and older divorcees (Kiernan, 1989). During the 1980s, the rise in numbers of lone mothers reflected both a real rise in numbers of separated and divorced women as well as a rise in the numbers of women living as cohabitees. There was a further shift in family formation among very young women. Among those who had left school early and faced limited job prospects, many young men remained single while young women began their child-bearing career as never-married mothers (Burghes and Brown, 1995). Some of these mothers increased the numbers seeking a route into social housing through the homelessness legislation.

The benefit which UK families have derived from the provision of social housing had largely protected women and children from the worst experiences of homelessness since 1977. Housing benefit payments have also raised the level of welfare payments received by families in the UK. In 1992, 1.3 per cent of UK's GNP was spent on housing benefit, raising the proportion spent on social assistance in the UK to 3.9 per cent. This is the highest figure spent on housing benefit payments in Europe, with only Sweden and France spending similar proportions on particular housing assistance (Eardley *et al.*, 1996). In the UK, provision of universal benefits through the National Health Service, Child Allowances and social housing have been especially important in protecting women from the worst excesses of benefit poverty. In a comparative study of social transfer rates within developed countries, the UK was found to be the only Northern European country whose poverty rates could be compared to those in the USA and Canada but, if the benefit of a universal health care system was included, then the position of welfare claimants was improved, especially that of lone mothers (Smeeding and Rainwater, 1991; Bradshaw *et al.*, 1993). Adding the benefits of the homeless persons' legislation and housing benefits improves the level of social transfer still further.

Although state support to lone mothers and children has not lifted them out of poverty, it has allowed women to 'de-familialize' themselves – that is, to free themselves from financial dependence on other family members without participating in the labour market. Now, however, in both the USA and the UK, governments have pressed forward with the construction of what they describe as 'new settlement' welfare policies for the twenty-first century. These 'new settlements' do not recognize social problems as arising from shifting patterns of family formation and the affordability crisis in family housing but, rather, as arising from personal decisions taken by individuals – not to seek work and/or to have children. As governments seek to reduce welfare budgets in the name of economic probity, this leads to the targeting of welfare and the renaming of welfare 'claimants' as welfare 'dependants'.

In the USA, the campaign for a new settlement of 'workfare', rather than welfare, preceded the signing of the Republican-inspired Personal Responsibility Act by President Clinton in August 1996. This Act has abolished federal control over the Aid to Dependent Children programme, which had been in place since the 1930s. It limited the amount of time a family could draw welfare to two years at any one time and to five years in a life-time and has gone further than any previously proposed welfare programme in time-limiting access to welfare and forcing mothers on welfare into work (Abramovitz, 1996; de Acosta, 1997).

The early image of a single-parent mother as a woman struggling to raise 'future citizens' – all our children – has been replaced by the image of a young mother deliberately using her children in order to be welfare dependent despite all evidence that this is not so (Bradshaw *et al.*, 1993; Duncan and Edwards, 1997). As with the Personal Responsibility Act in the USA, the 1996 Housing Act was preceded by a debate over the existence of an 'underclass' which, it was claimed, had been created through welfare dependency (Smith, 1992; Dennis and Erdos, 1992; Murray, 1994)].[11] Although this measure has now been modified by the new Labour government, it is to be replaced by a welfare-to-work programme particularly targeted on young single people and single-parent mothers. All of these measures, encouraging young mothers to work for low wages or encouraging them to declare the father of the child to the Child Support Agency (which carries a benefit reduction penalty), are justified by the argument that 'welfare dependency' should be abolished.

In both countries, anxieties about social disorder have been displaced onto young never-married mothers. As Abramovitz (1996) writes:

... Attacking welfare and the women who receive it eases the economic, moral and racial panics provoked by economic insecurity, changing family structures and racial progress ... projecting fears about society-wide changes in family structures and women's roles onto the poor.

## Conclusions

There are many reasons why Western societies are facing an upsurge in youth homelessness, including homelessness among young people responsible for children. First, families have changed. The increasing numbers of disrupted families mean that more young people are likely to leave home before they can support themselves (Jones, 1995). Second, the social milieu in which young people grow up has changed – young people are more at risk from substance misuse, early sexuality as well as criminalization and some will leave non-disrupted homes because of these factors. Third, young people are poorer than they were, both because they are more likely to be unemployed and because youth wage rates are now falling in relation to adult wage rates (Kumar, 1993). Fourth, both the private housing market and social housing provision have changed. Housing has become less affordable and/or appropriate to the needs of young single people and young single parents. For all these reasons, there has, not surprisingly, been an upsurge in homelessness, particularly youth homelessness, in France, Germany and the UK.

The social context of this upsurge of homelessness among the past two generations of young people becomes obscured by the separation of the study of single homelessness and of family homelessness which, in the UK, has been reinforced by the provisions of the homeless persons legislation. In the study of single homelessness, researchers have concentrated on the 'downward spiral' facing the young single homeless, the life-histories and personal and family circumstances which are associated with single young people leaving home 'early'; whereas the study of family homelessness has concentrated on unemployment, poverty and the housing stress facing young families. However, many young single people and young families, particularly those headed by single mothers, are homeless for the same reasons and in the same circumstances.

The study of single homelessness, as distinct from family homelessness, has given rise to a picture of homelessness drawn principally from the experiences of young single homeless men (mostly white) who are likely to have slept rough. This picture has two consequences. First, it provides a justification for the Rough Sleepers Initiative, adopted by the government in the early 1990s, and its expansion in the late 1990s. This Initiative has been an extremely cheap policy option for the government. It has given the appearance of activity against youth homelessness while, in reality, huge tranches of public funds have been cut from social housing. Often, in the same policy announcement, much more has been cut from the social housing budget than was being provided to fund night shelters. Second, it helps shift the definition of homelessness, from one in which those without secure accommodation can apply as homeless, to one in which having slept rough the night before is privileged evidence of being homeless.

Young women, in particular, are caught between two policies which are increasingly closing the route into social housing for themselves as single women and for themselves and their children as single parent families. On the one hand, young women are less likely to sleep rough than young men and so are seen as 'less homeless' than male rough sleepers. If homelessness is increasingly defined as 'rooflessness', those young women and men from an ethnic background other than white European who avoid sleeping rough will also be seen as less eligible to qualify for services. On the other hand, as welfare is re-moralized, single mothers and their children will face additional scrutiny in their application for social housing. Moreover, the ability of some to pay the new market rents for social housing will be compromised by benefit claw-backs as well as by their employment in low-wage occupations (Joshi, 1991).

The 'underclass' argument provided a ready-made cloak for the homeless and housing crisis that lay behind the changes in housing legislation in 1996 and for the rising social security bill which lies behind the 'welfare to work' budget of 1997. Although the reasons for this crisis were to do with the shortage of social housing set against changes in household structure together with the increasing prevalence of unemployment, the language was moralistic, and young women have born the brunt of legislation which is based on the assumption that they choose to leave home and become homeless, they choose not to work and they choose to have children as lone mothers. Reversing the family ethic, which once protected women with young children, may appear an efficient source of saving on public funds in the short-term but in the long-term it may prove very costly indeed.]

## Notes

1. The research on gender differences reported in this chapter derives from projects undertaken by a team of researchers in the Housing and Community Research Unit, Staffordshire University – *The Family Background of Young Homeless People*, funded by the Joseph Rowntree Foundation, and *Bright Lights and Homelessness*, the report on an agency count of youth homelessness for The National Inquiry into Youth Homelessness, funded by YMCA, England. Sheila Gilford, Pauline Ing and Ann O'Sullivan worked on both research projects. Perpetua Kirby and Andrew O'Reilly worked on the latter project.

2. In a recent paper, analyzing the odds of new households entering social housing, Burrows (1997, Table 5) has calculated that the odds of new lone parents with dependent children entering social housing increases by a factor of 3.6.

3. In group interviews, undertaken by the Housing and Community Research Unit, young single mothers were very clear about which streets, on local authority housing estates, they wanted to avoid.

4. In 1988, a Department of Environment study reported that 40 per cent of homeless applicants were rejected (Evans and Duncan, 1988). Homeless acceptances peaked in 1991 and 1992 (Balchin, 1995, p. 271).

5. Sir George Young was particularly active in pushing this view on a BBC 2 phone-in in July 1994.

6. The research reported in *Bright Lights and Homelessness* (Smith *et al.*, 1996), published by YMCA, England, was undertaken on behalf of the National Inquiry into Youth Homelessness 1996.

7. Previous research undertaken in Birmingham in 1993 had found that homeless single young women were as likely to approach a housing department or a housing association as a hostel or shelter (Smith and Gilford, 1993).

8. Evans (1996) also produced a national estimate of youth homelessness based on her study of single people applying to local authority housing departments as homeless.

9. The percentage of young homeless people in London from ethnic origins other than white European was very high – nearly half of the study. In the Inner London boroughs which took part, nearly one in five young homeless people were of Black British/African-Caribbean origin; one in seven were of African origin (including many refugees); and one in twenty of Asian origin. Outside London, Birmingham had the highest proportion of young people from ethnic backgrounds other than white European (35 per cent). Comparing these proportions with the pattern of ethnic affiliation reported in the 1991 census, young women and men of British African-Caribbean/African origins are over-represented among homeless young people in London and Birmingham (Smith *et al.*, 1996). In London, however, young people from ethnic origins other than white had the lowest percentage of reported rough sleeping, and this also demonstrated how the Rough Sleepers Initiative not only renders

homelessness among young women invisible but also homelessness among young people of ethnic origins other than white European. Young white Irish people shared the characteristics of other young white Europeans with respect to rough sleeping.

10. The study *Family Background of Young Homeless People* (Smith *et al.*, 1997), funded by the Joseph Rowntree Foundation, was based on interviews with 56 young homeless people from Staffordshire (30 young men and 26 young women) who were interviewed in depth about their family background as were their parents, wherever possible. The stories of leaving home which they told were then compared with the experiences of young people living on local authority council estates in the local area. The group of young people were, with one exception, of young white European ethnic origin and the discussion in this chapter applies only to this group of young homelessness people.

11. Murray ( 1994) turned Wilson's argument of the shrinking marriageable pool on its head – blaming never-married mothers as the begetters of a new band of unemployed, unemployable welfare-dependent young men, a 'new rabble'. He argued that, just as the existence of Aid to Dependent Families was the cause of the black 'underclass' in the United States, so the right to social housing and housing benefit, in the UK, was creating a white underclass who were living in local authority housing estates on Income Support. He further claimed that women became single-parent mothers to gain social housing.

## References

Abel-Smith, B. and Townsend, P. (1965) *The Poor and the Poorest*, London: Longman Green.

Abramovitz, M. (1996) *Under Attack, Fighting Back: Women and Welfare in the United States*, New York: Cornerstone Books.

Anderson, I., Kemp, P. and Quilgars, D. (1993) *Single Homeless People*, London: HMSO.

Audit Commission (1989) *Housing the Homeless: The Local Authority Role*, London: HMSO.

Balchin, P. (1995) *Housing Policy: An Introduction*, 3rd edn, London: Routledge.

Bradshaw, J., Ditch, J., Holmes, H. and Whiteford, P. (1993) *Support for Children: A Comparison of Arrangements in Fifteen Countries*, Department of Social Security Research Report no. 21, London: HMSO.

Bramley, G. (1994) 'The affordability crisis in British Housing: Dimensions, causes and policy impact', *Housing Studies*, vol. 9, no 1.

Burghes, L. and Brown, M. (1995) *Single Lone Mothers: Problems, Prospects and Policies*, London: Family Policy Studies Centre.

Burrows, R. (1997) *Powers of Exclusion: Residential Mobility and the Dynamics of Residualisation*, paper to the British Sociological Association, April 1977, contact Centre for Housing Policy, University of York.

Carlen, P. (1996) *Jigsaw: A Political Criminology of Youth Homelessness*, Buckingham: Open University Press.

de Acosta, M. (1997) 'Single mothers in the USA: Unsupported workers and mothers', in S. Duncan and R. Edwards (eds) *Single Mothers in an International Context: Mothers or Workers?* London: UCL Press.

Dennis, N. and Erdos, G. (1992) *Families without Fatherhood*, London: IEA.

Department of the Environment (1994) *Access to Local Authority and Housing Association Tenancies*, consultation document, London: Department of the Environment.

Department of Health and Social Security (1974) *Finer Report 1974: Report of the Committee of One-Parent Families*, vol. II, 'Evidence', London: Department of Health and Social Security.

Douglas, A. and Gilroy, R. (1994) 'Young women and homelessness', in R. Gilroy and R. Woods (eds) *Housing Women*, London: Routledge.

Drake, M. (1981) *Single and Homeless*, London: Department of the Environment.

Duncan, S. and Edwards, R. (1997) 'Single mothers in Britain: Unsupported workers or mothers?', in S. Duncan and R. Edwards (eds) *Single Mothers in an International Context: Mothers or Workers?*, London: UCL Press.

Eardley, T., Bradshaw, J., Ditch, J., Gough, I. and Whitford, P. (1996) *Social Assistance in OECD Countries*, vol. 1, Department of Social Security Research Report no. 46, London: HMSO.

Evans, A. (1996) *We Don't Choose to be Homeless*, a report for the National Inquiry into Homelessness, London: CHAR.

Evans, A. and Duncan, S. (1988) *Responding to Homelessness: Local Authority Policy and Practice*, London: HMSO.

Garside, P, Grimshaw, R. and Ward, F. (1990) *No Place Like Home: The Hostels Experience*, Department of the Environment, London: HMSO.

Golden, S. (1992) *The Woman Outside: Meanings and Myths of Homelessness*, Berkeley: University of California Press.

Greve, J. and Currie, E. (1990) *Homelessness*, York: Joseph Rowntree Foundation.

Hills, J. (1993) *The Future of Welfare. A Guide to the Debate*, York: Joseph Rowntree Foundation.

Hutson, S. and Liddiard, M. (1994) *Youth Homelessness: The Social Construction of an Issue*, London: Macmillan.

Jones, G. (1995) *Leaving Home*, Buckingham: Open University Press.

Joshi, H. (1991) 'Sex and motherhood as handicaps in the labour market', in M. Maclean and D. Groves (eds) *Women's Issues in Social Policy*, London: Routledge.

Kemp, R. and Kemp, C. (1969) *The Battered Child*, London: Penguin.

Kiernan, K. (1989) 'The Family: Formation and Fission', in H. Joshi (ed.) *The Changing Population of Britain*, Oxford: Blackwell.

Kumar, V. (1993) *Poverty and Inequality in the UK: The Effects on Children*, London: National Children Bureau.

Murray, C. (1994), series of articles in *Sunday Times*, May–June 1994.

Pizzey, E. (1974) *Scream Quietly, the Neighbours Will Hear*, London: Penguin.

Power, A. and Tunstall, R. (1995) *Swimming against the Tide: Polarisation or Progress on 20 Unpopular Council Estates 1980–1995*, York: Joseph Rowntree Foundation.

*Roof* (1994) *Roof*, April/May.

Smeeding, T. and Rainwater, L. (1991) 'Cross-national trends in income poverty and dependency: The evidence of young adults in the eighties', in *Luxembourg Income Study*, Working Paper no. 67, Luxembourg.

Smith, D. (ed.) (1992) *Understanding the Underclass*, London: Policy Studies Institute.

Smith, J. and Gilford, S. (1991) *Homelessness among Under 25 Year Olds*, Housing Findings Briefing Paper no. 48, York: Joseph Rowntree Foundation.

Smith, J. and Gilford, S. (1993) *Young and Homeless in Birmingham*, London: Barnardos.

Smith, J., Gilford, S., Kirby P., O'Reilly, A. and Ing, P. (1996) *Bright Lights and Homelessness: Family and Single Homelessness among Young People in Our Cities*, London: YMCA.

Smith. J., Gilford, S. and O'Sullivan, A. (1997) *Family Background of Young Homeless People*, London: Family Policy Studies Centre.

Stockley, D., Bishopp, D. and Canter, D. (1993) *Young and Homeless*, Final Research Report, Guildford: University of Surrey, Department of Psychology.

Thomas, A. and Niner, P.(1989) *Living in Temporary Accommodation: A Survey of Homeless People*, London: HMSO.

Wilson, E. (1976) *Existing Research into Battered Women*, London: National Women's Aid Federation.

Wilson, W. (1987) *The Truly Disadvantaged: The Inner City, the Underclass and Public Policy*, Chicago: University of Chicago Press.

Woods, R. (1996) 'Women and housing', in C. Hallett (ed.) *Women and Social Policy*, Hampshire: Prentice Hall.

# 7 Rationing device or passport to social housing? The operation of the homelessness legislation in Britain in the 1990s

*Angela Evans*

## Introduction

The 1996 Housing Act represents the culmination of growing ministerial concerns over access to social housing. The Act, introduced by the last Conservative government, consolidates the controversial Awua judgement of 1995, which found that the homelessness legislation (Part III, Housing Act 1985) did not confer on housing authorities a duty to rehouse permanently, but simply to provide 'suitable' accommodation (*R.* v. *London Borough of Brent, ex parte* Awua (1995)). The 1996 Act clearly states that eligible homeless applicants have a right to only temporary accommodation and also introduces a single access channel to social housing. In support of the reforms, the government has argued that the homelessness legislation,[1] first introduced in 1977, was providing a major route into social housing rather than the limited safety net originally envisaged. Ministers also claimed that the priority awarded homeless people was being abused by applicants looking for a 'fast track' to social housing and that those on the waiting list, who often had 'comparable underlying needs',[2] were being disadvantaged by the 'two track' system.

In many ways, the controversy surrounding the homelessness legislation is unsurprising. Since its inception, the legislation has sought to strike a difficult balance between improving the housing situation of homeless people and, because of the limited supply of social housing, keeping the demand it generated within manageable limits. The concepts of relative need and desert were introduced as rationing devices. The legislation designates priority groups (for example, applicants with children, pregnant women) who are considered to be most vulnerable when homeless or threatened with homelessness and, therefore, more needy of assistance.

the original legislation. Concerns that the legislation would become a 'charter for scroungers and scrimshankers'[3] led to the introduction of the concepts of intentionality and local connection. Applicants would only have a right to permanent housing if their homelessness was unintentional and if they had a connection with the area in which they were applying as homeless. The homelessness legislation was always, therefore, a compromise which sought to balance the housing rights of homeless people with safeguards against abuse and the creation of excessive demand.

Views on how well the homelessness legislation has operated have varied over time as well as between groups. Campaign groups have argued that, although the legislation has significantly improved the situation of many homeless people, it should be better resourced and extended to cover non-priority groups such as single people. In the past, the government has also been generally supportive of the legislation. For example, following a review of the legislation in 1988, it concluded that the legislation 'has worked reasonably well and should remain in place as a long-stop to help those who through no fault of their own have become homeless' (Department of the Environment, 1989b) and that the Act struck 'a reasonable balance between the interests of the genuinely homeless and others in housing need'.[4]

However, the government's view of the legislation has clearly shifted since this time. From the early 1990s, ministers began to refer to the legislation, not as a valuable safety net for a minority of the most needy and urgent cases, but as the main route to social housing. It was argued that the growing dominance of homeless lettings was distorting the distribution of social housing and disadvantaging waiting list applicants. For example, in a House of Commons debate in 1994, the Housing Minister said that 'the homelessness legislation also provides people, once they are accepted as statutory homeless, with access to a permanent home ahead of others in as great or greater need who are on the housing waiting list. The tenancy of a council or housing association property is a great asset. We want to ensure that these tenancies go to those with the best claim to them'.[5]

There were also suggestions that the statutory homelessness system was being abused by applicants who were manipulating or misrepresenting their circumstances in order to qualify for assistance. Notions of who most and least deserved social housing formed a critically important backcloth to the government's plans to reform the legislation, although they were not explicitly given as the reasons for the changes. For example, there were a number of ministerial condemnations of young women becoming pregnant in order to qualify under the homelessness legislation, but these were usually voiced as part of a broader ideological campaign aimed at stemming the dependency culture and encouraging families to shoulder more of the welfare burden. The government's official justification for the legislation focused on issues of housing need. One of the main strands of their argument was the removal of the right of eligible homeless applicants to permanent housing, and the introduction of a single access channel would ensure that 'social housing goes to those households with the greatest underlying needs'.

So, was the pre-1997 statutory homelessness system as open as the Conservative government believes it was? Was it really a passport to social housing or more a rationing device strictly controlling access to a scarce resource? This chapter contributes to the debate on these issues by examining how the statutory homeless system operated, who applied to local authorities as homeless and who made it through the process to be permanently rehoused. The first section outlines the homeless application process, the second describes the characteristics and housing circumstances of homeless applicants, while sections three and four compare those who were accepted and rehoused as homeless with those who were rejected and those who withdrew from the application process. The chapter also examines some of the ways in which access to social housing, via the homeless route, can be rationed through, for example, the type and amount of evidence required, the interpretations of the legislation, the attitude of staff and the type of accommodation provided. These are laid out in section six.

The chapter concludes with an evaluation of the implications for the operation of the new statutory homelessness framework introduced by the 1996 Housing Act. Although the Awua judgement and the1996 Act significantly alter the legal position of homeless people, an appreciation of how the old system operated is still important. Many statutory definitions and duties remain the same (for example, most of the eligibility criteria are unchanged), and we can only assess the impact of the new arrangements if we fully understand the operation and outcomes of the earlier system.

The chapter draws heavily on findings from the largest ever cohort study of homeless applicants to local authorities in England. The study, which was undertaken in nine local authorities between 1992 and 1995, was commissioned by the Department of the Environment and undertaken by the Centre for Housing Management and Development at the University of Wales, Cardiff, in conjunction with Social and Community Planning Research (O'Callaghan et al., 1996). Almost 2,500 homeless applications across nine local authorities were recorded and their outcomes were monitored over a two-year period. In addition, homeless applicants were interviewed twice during the course of the study.

Since only nine local authorities were included, it is important to note that the cohort study is not nationally representative, but it is, nevertheless, indicative of wider trends and influences. It is referred to extensively in this chapter because of its significance as the only longitudinal examination we have of outcomes under the 1977 homelessness legislation.

## The homeless application process

The homeless application process is complex for applicants and local authorities alike. Local authorities have to check the eligibility of applicants and undertake investigations, to establish homelessness or threatened homelessness, priority need, local connections and whether or not homelessness was intentional, all of which can be both involved and time consuming. The process is likely to be even more protracted if an applicant's situation is a complex one, if there is little or no documentary evidence to support an application or if the local authority suspects that an application may be fraudulent. In addition, the need to accommodate applicants temporarily, either while enquires are being undertaken or until permanent housing becomes available, increases the administrative burden as well as prolonging the rehousing process.

The movement of applicants through the various stages of the application process can also be complicated. Applications can end at any stage of the process by the authority deciding to reject an applicant because she/he is ineligible or by the applicant withdrawing their application, either expressly or by not contacting the authority. Many authorities reject a proportion of applicants at the point of application without giving them a full assessment interview. Rejection at this early stage is nearly always because applicants are single and judged not to be in priority need. Local authority staff, interviewed for the cohort study, said that early rejections reduced officers' workloads to more manageable levels and meant that applicants' expectations were not unrealistically raised. However, rejection without an assessment interview does not necessarily mean that applicants do not receive any advice about their housing options. Applicants are also rejected following an assessment interview and a more detailed investigation of their application.

Applicants can withdraw or 'drop out' of the application process at one of four stages – before their assessment interview, after the interview but before a decision on their application is taken, after acceptance but before they receive an offer of permanent accommodation and, finally, following an offer of permanent housing. The process can be further complicated by applicants who have been rejected or have withdrawn their application re-applying as homeless.

Figure 7.1 shows the flow of applicants through the application process. Only the main stages of the application process are shown, since the intricate pathways taken by applications vary considerably. Just as no two homeless applicants will be in exactly the same situation, so no two housing authorities will organize their homelessness services in precisely the same way. The homelessness legislation, and guidance that accompanied it, provided local authorities with considerable latitude to determine the most appropriate way to respond to homelessness.

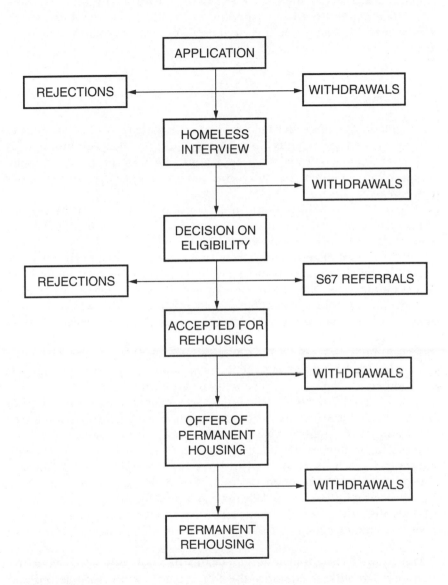

Figure 7.1  The flow of applicants

**Who applied as homeless?**

This section describes the characteristics and circumstances of homeless applicants included in the Department of the Environment cohort study. In particular, applicants are compared in terms of their household type, age, employment, income, housing circumstances and reasons for homelessness.

*Household type*

Although households with children were the largest group of applicants (44 per cent), they represented a smaller proportion of applicants than is popularly imagined. Even when applicants who were pregnant (with no children) are included, they still accounted for only just over a half (54 per cent) of all applicants.

Single applicants (including couples) made up over two fifths (41 per cent) of all applicants and, in the three metropolitan areas included in the cohort study, the proportion was even higher at over a half.

The high level of applications from single people is surprising since the legislation so clearly favours those with dependants. Although there is no direct evidence to suggest why these applications were made, there are a number of possible explanations, some relating to applicants' circumstances and understanding of their legal position, others to local authority responses.

First, some single applicants will have been eligible because they were vulnerable due to old age, mental illness or handicap, physical disability or for another 'special reason'. Second, some authorities, usually those with a reasonably plentiful supply of lettings, accept single applicants who are ineligible under the legislation on a discretionary basis. The high number of applications from single people to the metropolitan authorities in the study appears to be due to the relatively liberal acceptance policies of those authorities which, in turn, depend on a ready supply of social lettings. Third, there may also be an incentive for single applicants to apply as homeless even if they are unlikely to be accepted for rehousing. A number of study authorities provided comprehensive advice and assistance to single people, sometimes helping them find accommodation in the private sector.

Fourth, it is clear that some applicants did not fully understand the statutory eligibility criteria since the cohort study found that rejected and accepted applicants were almost equally as confident of their chances of being accepted. Sixty-two per cent of rejected applicants said that, when they first applied, they had thought it likely that they would be accepted, compared with 66 per cent of those who were later accepted. However, it is important to bear in mind here that, even if an applicant had anticipated rejection, they might still have considered it worthwhile applying since there was always a possibility that they might be accepted and, if not, they might have hoped for some other sort of assistance.

There was a high incidence of lone parents among applicants. Over a quarter (27 per cent) of all applicants and around three-fifths (61 per cent) of households with children were lone-parent families. The relatively large number of lone parents and single applicants was reflected in small household sizes. Four in ten applicants wanted housing for just themselves and a further 27 per cent wanted housing for two people. The mean household size was 2.2 people, while households with children had a median of one child.

*Age*

The great majority of cohort applicants were young. Three-quarters were under 35 years of age, while over two-fifths (42 per cent) were under 25 years of age. The young age profile is likely to reflect the fact that young people, especially those who have not started their own family, are often in transient housing situations and more vulnerable to homelessness. A disturbingly high proportion of applicants were very young – over a tenth (11 per cent) were between 16 and 18 years of age. However, it seems that the government's concern that young women were becoming pregnant in order to qualify under the homelessness legislation was unfounded. Only three per cent of applicants were single pregnant women or lone parents under 19 years of age. As one would expect, the children of applicants were also young – seven in ten households with children contained children under five years of age.

*Employment*

Only a minority (29 per cent) of cohort applicant households contained someone in paid work. Over a third (36 per cent) of applicants were registered unemployed and a further tenth (9 per cent) were unemployed but not registered. More than four in ten (44 per cent) of those under retirement age, and not in work, had not had a full-time job in the previous five years.

*Income*

Most homeless applicants had low incomes. Almost a fifth had a gross household income of under £39 a week (including benefits other than housing benefit), and more than eight in ten (82 per cent) received less than £154 a week. Single people had the lowest household incomes with over two-fifths (44 per cent) of single pregnant women and over a third (35 per cent) of single applicants receiving less than £39 a week. Almost all households (86 per cent) received one or more type of welfare benefit, the most common being income support (61 per cent), child benefit (40 per cent) and housing benefit (34 per cent).

*Housing circumstances*

Only two-fifths of applicants had their own independent accommodation when they applied as homeless (32 per cent were renting and 9 per cent were buying or owned their property), while over half (51 per cent) were staying in someone else's home (evenly divided between those living with their parents and those living with other relatives or friends). Older applicants were most likely to have their own accommodation – for example, the peak age range for owner-occupiers was 35 to 44 years (26 per cent) and, for those living in rented accommodation, it was 45 to 54 years (42 per cent). Almost two-fifths of applicants had no experience of renting or owning their own property, reflecting the large proportion of applicants who were young and only just beginning their housing 'careers'. A significant proportion of those sharing their accommodation had previously had their own accommodation but had moved in with someone else on a temporary basis.

*Reason for homelessness*

The cohort study found that only in a minority of cases was homelessness the outcome of an isolated event or situation (see Table 7.1). It was more usually the consequence of a number of problems which occurred either simultaneously or sequentially. Changes in family relationships and structures were often part of the equation and were mentioned by over half (55 per cent) of cohort applicants. However, this is likely to underestimate the true incidence, since some of the accommodation-related problems, mentioned by applicants, will have followed on from more personal problems. It is reasonable to assume that many applicants, who have no choice but to leave their stable accommodation, will make temporary accommodation arrangements until they are able to find something more suitable. For example, a woman may leave the marital home because of relationship difficulties and move with her children to her parents' home and then have to move out because of overcrowding and other pressures. The fact that relationship and family breakdown were far more common problems among study applicants mentioning a series of events leading to homelessness than those mentioning just one event would seem to confirm the prevalence of this pattern. Also, as we have seen, over half of cohort applicants were living in someone else's home when they applied as homeless. This strongly suggests that family/relationship problems are frequently followed by accommodation problems and that many applicants do attempt to make their own accommodation arrangements. However, it appears that these make-shift solutions are not usually suitable in the longer-term and in most cases merely delay, rather than avert, the need to apply as homeless.

Table 7.1 Immediate causes of housing difficulties

| Cause | % |
| --- | --- |
| **Relationship breakdown** | **17** |
| Divorce, separation, split with partner | 11 |
| Arguments/rows with partner | 1 |
| Domestic violence | 4 |
| Asked to leave by partner | 4 |
| **Family breakdown** | **21** |
| Arguments/rows with family | 9 |
| Asked/told to leave by family | 16 |
| **Relationship or family formation/expansion** | **17** |
| Pregnancy | 9 |
| New baby/children | 8 |
| Marriage/new partner | 1 |
| **Accommodation problems** | **51** |
| Overcrowding or no privacy | 19 |
| Needs or wants own home | 11 |
| Temporary arrangement | 6 |
| End of tenancy/house owner moving | 4 |
| Rent/mortgage arrears | 2 |
| Repossession | 4 |
| Other accommodation problems | 7 |
| **Other Causes** | **25** |
| **Refused/don't know** | **6** |

Base = 1,497 homeless applicants. Percentages total more than 100% as more than one answer was possible.

Many of the personal situations that create a need for alternative accommodation are the consequence of life-cycle transitions. For example, the large number of young single applicants in the cohort reflects the fact that many young people are on the threshold of establishing an independent home and so their housing situations at this time are often fluid, to the extent of being precarious, particularly if a young person has few resources and little support. Family conflict and family formation were given as the main reasons for homelessness among young cohort applicants. In contrast, relationship breakdown was the most common reason for homelessness among the 25 to 44 age group. However, the need for alternative accommodation usually only becomes problematic if a household lacks the resources to be able to secure suitable accommodation. The very low incomes of the majority of applicants (see above) may, therefore, be as much a cause of homelessness as the more immediate accommodation and relationship-related problems mentioned by applicants.

The next two sections describe and compare the characteristics, circumstances and outcomes of cohort applicants who were rehoused as homeless by study authorities as well as those applicants who were either rejected as homeless or who withdrew from the application process. These comparisons are important measures of the effects of the statutory homelessness system on the outcomes for applicants.

**Who was rehoused as homeless?**

Less than a third (31 per cent) of cohort applicants were accepted for rehousing under the homelessness legislation and rehoused by the end of the study period (some 18 months after the recording of applicants commenced). A further eight per cent of applicants were awaiting either a decision on their application or permanent rehousing.

Compared to rejected applicants, applicants who were accepted for rehousing were twice as likely to live in a household with children or a pregnant woman, which reflects the priority need categories of the legislation. Accepted applicants were more likely than other applicants to have been living in someone else's home when they applied as homeless and were most likely to think that their accommodation was overcrowded. However, a significant proportion of these applicants had previously had their own independent accommodation.

Local authority housing was the main source of permanent accommodation for those rehoused under the homelessness legislation. The great majority (80 per cent) were rehoused in local authority stock, 17 per cent in housing association housing and just 2 per cent in the private sector. The majority (56 per cent) were rehoused in a flat or maisonette and two-fifths (39 per cent) in a house. Although permanently rehoused applicants were generally satisfied with their accommodation (86 per cent), a significant proportion (73 per cent) reported problems. Table 7.2 shows that two-fifths of applicants described problems with the physical condition of their accommodation, while others identified problems with the area or neighbourhood, the inadequate size of the accommodation or the type of accommodation they had been allocated.

Table 7.2 Main problems with accommodation following rehousing

| Problems/no problems | % |
| --- | --- |
| Physical problems with accommodation | 42 |
| Area and neighbourhood problems | 17 |
| Too small/overcrowded | 12 |
| Unsuitable type of accommodation | 11 |
| Rents/bills too high | 2 |
| Other problems | 27 |
| No problems | 27 |

Base = 330 homeless applicants rehoused in local authority-provided permanent accommodation. Percentages total more than 100% as more than one answer was possible.

Although a majority (61 per cent) of permanently rehoused applicants said they were living in better accommodation following their application, a substantial minority thought the accommodation was worse (21 per cent) or of about the same standard (16 per cent). In addition, a third (32 per cent) of all rehoused applicants were either already on the transfer list or said they were likely to join it. Two-thirds of those wishing to transfer wanted to move because of accommodation-related reasons, most often because they wanted a different kind of accommodation (typically, a house rather than a flat) or because they felt the accommodation was too small. Just over a half wanted to move out of the area they had been rehoused in – a quarter mentioned crime or violence in the area and just over a tenth mentioned distance from family, friends and amenities.

## Who was rejected or withdrew from the process?

This section describes the characteristics, circumstances and, where it is known, the outcomes for cohort applicants who withdrew their application or were rejected for rehousing.

### Applicants who withdrew

The majority (55 per cent) of applicants were either rejected under the legislation (36 per cent) or had 'dropped out' of the application process (19 per cent). Of those who withdrew, three-fifths (60 per cent) did so before the local authority had reached a decision on their application (including 7 per cent who did not attend their assessment interview), a fifth after being accepted but before receiving an offer of accommodation and another fifth after they were offered accommodation.

It was not always easy for the study to establish reasons why applicants withdrew their application. Applicants did not always notify the authority that they no longer wished to be rehoused and it was often a lack of response to an authority's attempts to progress an application that suggested that the application had, in effect, been withdrawn. Despite these difficulties, information was available for around a fifth of those cohort applicants who withdrew their application. These applicants were roughly evenly divided between those who no longer wanted or needed to move (54 per cent) and those who had found alternative accommodation (51 per cent). The most common reasons for wanting to stay put were reconciliation with a partner (13 per cent), another change in personal circumstances (13 per cent) and a decision that local authority accommodation was no longer wanted (13 per cent).

Applicants who had withdrawn their application[6] had a similar household profile to those who were accepted for rehousing. Two-thirds of applicants lived in a household with children or a pregnant woman. However, applicants who withdrew were, on average, slightly older than other applicants. Applicants who withdrew also had slightly higher incomes and were more likely to have assets in the form of savings or property. However, they were also more likely to have a mortgage debt.

Applicants who withdrew their application were more likely than other types of applicant to have owned or have been buying the accommodation they applied from and to have been a local authority or housing association tenant. For example, 15 per cent were council or housing association tenants at the point of application compared with 8 per cent of other applicants. Withdrawals also tended to have lived in the place they applied from for longer than other applicants, were least likely to have problems with the accommodation and were most likely to view it as a settled home. Applicants who withdrew their application generally had experienced similar problems to applicants who were accepted, although they were slightly more likely than other applicants to have experienced relationship breakdown, especially where this involved domestic violence, and to have become homeless because of rent or mortgage arrears.

Findings on the housing outcomes of applicants who had withdrawn their application need to be treated with caution since the numbers involved are small. By the end of the study period, of the 53 applicants who were found and interviewed, 17 had remained in the accommodation they had occupied at the time of their first interview, 21 had moved into new accommodation they had found for themselves and 15 had been provided with accommodation by a local authority, either following a further homeless application or through the housing waiting list. Although the numbers are small, it does appear that applicants who withdrew their application were more likely than rejected applicants to have found alternative accommodation themselves and, in many cases, this may account for why they had withdrawn from the application process.

*Applicants who were rejected*

Cohort applicants who were rejected were divided evenly between those who were rejected at the point of first contact with the authority and those who were rejected following an assessment interview. As one would expect, rejected applicants were significantly more likely to be single and childless than applicants who were accepted for rehousing or had withdrawn. Over half (57 per cent) of rejected applicants consisted of a single person or childless couple compared with under a third of other applicants. These household profiles reflect the impact of the priority need categories as criteria for acceptance under the homelessness legislation.

However, the indications are that rejected applicants were also in housing need. They had low incomes, around a half were sharing their accommodation with another household, a larger than average proportion expressed dissatisfaction with their accommodation and it appears that many had unsuccessfully attempted to resolve their housing difficulties (see Chapter 8). For example, rejected applicants were most likely to have a household income of less than £39 a week or £2,000 a year. Around a fifth (21 per cent) received as little as this compared with 16 per cent of those who were accepted and 14 per cent of those who withdrew their application. However, the lower incomes of rejected applicants are likely to reflect the lower levels of benefit paid to single people.

Although almost half (47 per cent) of rejected applicants were sharing their accommodation when they applied as homeless, they were more likely than other applicants to have their own rented accommodation (37 per cent compared with 22 per cent of acceptances). However, the great majority of these were living in the private rented sector. For example, over a quarter (26 per cent) of applicants who were subsequently rejected had been living in private rented accommodation when they applied as homeless compared with just 11 per cent of applicants who were accepted.

Rejected applicants had also been living in the place they applied from for a shorter period than other applicants and were least satisfied with their accommodation. Almost a half expressed dissatisfaction compared with only a third of other applicants. They had also been most mobile between leaving their last settled home and moving into the place they applied from. Two-fifths of rejected applicants, who had stayed elsewhere between leaving their settled home and moving into the place they applied from, had moved at least four times a year. Rejected applicants were also significantly more likely than other groups to have moved from settled accommodation, in someone else's home, into independent accommodation, usually in the private rented sector. Although all groups were equally likely to have made a previous homeless application, rejected applicants were more likely to have made three or more previous applications.

By the end of the study period, the majority (55 per cent) of applicants who had been rejected or had withdrawn early in the application process had not moved from the accommodation they were in when they applied as homeless. Over a quarter (26 per cent) had moved to accommodation they had found themselves and the remaining 19 per cent were in permanent accommodation provided by the local authority (acquired either via the waiting list or a subsequent homeless application). Most of those who had moved and found their own accommodation were living in the private rented sector.

In summary then, although the majority (54 per cent) of cohort applicants were pregnant and/or had children, a very substantial minority (41 per cent) were single or couples. There was a high incidence of lone parenthood among applicants and family sizes were generally small, reflecting the fact that the great majority of applicants were young – three-quarters under 35 years of age and over two-fifths younger than 25. The great majority of applicant households were on low incomes. Almost three quarters (71 per cent) had no-one in paid work and 82 per cent received less than £154 a week.

Around a half (51 per cent) of applicants were sharing accommodation with another household and only two-fifths had their own independent accommodation. Homelessness was usually the outcome of a chain or collection of events, often including a change in family relationships or structure and, only in a minority of cases, was it a consequence of an isolated and specific event.

Applicant households accepted for housing were twice as likely to include children or a pregnant woman, compared with rejected applicants, reflecting the priority need categories included in the legislation. Applicants who were accepted were also more likely to be living in someone else's home at the time they applied as homeless, although a significant proportion had previously had their own independent accommodation.

Although the majority of rehoused applicants were satisfied with the permanent accommodation they had been allocated, a substantial minority (around a third) expressed dissatisfaction and a desire to move elsewhere.

Applicants who withdrew from the application process had similar profiles to those who were accepted for housing although they were on average slightly older, with higher incomes and were more likely to have assets in the form of savings or property. They were also more likely than other applicants to have owned their accommodation or to have rented from a housing association or council and to be homeless because of rent or mortgage arrears or relationship breakdown. It is possible that applicants who withdrew had more options available to them because of their higher incomes and assets or, having previously had their own accommodation, they may have been more selective in terms of the accommodation they were prepared to accept.

Rejected applicants were much more likely to be single or in couples, again reflecting the priority need categories covered by the legislation. Around a half of rejected applicants were sharing accommodation with another household and a higher than average proportion were renting privately owned accommodation. Rejected applicants were more likely than other applicants to express dissatisfaction with their accommodation and had been more mobile since leaving their last settled home.

## Rationing mechanism or passport to social housing?

Rather than a passport to social housing, it appears from the findings described above that the homelessness legislation has operated as a strict rationing mechanism. Only a third (31 per cent) of cohort applicants had been permanently rehoused as a consequence of their application by the end of the study period and, given that a third of these (32 per cent) wanted a transfer soon after moving in, it would seem that only around a fifth of applicants were rehoused to their own satisfaction.

It could be argued that the relatively small proportion of homeless applicants who are accepted and rehoused is evidence that the system has successfully weeded out the least needy cases. Indeed, the intention of government had always been for the legislation to operate as a rationing device, providing a limited safety net for specific priority groups who were perceived to be most vulnerable. However, in the light of the study findings described above, it is difficult to sustain the argument that only those accepted and rehoused as homeless were in housing need. The findings suggest that applicants who were rejected were also in housing need (see Chapters 6 and 8). For example, the great majority were out of work and on very low incomes, almost a half were sharing with another household and they were more likely than average to be dissatisfied with the accommodation they applied from. Many were rejected, not because of their lack of need, but because they were single and not vulnerable for any reason and so fell outside the priority need categories covered by the legislation. However, it appears that being single did not make the securing of suitable accommodation any easier. We have seen that rejected applicants were more likely to have looked for and secured accommodation in the private rented sector prior to their homeless application and the majority (55 per cent) were still in the accommodation they applied from at the end of the study period.

Also, it could be argued that the output from the statutory homelessness system, in terms of homeless applicants satisfactorily rehoused, should be commensurate with the effort put into the system. The homelessness system is complex, administratively burdensome and expensive to operate. A key issue is whether a fifth of applicants satisfactorily rehoused is an adequate outcome given the considerable effort and expense of operating the system.

**How is access rationed?**

It is important to examine the ways in which access to social housing through the homelessness route has been restricted. In some instances, it is the legislation itself which is the rationing device, while, in others it is the way in which a local authority interprets or administers the statutory requirements that is most influential. Rationing can be deliberate or it can be an unintentional by-product of an authority's policies and practices. Rationing can also occur in a number of different ways. Homeless people can be discouraged from applying in the first place, the way in which an authority responds to cases of homelessness can encourage applicants to withdraw from the application process or applicants can be rejected for rehousing.

Since this chapter draws heavily on a study of people who applied as homeless, the focus is on rationing through the rejection or withdrawal of applications. However, it is clear, from other homeless studies, that a significant proportion of homeless people do not approach a local authority at all about their problem. For example, a Department of the Environment survey of single homeless people who were sleeping rough or living in bed and breakfast hotels or hostels found that less than two-fifths had applied to the local council as homeless within the previous 12 months (Anderson *et al.*, 1993). Homeless people can be discouraged from applying in a number of different ways. For example, they may feel that it is not worth their applying since they are unlikely to be accepted (especially if they fall outside the priority need categories), they may not want the type of accommodation made available to homeless applicants or they may be deterred by a local authority's image for being tough and unsympathetic towards homeless applicants.

This 'non expression of legitimate demands for service provision' by clients has been described by Judge (1975) as 'consumer rationing'. In his analysis of the phenomenon, Judge makes a distinction between an unbiased decision not to express a legitimate demand and a lack of demand which emanates from the way in which a service is delivered. When resources are scarce, services are often provided, either consciously or unconsciously, in ways which will discourage clients from applying. Although most of these disincentives operate at the local level, much broader negative perceptions of services and service recipients can also discourage take-up. For example, the recent presentation of homeless applicants as undeserving and manipulative, together with the generally negative images of social housing portrayed by the media, are bound to lead to concerns among homeless people that they will be stigmatized by applying as homeless, that the application process will be demeaning and that, if 'successful', they will end up in a social housing ghetto. Some of the ways in which local authorities have controlled access to social housing through the homelessness channel are examined below.

*Interpretation of the legislation*

The homelessness legislation, and accompanying guidance, are themselves rationing devices, setting the legal parameters by excluding those who are not homeless, non-priority groups, those who were intentionally homeless and those without a qualifying local connection. Additionally, however, the law has left ample scope for local discretion and a number of studies have shown how local authorities have varied in their interpretation of key definitions and duties (Department of the Environment, 1988; 1989a; 1996a). For example, authorities have differed in terms of the stage at which applicants are accepted as homeless, their definition of 'vulnerable for some other reason', the type and duration of enquiries they undertake and the way in which intentionality is assessed.

It is important to note that the resource issue has been a very influential determinant of how strictly or liberally an authority interprets the legislation. For example, the cohort study found that metropolitan authorities, with a relatively plentiful supply of social lettings, were significantly more likely to accept applicants for housing. In London, where housing opportunities are more constrained, authorities were more likely than average to reject applicants. It is, therefore, possible for local authority officers and members to be sympathetic to the needs of homeless applicants but to be bound by a shortage of resources. A number of the local authorities, included in the cohort study, reported that they had adopted more restrictive eligibility criteria in response to increased demand, but , as we shall see below, this was less common than an insistence on more evidence of an applicant's situation.

We have seen that around half of the cohort applicants who were found to be ineligible were rejected by reception or 'front-line' staff, without a full assessment interview. Although there are some very good reasons for making such early decisions, it does inevitably mean that considerable discretion is exercised in ways that can be difficult to monitor.

*The application process*

The longer and more complex the application process, the higher the withdrawal or 'drop-out' rate will be. In the cohort study, most delays to the application process appear to have been unintentional and related mainly to a shortage of housing, the complexity of cases, administrative overload and system failures or inefficiency. For example, all study authorities used some form of temporary accommodation while enquiries into cases were being undertaken or because permanent accommodation was not immediately available. The use of temporary accommodation, especially the least desirable types like bed and breakfast accommodation, is bound to act as a deterrent to applicants and increase withdrawal rates, even if this is not the intention of the authority (see Chapter 11).

In other cases, study authorities had tightened up their investigation of cases in order to weed out the least genuine and urgent cases. In fact, authorities were more likely to have tightened up their investigation of cases than their interpretation of the legislation in response to the increase in homeless applications experienced up until the early 1990s. Typically they required more documentary evidence of an applicant's situation and undertook more thorough investigations. Study authorities reported that this had the effect of discouraging people from applying as well as increasing withdrawal and rejection rates. Authorities saw it as a fairer and more targeted way of reducing demand than applying stricter definitions of homelessness, priority need, intentionality and local connections. However, officers also reported that it had changed the nature of their work as well as their relationship with applicants.

Despite the complexities of the process, the majority of cohort applications were progressed relatively quickly. Overall, nearly half (49 per cent) of decisions were taken within a week of an application being received and almost two-thirds (64 per cent) within a month, with a median of six days. However, applicants who were rejected on the day they applied (without an assessment interview) are included in these figures. Also, two-fifths of applications in London and just under a fifth (18 per cent) of cases in metropolitan and non-metropolitan authorities were not determined within the Code of Guidance's recommended time limit of 30 working days.

The median time between application and permanent rehousing (for those who completed the process within the study period) was 16 weeks. Two-fifths (39 per cent) of applicants were rehoused within three months and nearly two thirds (65 per cent) within six months. In almost a third (30 per cent) of cases it took over six months to rehouse applicants permanently and, it should also be remembered, that eight per cent of applicants were still waiting for a decision or rehousing at the end of the study period.

*The attitude of staff*

The attitude of staff towards applicants, together with other indicators of how clients are viewed by an authority, such as the type and condition of reception facilities, can be a very influential rationing device. Indeed, the main reason for dissatisfaction among applicants interviewed for the cohort study was the uncaring attitude of staff. Almost a half (45 per cent) of applicants said they were dissatisfied with the way the council had handled their application and the main reason for being dissatisfied was because local authority staff had seemed unconcerned about the applicant's problems (41 per cent of dissatisfied applicants). Other reasons for being dissatisfied included being given inadequate assistance (26 per cent), dissatisfaction with council rules and requirements (20 per cent), difficulties over contacting the authority (18 per cent), being offered unsuitable accommodation (15 per cent) and having to wait too long to be rehoused (12 per cent). Although dissatisfaction rates were closely allied to outcomes, a significant minority (32 per cent) of applicants, who had been accepted for rehousing, also expressed dissatisfaction with the way in which their application had been handled.

It does appear that the homelessness system can be insensitive to the complex and urgent needs of applicants. We have seen that many applicants have problems in addition to their homelessness, but the statutory homeless system is narrowly focused on homelessness as a housing problem. Eligibility is usually determined by the most recent housing situation (see Chapter 6) and it is often assumed that permanent rehousing will be the solution to an applicant's problems. The stringent application of the statutory eligibility criteria, in combination with resource pressures, can also mean that applicants are processed rather than listened to. The more thorough investigation of cases, mentioned above, can also make the system more bureaucratic and less sensitive to the individual circumstances and needs of applicants.

*Housing outcomes*

If a council offers homeless applicants poor-quality accommodation in undesirable areas, homeless people will be deterred from applying and those who have applied will be more likely to withdraw from the application process. Almost a tenth of homeless applicants, who were offered permanent accommodation, were not rehoused because they refused or failed to respond to the offer. There is some evidence that homeless applicants do receive offers of less desirable properties. The majority (56 per cent) of cohort applicants were rehoused in a flat or maisonette and only two-fifths

(39 per cent) in a house. Also, almost two-fifths (37 per cent) of permanently rehoused applicants said their accommodation was no better than the accommodation they had applied as homeless from. The majority of councils operate one-offer only policies for homeless applicants and it is this limited choice which often results in homeless applicants being rehoused in the least popular housing types and areas.

We have seen that there is significant fall-out from the statutory homelessness system – the majority of applicants are either rejected or withdraw from the process. Access is regulated, not just by the legislation itself and the interpretation that is placed on it, but also through the way in which homelessness services are provided – for example, by the attitudes of staff, the nature of the application process and the type of accommodation offered. Although the 1996 Housing Act has significantly altered the rights of eligible homeless applicants, these rationing devices are likely to remain features of the statutory homeless system.

## Implications for the future

The findings on the operation and outcomes of the pre-1997 statutory homelessness system, described above, have a number of possible implications for future access to social housing. First, there is clearly considerable un-met housing demand among single people, and there is every indication that this type of need will continue, indeed grow, in the foreseeable future. We have seen that, in spite of the fact that the homelessness legislation favours households with dependants, over two-fifths of applicants were single. Recent housing demand and need studies, together with household projections to 2016, confirm this picture of housing need (Holmans, 1995; Department of the Environment, 1996b). Due to demographic and social changes, the greatest housing demand by far will come from single people and, although the private housing markets will meet some, or even most, of this demand, there will be many single people who cannot afford private housing options. An increasingly important issue will be the exclusion of single people from mainstream social housing when there is growing evidence of considerable housing need among this group (see Chapter 8).

We have seen that the complex rules and administrative procedures, associated with the pre-1997 statutory homeless system, meant that only a minority of homeless applicants were rehoused in social rented housing. Access under the 1996 legislation promises to be much more difficult. The new homeless legislation not only offers fewer rights, but the process of exercising those rights is likely to be more arduous and protracted. In addition to the well-established tests of homelessness, intentionality, priority need and local connection, local authorities are obliged to investigate whether applicants are 'eligible for assistance' (having the appropriate residential status) and whether there is other suitable alternative accommodation available in the district. These additional requirements are likely to lead to more detailed and time-consuming investigations of cases, additional bureaucracy, more rejections and a greater psychological distance between the homeless applicant and the local authority officer. The introduction of a single route to social housing is not inherently damaging to the interests of homeless people – indeed, it could be argued that an integrated system is fairer and less stigmatizing. However, any access system has to be capable of responding quickly and sensitively when applicants are homeless or threatened with homelessness. The added complexities of the new statutory homelessness system could well lead to a further deterioration in the already poor ratio between bureaucratic effort and the number of homeless people rehoused, and to fewer homeless people receiving the help they need.

## Notes

1.  The homeless legislation was first introduced in 1977 with the Housing (Homeless Persons) Act and was later included in the Housing Act 1985 for England and Wales, the Housing (Scotland) Act 1987 for Scotland and the Housing (Northern Ireland) Order 1988 for Northern Ireland.
2.  Sir George Young in a statement to the House of Commons, 18 July 1994.
3.  House of Commons debate, 18 February 1977.
4.  House of Commons debate, 25 November 1989.
5.  House of Commons debate, 20 January 1994.
6.  This information is only available for applicants who withdrew their application before a decision on their eligibility had been taken.

## References

Anderson, I., Kemp, P. and Quilgars, D. (1993) *Single Homeless People*, London: HMSO.

Department of the Environment (1988) *Responding to Homelessness: Local Authority Policy and Practice*, London: HMSO.

Department of the Environment (1989a) *Homelessness in Nine Local Authority Areas: Case Studies of Policy and Practice*, London: HMSO.

Department of the Environment (1989b) *The Government's Review of the Homelessness Legislation*, London: Department of the Environment.

Department of the Environment (1996a) *Evaluation of the 1991 Code of Guidance*, London: HMSO.

Department of the Environment (1996b) *The Government's Response to the Second Report from the House of Commons Select Committee on Housing Need*, London: Department of the Environment.

Holmans, A. (1995) *Housing Demand and Need in England 1991–2011*, York: Joseph Rowntree Foundation.

Judge, K. (1975) *Rationing Social Services*, London: Heinemann.

O'Callaghan, B., Dominion, L., Evans, A., Dix, J., Smith, R., Williams, P. and Zimmeck, M. (1996) *Study of Homeless Applicants*, London: HMSO.

# 8 Social housing or social exclusion? Non-access to housing for single homeless people

*Isobel Anderson*

## Introduction

This chapter reviews the evidence on the nature of single homelessness and the opportunities for single people to obtain social housing. It focuses on two empirical studies carried out by the author in partnership with other colleagues (Anderson *et al.*, 1993; Anderson and Morgan, 1997). The analysis highlights the contradictions in the approaches to tackling single homelessness which fail to deal with single people's wider exclusion from the social housing system. While the problem of 'single homelessness' in Britain is widely recognized, the homelessness legislation directly discriminates against most single people. Single people are also disadvantaged, relative to other household types, in other access routes into social housing. The legitimacy of single people's needs for secure, affordable housing is rarely acknowledged in housing policy, in legislation or in practice.

The chapter is presented in four parts. First a brief overview is given of the debates on social exclusion and legitimacy as a framework for examining single homelessness. Second, there is a discussion of single homelessness in relation to the position of single people in the wider housing system. Third, a summary of the nature of single homelessness is made. Fourth, there is as an evaluation of the opportunities for single homeless people to gain access to social housing. Finally, the conclusions draw together the ideas and evidence presented, demonstrating the extent to which single people experience sustained disadvantage in the social housing system.

In this chapter, 'single person' or 'single people' refer to individuals aged between 16 and 59 years who live, or wish to live, as a one-person household at a particular point in their lives. The term 'homelessness' is used to encompass a broad range of housing circumstances where individuals lack secure, habitable or affordable accommodation. The terms 'statutory' homelessness and 'single' homelessness or 'non-priority' homelessness are used to convey the legal status of households with reference to the homelessness legislation contained in the Housing Act 1996 and Housing (Scotland) Act 1987. 'Social housing' includes long-term, secure/ permanent council housing and housing association accommodation. 'Low income groups' can be taken to include those who are unable to afford housing, to buy or rent, on the private market. In practice, their incomes are likely to be around, or below, state benefit levels, whether they are in receipt of benefit or in low paid employment. 'Social exclusion' refers to exclusion from aspects of well-being and social participation (including housing) taken as 'usual' among the majority within society.

### Inclusion or exclusion: a question of legitimacy?

In the view of this author, access to housing of a reasonable quality, at a reasonable price, is a fundamental pre-requisite for both human well-being and meaningful participation in social life. At a time when politicians and commentators on social issues are increasingly concerned about the 'breakdown of the fabric of society', it is surprising that weaknesses in housing policy and the housing system have not been central to the evolving debates on social exclusion and social integration.

European Union agencies increasingly use the term 'social exclusion' with reference to both poverty and deprivation itself and to policies aimed at bringing about greater social cohesion (Room, 1995a; see also Chapter 3). While poverty is characterized as reflecting *distributional* issues (access to resources), social exclusion is described more broadly – reflecting *relational* issues of inadequate social participation, in particular exclusion from employment (Room, 1995a; 1995b). Berghman (1995) develops the concept of social exclusion as a process which is both comprehensive and dynamic. Social exclusion is *comprehensive*, in that it embraces a range of social experiences beyond work and income and *dynamic* in that poverty, or disadvantage, need not be fixed, unchangeable states (Berghman, 1995, pp. 21–2). On this interpretation, policies to combat exclusion, or to promote a cohesive society, should also be comprehensive and dynamic in nature. That is to say, to be effective, policies would need to tackle the multi-dimensional nature of social exclusion, with the aim of moving people from an excluded to an included position.

Social exclusion has also been associated with debates as to whether an 'underclass' of marginalized or excluded individuals can be identified in the developed nations in the late 20th century (Murray *et al.*, 1990; 1994). The notion of an identifiable, excluded 'class' is highly contentious and subject to interpretation according to different ideologies. For example,

Taylor-Gooby (1991) discusses neo-liberal and social-democratic ideologies in relation to social exclusion, which broadly coincide with individualistic and structural explanations of homelessness (Hutson and Liddiard, 1994). Housing policy has not been central to debates on social exclusion, but homelessness has been recognized as a crucial element of social exclusion across Europe (Council of Europe, 1993; Daly, 1993).

An increasingly important dimension of contemporary perceptions of social exclusion in Britain is the spatial concentration of 'the excluded poor' in social housing estates. Consequently, debates about housing and social exclusion in Britain have tended to focus on the changing role of social housing and the experiences of households living in this tenure (Forrest and Murie, 1983; Page, 1993; Malpass and Murie, 1994; Lee *et al.*, 1995). A succinct summary of the process of social exclusion in the council housing sector is provided by Malpass and Murie (1994, pp. 146–51). Since 1980, much of the highest quality and most desirable council stock has been privatized and transferred into owner occupation through sales to sitting tenants. The same period has seen continued disinvestment in building and repair of council housing and the allocation of vacant council dwellings to households considered to be in the greatest need of subsidized housing. By the 1990s, the overall quality of the remaining council sector had declined substantially – in terms of age, design, type, condition and the desirability of properties. The characteristics of council tenants had also changed – from the affluent, employed working-class to a lower-income, benefit-dependent, group. The term 'residualization' is used to describe the pattern of change in the council housing sector and the term 'marginalization' is used to convey the degree of social exclusion experienced by the residents of council housing (Malpass and Murie, 1994).

The housing policies which led to these changes in the social housing sector represented the housing dimension of a Conservative government ideology, which sought to reduce state intervention and the public expenditure on the collective provision of welfare (see Chapter 2). The lack of any prevailing consensus regarding rights to housing, or housing provision, as a welfare service meant that there was less political opposition to cuts in social housing investment, compared to other aspects of welfare provision. By the mid-1990s, council housing increasingly operated as a safety net for the poorest, most disadvantaged households in society, including many who had experienced homelessness. Even among these marginalized groups, however, important demarcations can be identified and the processes by which council housing is allocated dictate that certain individuals have fewer opportunities to gain access, even to this residualized tenure. A key argument of this chapter is that debates on housing and social exclusion have neglected a significant group of people who have *no* accommodation, or who have shelter which is much less secure than council housing – single homeless people.

Access to any aspect of welfare is, to some extent, determined by the notion of legitimacy, which gives entitlement to assistance. Unlike some other aspects of welfare, access to social or welfare housing has never been explicitly determined by an income-related means test. Rather, assistance is determined by bureaucratic procedures ostensibly based on the concept of 'housing need'. There is no official definition of housing need, although legislation has prescribed certain priority housing circumstances (such as overcrowding or disrepair) which should be taken into account in prioritizing applicants for social housing. Importantly, the systems which measure housing need and determine access to social housing are constructed from prevailing ideas as to which housing circumstances *and household characteristics* merit assistance.

Successive central government policy and legislative statements since 1971, have emphasized the state's responsibility to *families* in housing need – rather than to all citizens (Holmans, 1995). Referring directly to single people, Holmans (p. 5) points out that where they have sufficient funds to obtain housing in the market, no practical questions arise as to whether single people 'really need' to live independently. If, however, they cannot provide for themselves, questions are raised as to whether they have a legitimate claim to social rented housing, irrespective of need. The House of Commons Environment Committee (1996) acknowledged the problems and the contradictions arising from the lack of a clear definition of housing need. With respect to different household types, the Committee accepted that covert 'moral judgements' should be avoided in determining housing needs (House of Commons Environment Committee, 1996) – but no change in attitudes has, as yet, filtered into official policy statements from central government.

## Single people and single homelessness

Trends in housing need and homelessness reflect both patterns of household formation and opportunities to gain access to suitable accommodation. The significant rise in single homelessness and street homelessness, which occurred in Britain in the late 1980s and early 1990s, took place following a long period of growth in the formation of single-person households. During the same period, the procedures by which low-income groups gained access to social housing tended to discriminate against single people.

The proportion of people living alone in Britain has almost doubled since the 1950s (HMSO, 1995, p. 65) as a result of people choosing to live alone and people remaining on their own following the dissolution of a relationship or a bereavement. By 1991, more than a quarter (27 per cent) of households in Great Britain were one-person households (HMSO, 1995,

p. 74), most of which were over pensionable age. Only four per cent of the 16–24 age group and eight per cent of those aged 25–44 lived in officially recognized single-person households in 1993 (HMSO, 1995, p. 72). It is therefore important to differentiate 'single-person households' from 'single people'. The proportion of single adults in the population also increased by around 50 per cent between 1961 and 1991 (HMSO, 1995, p. 72). Although there was an increase in independent living among single adults, the period also saw growth in the proportion of men and women in their mid- and late twenties who remained in the parental home or in shared accommodation (HMSO, 1995, p. 73).

Looking to the future, the House of Commons Environment Committee (1996) reported that the total number of households in England was expected to rise by 4.4 million (23 per cent) over the period 1991–2016, and one-person households are expected to make up 80 per cent of this anticipated increase (Town and Country Planning Association, 1996). Holmans (1995, p. 43) has shown that growth in household formation will mainly take place among those aged 30 years and above, and that the number of single people, aged 20–29 is likely to decline, due to the fall in the birth rate in the late 1960s and early 1970s.

Throughout the 1980s and 1990s, there have been two main access routes to social housing – housing waiting lists and the homelessness procedures. A detailed review of the legislation relating to the allocation of local authority and housing association tenancies in Scotland, England and Wales is presented in Anderson and Morgan (1997). Broadly, waiting lists tended to prioritize family and older households, but they did not systematically exclude single people, while the homelessness provisions did directly discriminate against single people.

Legislative provisions for local authorities to deal with homelessness were first introduced in 1977 and consolidated in the Housing Act 1985 and the Housing (Scotland) Act 1987. Until the implementation of the Housing Act 1996, the terms of the legislation were identical across Scotland, England and Wales. Briefly, local authorities were obliged, by law, to secure accommodation for households which were found to be: homeless; in a priority need group; not intentionally homeless; and having a local connection. The priority need groups included: households with dependent children; households with an expectant mother; households homeless in an emergency (such as a fire or flood); and households containing a 'vulnerable' person. The principal categories of vulnerability in the legislation are: old age; physical disability; mental illness/handicap (learning difficulties); and other special reasons. The homelessness provisions effectively created the circumstances in which the majority of single people who became homeless had no priority for council housing, due to their exclusion from the main priority need groups. The same situation applied to childless couples, where neither person qualified for another category of priority need.

Despite the discrimination against single people, which is inherent in the homelessness legislation, successive codes of guidance have given consideration to specific groups of homeless single people who may be vulnerable and, therefore, eligible for assistance, such as young care-leavers or those at risk of violence and/or harassment. The difficulty with this has been that the guidance did not clearly stipulate the circumstances in which single people should be deemed vulnerable. Local authorities retained a much greater degree of discretion in dealing with homelessness applications from single people than with regard to other household types, such as those with older people, families with children or households containing a pregnant woman. The new homelessness provisions in the Housing Act 1996 do not incorporate any substantial changes to the groups considered to be in 'priority need'.

Despite their lack of priority under the legislation, homeless single people account for a substantial proportion of homelessness *applications*. Unsurprisingly, only a very small proportion of households *accepted* as homeless are likely to be single people of working age. A survey of homeless applicants in six local authority areas in Scotland demonstrated that some 22 per cent of all applicants were single adults, with the proportion varying between 13 to 40 per cent in different districts (Evans *et al.*, 1994, p. 70). A similar study in England found that almost 35 per cent of applicants were single people, almost all of whom were of working age (O'Callaghan *et al.*, 1996; see also Chapter 7). In contrast, only three per cent of homelessness acceptances in England, in 1995, were in the non-priority need category (Wilcox, 1996, p. 87).

Housing associations have had more freedom than local councils to determine their own allocations policies, within the broad frameworks set out by their regulatory bodies. During the 1970s and 1980s, housing associations (particularly in England) were encouraged to provide for the housing needs of those given a low priority by local authorities, including single people (Parker *et al.*, 1992; Garside, 1993). During the 1990s, central government, through its regulatory agencies, expected associations to house increasing numbers of statutorily homeless households (Withers and Randolph, 1994), a change in emphasis which is likely to result in a squeeze on housing opportunities for single people. Despite recent expansion of the housing association sector, by 1995 they accounted for only 4.5 per cent of the total dwelling stock of Great Britain (Wilcox, 1996, p. 96).

The exclusion of single people from the homelessness priority groups has also resulted in a lack of reliable data on the extent of single homelessness, as they are not adequately recorded in official homelessness statistics. Nevertheless, a substantial increase in single homelessness in the late 1980s was acknowledged by central and local government, as well as by voluntary sector agencies (Anderson, 1993; 1994). The 1990s have seen efforts to improve estimates of single homelessness (OPCS, 1991; Shaw *et al.*, 1996) but a rigorous measure remains elusive. Moreover, these attempts to quantify single homelessness have tended to focus, almost exclusively, on counting 'people sleeping rough', at the expense of the undoubtedly much greater number of single homeless people living in inadequate and insecure accommodation (see Chapter 6).

Single people's housing needs are routinely neglected in national estimates of housing need, despite the recognition that single-person households will comprise the main element of growth in household formation in the next two decades. For example, Holmans (1995) excluded sharing single adults from housing needs estimates on the grounds that there was no consensus about their having a *legitimate* expectation of access to subsidized rented housing (emphasis added). Interestingly, 'would-be couples living apart' were included in Holmans' estimates. The notion that single people are adequately housed in shared accommodation was made explicit in recent government proposals to restrict housing benefit in private sector tenancies to the rent level for shared accommodation (Social Security Advisory Committee, 1996). However, this idea is challenged by research (Holmans, 1995, p. 24) which showed that single people rarely choose shared accommodation if they have sufficient purchasing power to obtain their own housing.

Access to housing is not solely determined by 'housing' policy. Other policy areas, such as social security, social care and employment, also influence single people's access to housing (see Anderson, 1993; 1994). Conservative government policies, since 1979, have consistently sought to contain expenditure on social security by imposing successive reductions in the value and scope of a range of welfare benefits. The rise in single homelessness in Britain, since 1988, was associated with the impact of long-term unemployment, reductions in income support (replaced by Job Seekers Allowance in 1996), cuts to housing benefit as well as the exclusion of single people from the social housing system (Anderson, 1993; 1994).

## The nature of single homelessness

This section reflects on some of the key findings from the Department of the Environment's 1991 survey of single homeless people. The survey comprised structured interviews with a sample of more than 1,800 single homeless people who were living in hostels or bed and breakfast accommodation or who were sleeping rough. All data quoted in this section are taken from the published report of the survey *Single Homeless People* (Anderson, Kemp and Quilgars, 1993).

*Gender, age and ethnic group*

The survey revealed that single homelessness was largely a male experience – 77 per cent of hostel respondents and around 90 per cent of street homeless respondents were men. The survey effectively excluded pregnant women and people with children in their care – groups who should receive priority for assistance with housing in the event of homelessness. Nevertheless, writers such as Watson and Austerberry (1986) and Webb (1994) have argued that the experience of homelessness among single women is likely to be more widespread than is indicated by large scale surveys, but that their homelessness tends to be more concealed in nature (see Chapter 6).

Three-quarters of street homeless respondents and over half of those in hostels were in the age range 25–59 years. Although a minority of single homeless people were aged under 25 years, this younger group was over-represented compared to the general population and women outnumbered men in this age-range. Most single homeless people were white, but people from minority ethnic groups were over-represented among those living in hostels, relative to the proportion of black people living in the survey areas. This was especially the case for women from minority ethnic groups.

*Housing circumstances*

Single homeless people were living with a very high degree of uncertainty about their housing situation. The vast majority had nowhere else where they could stay, even for a short time. Most people had been in their present accommodation for less than 12 months, and many had moved twice or more within that period. People had stayed in a range of accommodation – from sleeping rough, through hostels and lodgings, to their own or parents' homes. A substantial proportion considered that they had had a home one year before the survey – reflecting the dynamic nature of the housing dimension of social exclusion. While it was clear that single homeless people had not always been homeless, the survey method could not satisfactorily examine the process of moving from homelessness into more secure housing (see also Chapter 7). Single homeless people were asked why they left their last home and reported a diverse and complex range of reasons relating to families and relationships, accommodation problems, employment, leaving institutions and other reasons. The range of influencing factors suggests housing and other aspects of social well-being do indeed interact to result in a comprehensive process of exclusion (see Chapter 9).

The reasons why people left their previous accommodation do not fully explain why people become homeless. The decision or requirement to move from one's 'home' needs to be considered in the light of opportunities to gain access to other accommodation. It is at this point that individual circumstances and structural barriers may combine, resulting in homelessness for those who cannot secure alternative accommodation. Single people on low incomes, who cannot provide for themselves in the market, but have low priority for social housing, will be particularly vulnerable to homelessness at times when they have to move accommodation. Most single homeless people surveyed by Anderson *et al.* (1993) were, indeed, actively looking for other accommodation but they reported that their options were severely constrained. Either their financial circumstances prevented them from renting in the private sector, or they did not meet the bureaucratic criteria for access to council housing. Single people still, however, tended to look to social housing as a solution to their housing problems. Group discussions among homeless people, conducted in addition to the structured survey, revealed that many single people were aware of their low priority for social housing. Nevertheless, they viewed social housing as more secure and more affordable than privately rented housing.

*Employment and income*

Apart from their lack of housing, unemployment and low incomes were the most striking indicators of social exclusion among single homeless people. Only around 10 per cent of single homeless people were in paid work during the week prior to the survey and a high proportion had very little or no previous experience of working. More than half of those interviewed had no formal qualifications and low levels of education and training meant that single homeless people would be disadvantaged in competing for any available jobs, relative to those with higher educational attainment. The survey did not test respondents' attitudes to work but qualitative group discussions indicated that single homeless people were put off job searching by disillusionment and the difficulties they faced in both finding and keeping work while homeless.

Commensurate with the extent of exclusion from the labour market, single homeless people had very low incomes. Among the 10 per cent in paid employment, average incomes were only slightly above state benefit level. The most common source of income was income support, the basic level of welfare benefit available at the time. Among those who were sleeping rough, a fifth said they had no income in the previous week, not even state benefits. Although this may have reflected fortnightly payments, it could also be explained by the difficulties people faced in claiming benefit when they have no fixed address. Begging or asking for money on the street was an alternative source of income for a minority of respondents. Among those living in hostels, only two per cent had received income from this source in the previous week, although 20 per cent of those sleeping rough had done so. The reported incomes received from begging were typically very low, at between £10 and £20 per week.

*Dimensions of disadvantage*

The survey collected data on some other dimensions of well-being which can be included in a comprehensive definition of social exclusion. In particular, a high proportion of single homeless people were excluded from the experience of good health and many were not receiving treatment for their illnesses. The incidence of health problems was higher among those sleeping rough and many reported conditions which would be exacerbated by sleeping out. Significant numbers of single homeless people had spent time in psychiatric care or had experienced a long stay in hospital, with the experience of those sleeping rough again being more acute than that of those living in hostels. The same pattern emerged with respect to time spent in an alcohol unit. The reported incidence of stays in drug units was low, possibly reflecting under-reporting and the lack of specialist provision for this problem.

A high proportion of respondents had some experience of a stay in prison, remand or young offenders' institutions, but no data were collected on the nature of the crimes or the detail of convictions or stays in prison. It is important to note, however, that sleeping rough remains a crime under the vagrancy laws in Britain and that a person can be arrested and detained merely for sleeping rough or for begging. Finally, a significant proportion of single homeless people had experienced being in a children's home or in foster care – a factor particularly associated with youth homelessness.

**Access to social housing?**

This section draws on a study of local authority and housing association policy and practice with respect to providing housing for single-person households (Anderson and Morgan, 1997). Acknowledging their limited statutory obligations, the study sought to establish whether social housing providers were developing more progressive policies towards single people in the light of demographic changes and the growth of single homelessness. While the research considered access to housing for all single people, those who had experienced homelessness were the particular focus of enquiry. Given the acknowledged difficulties in defining and quantifying single homelessness, the findings pertaining to all single people are considered below. The research methods included: analysis of published literature and statistics; providers' information on allocation policies and homelessness procedures; a postal questionnaire survey of local housing authorities; and five local case studies of policy and practice. The study investigated provision by both housing associations and local authorities. While there are important differences in the scale and nature of provision by the two types of agencies, space does not permit a detailed comparison between them in this chapter.

*The housing needs of single people*

The survey of single homeless people (Anderson *et al.*, 1993) focused on those who were roofless or living in hostel/bed and breakfast accommodation. The later study, by Anderson and Morgan (1997), found that a broader group of single people on local authority and housing association waiting lists also experienced a relatively high degree of insecurity in their housing circumstances. The trend which emerged was that single people's housing need tended to reflect the insecurity of current accommodation, which was sometimes insecure to the point of moving between a number of different addresses or even absolute rooflessness. However, this common trend of insecurity did not mean that all single people experienced the same degree of housing need. There were variations in the degrees of insecurity experienced by single people and the housing opportunities of single people were affected by the degree of sensitivity of allocation systems to these different needs. As in the 1993 study, single homeless people were identified as a diverse group, although increasing numbers of single people with special needs were applying for social housing (see Chapter 10)

   The perception that the needs of single people for independent housing were, somehow, less than those of couples or families remained widespread, although there was some evidence that this irrational perspective was beginning to be challenged at the local level. In assessing single people's housing needs, about half of all local authorities still used the housing waiting list, although survey respondents could not always identify the proportion of *single* people on their lists. From the postal survey, single people accounted for 36 per cent of all waiting list applicants on average, but case study evidence indicated that waiting list data underestimated the demand from single people. Similarly, authorities could not always accurately estimate single homelessness applications, but, on average, single people accounted for nearly one third of applications. Local authorities were, however, increasingly aware of the limitations of traditional mechanisms for measuring housing need and efforts were being made to improve data collection with respect to single people, for example by conducting housing needs surveys.

*Eligibility and priority for social housing*

Single people were disadvantaged by certain common eligibility criteria for access to council waiting lists and for tenancy allocations. In England and Wales, the most significant factor was age, with vulnerable young people aged 16 and 17 years tending to experience the most severe barriers to waiting list registration (a criterion which is illegal in Scotland). Single people experienced a greater degree of disadvantage in the systems for prioritizing applicants on the waiting list, including commonly used measures of housing need and points weightings for priority criteria. Given similar housing circumstances, single people often experienced a slight disadvantage relative to couples without children and a more significant disadvantage relative to families.

A key issue determining the housing opportunities of single people was whether priority systems took account of the insecure housing situations they commonly experienced. The study revealed that many providers failed to take adequate account of the specific housing needs of substantial numbers of single applicants in their allocation priority schemes. To remedy this situation, housing providers would need to recognize insecure housing situations as housing need factors and weight their importance in the same way as the other factors in the system. A spectrum of needs, such as rooflessness, bed and breakfast accommodation, lodgings or living with parents, could be taken into consideration.

In line with their traditional role in housing, of providing for those who have low priority for council housing, housing association policies were generally sensitive to the needs of single people. For example, virtually all of the associations in the study had points schemes which took some account of insecurity of tenure. The research sought to establish whether associations were increasingly housing those in the homelessness priority need groups. While practice was quite variable, it appeared that a high percentage of local authority nominations were being used to meet the needs of statutorily homeless households, rather than non-priority single homeless people.

*The homelessness procedures*

Local authority officers continued to exercise a great degree of discretion in making decisions about priority need for potentially vulnerable single homeless applicants. For categories such as mental illness, learning difficulties and physical disability, some authorities did not routinely meet their statutory duty to award priority need in these circumstances. Young people were most likely to be considered vulnerable if they were in the 16–17 age group or had recently left care. Those least likely to be awarded priority need status at the discretion of local authorities included: people with alcohol or drug problems, people leaving prison, people sleeping rough, people leaving the forces and people who were refugees or asylum seekers – a range of characteristics common among homeless single people (Anderson *et al.*, 1993).

*Housing outcomes*

In the postal survey of local authorities, single people accounted for more than one third (36 per cent) of waiting list applicants, on average. In terms of outcomes, however, they were allocated an average of only 26 per cent of annual lettings, despite the fact that some 35 per cent of vacancies were one-bedroom properties. The study also examined possible alternative routes into social housing, such as referrals from specialist agencies or under the Community Care or Children Act legislation. While these routes could be favourable to low-income and homeless single people, they did not account for a substantial proportion of social housing lettings. Moreover, the least successful groups were the same as for the main access routes, namely those with drug and alcohol problems and ex-offenders/people leaving prison.

Overall, the study indicated only limited progress towards positive policy and practice on access to social housing for single people. There was evidence of greater acknowledgement of single homelessness and improved assessment of single people's housing needs, but this had not been adequately translated into practices to counter the disadvantage single people experienced in the systems which control access to social housing.

## Conclusions

This chapter aimed to incorporate empirical studies of single homelessness and the policies of social housing providers into a broad analytical framework focusing on the concepts of social exclusion and inclusion. Social exclusion is thought to be a helpful concept in so far as it moves beyond notions of poverty and inequality to embrace the comprehensive, dynamic and inter-related nature of a set of social processes which combine to prevent certain individuals from experiencing the degree of well-being taken for granted by the majority in contemporary British society.

Housing policies, and the housing system, play an important role in creating and sustaining the conditions whereby certain groups are excluded from fundamental aspects of well-being. The impact of prevailing ideologies, which prioritize the housing needs of nuclear families, retired people and those deemed 'vulnerable' has resulted in discrimination against most single people in the social housing system. The problem of single homelessness needs to be understood in the wider context of this sustained discrimination against lower income single people applying for social housing, combined with the growth in single person households. As there is only limited evidence that access policies are changing, while household formation among single people is expected to continue expanding, the problem of single homelessness is unlikely to be resolved in the foreseeable future.

The survey of single homeless people (Anderson *et al.*, 1993) demonstrated that, for the poorest homeless single people, their exclusion from housing was associated with a wider experience of exclusion from the labour market and from other aspects of health and well-being. This author believes, however, that social exclusion must be understood as exclusion from important elements of social life – not just as exclusion from society *per se*. Single homeless people remain part of the totality of contemporary British society, in a relationship of interdependence with better-off, better housed groups. Their disadvantaged position in the housing system results from the prioritization of others as having a more legitimate claim on available social housing. This wider housing system does not address the issue of inequality of opportunity for access to reasonable accommodation, which should form a basis for a cohesive society.

Since 1990, the government's main response to single homelessness has been its Rough Sleepers Initiative (Anderson, 1993). For the first six years of operation, the Rough Sleepers Initiative targeted resources exclusively on people who were, literally, sleeping rough, in a small area of central London. By March 1996, £182 million had been allocated to the central London initiative – funding permanent accommodation, hostel places, a winter-shelter programme and outreach and support workers (Department of the Environment and Welsh Office, 1995). Independent evaluation suggested that the initiative was reasonably successful in reducing the numbers of people sleeping rough in central London (Randall and Brown, 1993; 1995; 1996). In 1996, plans were announced to extend the Rough Sleepers Initiative to Bristol and some other English cities, with a Scottish initiative also announced at the end of that year. Despite the practical value of additional resources for single homeless people, the programme continued to focus on limited geographical areas and to address only the visible problem of street homelessness while ignoring the wider needs of single homeless people. The Rough Sleepers Initiative represents a responsive, fragmentary approach to mitigating the most severe consequences of single homelessness. Were the government and local housing providers to implement preventative, inclusive housing policies, which recognized the legitimate needs of low-income single people for fair access to social housing, there would be no requirement for special initiatives.

Section 167 of the Housing Act 1996 lists the housing circumstances which local authorities in England and Wales should prioritize in their new allocations policies. Families with dependent children and households including pregnant women are still prioritized, while no specific mention is made of single-person households. Nevertheless, authorities are required to give reasonable preference to those in unsatisfactory housing, including temporary or insecure accommodation, and to households whose social or economic circumstances make it difficult for them to secure settled accommodation. These latter criteria offer scope to develop more progressive policies towards single people, but the extent of such practice will only be evident after some evaluation of the impact of the new legislation.

For single people on low incomes, the main alternative to social housing is privately rented accommodation. During the late 1980s and early 1990s, the key barriers to obtaining such accommodation were the high access costs of deposits and rent in advance which are required to secure such accommodation. While subsidy, in the form of housing benefit, has been available to cover rental costs in the private sector, since 1988 the Department of Social Security has provided virtually no assistance to low-income single people for initial access costs. Rugg (1996) has evaluated the development of locally based schemes to assist single people's access into privately rented housing and found that such projects proved reasonably effective in overcoming initial barriers to access. During 1996, however, the government announced its proposals to limit single people's entitlement to housing benefit in the private sector to the level of the average local rent for shared accommodation (Social Security Advisory Committee, 1996). Following a consultation exercise, the restrictions were imposed upon young single people aged under 25. Reductions in the availability of housing benefit for private tenancies are likely to result in young single people living in poorer housing conditions or becoming homeless, as well as a further increase in their demand for social housing.

The restrictions of young single people's housing benefit to an amount which will purchase shared accommodation is directly designed to minimize any increase in the costs of housing benefit resulting from household formation among young single people (Social Security Advisory Committee, 1996). As such, these proposals represent a new legislative mechanism which directly discriminates against young single people – for no reason other than that they are not part of a couple or a nuclear family. Holmans (1995) has argued, however, that government policy has very little impact on household formation in practice. Nevertheless, reductions in assistance for low-income groups do have an impact on their ability to meet their housing needs. The outlook for low-income single people in the housing system is gloomy. Without a change in the direction of policy, towards a more inclusive approach, low-income single people will continue to experience 'non-access' to social housing, exacerbated by 'non-access' to independent accommodation in the private rented sector. The persistence of single homelessness seems a predictable outcome of these circumstances.

## Acknowledgements

I would like to acknowledge the contributions of Peter Kemp, Deborah Quilgars and James Morgan as co-authors of the empirical studies on which parts three and four of this chapter are based. The studies were funded by the Department of the Environment and the Joseph Rowntree Foundation, respectively. The arguments presented reflect my own interpretation of the findings from the research.

## References

Anderson, I. (1993) 'Housing policy and street homelessness in Britain', *Housing Studies*, vol. 8, no. 1, pp. 17–28.

Anderson, I. (1994) *Access to Housing for Low Income Single People*, York: Centre for Housing Policy, University of York.

Anderson, I., Kemp, P. and Quilgars, D. (1993) *Single Homeless People*, London: HMSO.

Anderson, I. and Morgan, J. (1997) *Social Housing for Single People? A Study of Local Policy and Practice*, Research report no. 1, Housing Policy and Practice Unit, University of Stirling.

Berghman, J. (1995) 'Social exclusion in Europe: Policy context and analytical framework', in G. Room (ed.) *Beyond the Threshold: The Measurement and Analysis of Social Exclusion*, Bristol: Policy Press, pp. 10–28.

Council of Europe (1993) *Homelessness*, Strasbourg: Council of Europe Press.

Daly, M. (1993) *Abandoned: Profile of Europe's Homeless People*, second report of the European Observatory on Homelessness, FEANTSA, Brussels: FEANTSA.

Department of the Environment and Welsh Office (1995) *Our Future Homes: Opportunities, Choices, Responsibility*, London: HMSO.

Evans, R., Smith, N., Bryson, C. and Austin, N. (1994) *The Operation of the 1991 Code of Guidance on Homelessness in Scotland*, Edinburgh: Scottish Office.

Forrest, R. and Murie, A. (1983) 'Residualisation and council housing: Aspects of the changing social relations of housing tenure', *Journal of Social Policy*, vol. 12, no. 4, pp. 453–68.

Garside, P. (1993) 'Housing needs, family values and single homeless people', *Policy and Politics*, vol. 21, no. 4, pp. 319–28.

HMSO (1995) *Population*, London: HMSO.

Holmans, A. (1995) *Housing Need and Demand in England 1991–2011*, York: Joseph Rowntree Foundation.

House of Commons Environment Committee (1996) *Second Report. Housing Need*, vol. 1, London: HMSO.

Hutson, S. and Liddiard, M. (1994) *Youth Homelessness: The Construction of a Social Issue*, London: Macmillan.

Lee, P., Murie, A., Marsh, A. and Riseborough, M. (1995) *The Price of Social Exclusion*, London: National Federation of Housing Associations.

Malpass, P. and Murie, A. (1994) *Housing Policy and Practice*, 4th. edn, London: Macmillan.

Murray, C., with Field, F., Brown, J., Walker, A. and Deakin, N. (1990) *The Emerging British Underclass (with Commentaries)*, London: IEA Health and Welfare Unit.

Murray, C., with Alcock, P., David, M., Phillips, M. and Slipman, S. (1994) *Underclass: The Crisis Deepens (with Commentaries)*, London: IEA Health and Welfare Unit.

O'Callaghan, B., Dominion, L., Evans, A., Dix, J., Smith, R., Williams, P. and Zimmeck, M. (1996) *Study of Homeless Applicants*, London: HMSO.

OPCS (1991) *1991 Census Preliminary Report for England and Wales: Supplementary Monitor on People Sleeping Rough*, London: HMSO.

Page, D. (1993) *Building Communities: A Study of New Housing Association Estates*, York: Joseph Rowntree Foundation.

Parker, J., Smith, R. and Williams, P. (1992) *Access, Allocations and Nominations: The Role of Housing Associations*, London: HMSO.

Randall, G. and Brown, S. (1993) *The Rough Sleepers Initiative: An Evaluation*, London: HMSO.

Randall, G. and Brown, S. (1995) *Outreach and Resettlement Work with People Sleeping Rough*, London: Department of the Environment.

Randall, G. and Brown, S. (1996) *From Street to Home: An Evaluation of Phase 2 of the Rough Sleepers Initiative*, London: Stationery Office.

Room, G. (ed.) (1995a) *Beyond the Threshold: The Measurement and Analysis of Social Exclusion*, Bristol: Policy Press.

Room, G. (1995b) 'Poverty and social exclusion: The new European agenda for policy and research', in G. Room (ed.) *Beyond the Threshold: The Measurement and Analysis of Social Exclusion*, Bristol: Policy Press, pp. 1–9.

Rugg, J. (1996) *Opening Doors: Helping People on Low Income Secure Private Rented Accommodation*, research report, York: Centre for Housing Policy, University of York.

Shaw, I., Bloor, M. and Roberts, S. (1996) *Without Shelter: Estimating Rooflessness in Scotland*, Edinburgh: Scottish Office.

Social Security Advisory Committee (1996) *Memorandum: Housing Benefit Changes for Private Sector Tenants*, London: Social Security Advisory Committee.

Taylor-Gooby, P. (1991) *Social Change, Social Welfare and Social Science,* Hemel Hempstead: Harvester Wheatsheaf.

Town and Country Planning Association (1996) *Land Use Planning Implications of Housing Projections,* Housing Research Findings 187, York: Joseph Rowntree Foundation.

Watson, S. and Austerberry, H. (1986) *Housing and Homelessness: A Feminist Perspective,* London: Routledge.

Webb, S. (1994) *My Address Is Not My Home: Hidden Homelessness and Single Women in Scotland,* Edinburgh: Scottish Council for Single Homeless, and Glasgow: Glasgow Council for Single Homeless.

Wilcox, S. (1996) *Housing Review 1996/7,* York: Joseph Rowntree Foundation.

Withers, P. and Randolph, B. (1994) *Access, Homelessness and Housing Associations,* Research report 21, London: NFHA.

# 9 Homelessness and young people

*Suzanne Fitzpatrick and David Clapham*

## Introduction

The aims of this chapter are threefold. First, a framework is outlined, based on the idea of a housing pathway, and this is suggested as an appropriate way of analysing the dynamic experiences of young homeless people. Second, examples are given of the pathways of some young people in Glasgow. These histories are taken from research undertaken in Glasgow by one of the authors as part of a PhD thesis. Third, some conclusions are drawn on the general factors which influenced the pathways and affected the experience of these young people over time. Areas for future research are then suggested.

The existence of homelessness among young people has been an important focus of media attention as well as research in the past few years. This is partly the result of the large growth in the numbers of homeless young people over the last decade, and, as other contributions to this volume show, the highly visible nature of some of this homelessness. There have been a number of research studies which have examined the response to youth homelessness by housing departments (Thornton, 1990; Caskie, 1993), and by social work services (Bannister *et al.*, 1993) and which have evaluated specific policy measures which have been implemented, such as the Rough Sleepers Initiative and foyers (Randall and Brown, 1993; Anderson and Quilgars, 1995).

The aim of this chapter is to build on our current knowledge of the causes of homelessness among young people and their experience of it (Hutson and Liddiard, 1994; Jones, 1993). Furthering our understanding of the phenomenon of homelessness is necessary if policy prescriptions are to be well targeted and effective. In particular, the chapter argues for a conceptual framework which is dynamic, viewing the homeless experience as part of a process which can only be understood by examining it over a period of time, as well as holistic – seeing homelessness as one part of the multi-faceted lives of young people.

## The framework

The framework proposed in this chapter uses the concept of a 'housing pathway'. Essentially this charts the progress over time of an individual or household through the housing system. This pathway may involve moving house or it may involve the household staying in one house for a long time. As we have argued elsewhere, immobility is just as important and interesting a phenomenon as mobility, although it has received far less attention in the housing literature (Clapham et al., 1993). The key issue for this chapter is that a housing pathway may involve episodes of homelessness. A principal strength of the pathways perspective is that these episodes can be related both to each other and to the housing circumstances both before and after.

Therefore the approach encourages a dynamic perspective, which is in stark contrast to much housing research, which takes a static, cross-sectional snapshot of a person's current position without attempting to understand how that situation was reached. Previous research on young people's housing circumstances has shown that homelessness is often not an isolated experience, or necessarily a long-lasting position. Young people can move in and out of homelessness as part of a pathway that can involve returning to the family home, staying with other relatives and friends or in their own tenancy, as well as sleeping rough, squatting or living in temporary accommodation such as hostels. Of course, which of these situations qualifies as homelessness depends on the definition adopted, as other chapters show. The key point is that the circumstances of a young person can only accurately be judged if all the housing situations are considered together and their relationship understood.

This housing pathways approach builds on the work of Forrest and Kemeny (1984) who discussed the concept of a 'housing career' (for a review see Clapham et al., 1993). They dismissed the term as having the connotations of a progressive upward movement as in a middle-class occupational career. They argued that housing trajectories could be downward as well as upward and so the more neutral concept of a pathway is more suitable. The housing pathway perspective also takes into account the future direction of a household, in contrast to a housing histories' approach, which is backward-looking (Forrest and Murie, 1991). There has been some research which has argued that the experience of homelessness is a downward trajectory in which the housing situation of young people progressively deteriorates, with episodes of rooflessness, residence in traditional hostels and migration between cities occurring more often in the later stages of a homelessness pathway (Hutson and Liddiard, 1994; Jones, 1993). However, based on research in Glasgow, we shall demonstrate that some young homeless people's pathways have a downward trajectory, some an upward one, and many move from one to the other, sometimes over a short space of time.

The pathways approach recognizes that various life course events influence a housing trajectory. Marriage, the birth of children or retirement from employment can have important housing impacts through changing income or housing requirements. This may trigger a move or lead to a re-adjustment of housing expenditures. In the case of young people, arguably the most important change is leaving home and the creation of a newly independent household. Leaving home is increasingly being viewed as a process which can take place over a considerable period of time (Jones, 1995). Indeed it is sometimes difficult to identify any single point at which it is possible to say that someone has left home. Leonard (1980) has drawn a distinction between young people who have 'left home' and those who are 'living away from home'. The latter group may have moved out of the family home into another house, but retain the option of returning at any time for periods of a few weeks or months to 'recharge their batteries', or even to move back in on a longer-term basis. During this process of transition it is normal for young people to receive a great deal of emotional and practical support from their families (Bannister et al., 1993).

The transition into an independent household is usually successfully undertaken, but sometimes it can go wrong and homelessness may result. Jones (1993) has demonstrated the significance of the process of leaving home in understanding how some young people become homeless.

The importance of the process of leaving home underlines the need to take a holistic view of a housing pathway. Leaving home is a complex process which touches on many aspects of a young person's life. The interaction of these elements needs to be considered as housing decisions are not taken in isolation:

Youth can be seen as a series of processes of transition to adult life, roughly parallel longitudinal processes which take place in different spheres, such as at home or in the labour market, but which must be understood together because they relate closely to one another. (Jones and Wallace, 1992, p. 13)

Thus, public policies in many fields can impact on housing decisions. The key ones for many young people are employment and social security policy. There is evidence that the effect of changes in these policies in recent years has been to extend the process of leaving home for many young people. For example, Jones and Wallace (1992) argue that the last Conservative government's approach was to:

... encourage young people to delay leaving home by withdrawing their social security entitlement so that they remain economically dependent upon their parents and live in the parental home rather than by providing young people with realistic incomes and housing.

No fundamental shift in the approach seems likely under New Labour.

The pathways approach places emphasis on the individual household and seeks to understand their progress in the housing system by exploring their experiences, attitudes and behaviour. In the previous literature on housing histories and careers there has been an attempt to understand household behaviour through the concepts of 'strategy' and 'coping mechanism' (Pickvance and Pickvance, 1994; Forrest and Kemeny, 1984). This relates to a wider sociological debate on the definition and use of the term 'strategy'. A strategy is generally taken to imply 'conscious and rational decisions involving a long-term perspective' (Crow, 1989, p. 19), though some authors argue that unconscious strategies are also possible (Pickvance and Pickvance, 1994).

In the housing literature the concept of strategy has been used mainly as a tool to describe the positive, goal-directed behaviour that some people exhibit in searching out and choosing housing. Thus young people may have a clear plan on leaving home which may include, for example, spending time in the private rented sector while saving a deposit to enter owner-occupation. In contrast, some young people may not have a clear goal and, perhaps more importantly, may not have housing choices available to them because of a lack of resources. In these circumstances the housing pathway may consist of a series of short-term, highly constrained coping mechanisms. There is little long-term planning; rather the preoccupation is to survive from one day to the next. In practice, individual young people may act in both these ways at different times and in different circumstances.

The concepts of strategy and coping mechanism are crude and difficult to define precisely. They are over-simplifications of what are often complex motives and behaviours. Nevertheless they provide useful aids to understanding the housing pathways of young people. In particular, this type of analysis brings into sharp focus the nature of people's decision-making and the housing choices which they have open to them. Thus these concepts offer a starting point which should be explored further, possibly using ideas derived from social psychology.

Finally, a criticism which could be made of this pathways approach, which focuses on the attitudes and behaviour of individual households, is that it neglects the social structures which frame behaviour. One way to address this point is to adopt the 'structuration' perspective of Giddens (1984). His framework acknowledges that structure has a major impact upon the attitudes and behaviours of individuals who are socialized into an existing social structure. However, social structures are not independent of individual actions and only continue in so far as individuals reproduce them through their actions. In most cases the effect of individual actions is to continue pre-existing structures unchanged, but there is some scope for changes in social structures, usually brought about by the unintended consequences of many people's actions.

In the study of housing pathways, the key lessons to be drawn from structuration theory are that the social structures which frame attitudes and behaviour need to be studied as well as the attitudes and behaviours themselves. The research technique used to discover and describe housing pathways is the biographical interview in which individuals recount in their own words their experiences, behaviour and motivations. However, according to Giddens, individuals may not be fully conscious of what they are doing and therefore cannot give a complete account of their actions. Thus the researcher has a key role in interpreting the meanings and actions of individuals in the light of structural forces.

## Leaving home and homelessness

It was mentioned earlier that leaving home is a key process for understanding how some young people become homeless. This process has become more difficult and elongated in recent years as a result of housing and social security policies, as well as adverse labour market conditions, in particular the high level of youth unemployment (Coles, 1995; Jones, 1995). The factors which influence the decision to leave home by young people have been divided into push and pull factors. The pull factors are the positive attractions of forming a new household. These may include getting married or setting up home with a partner; taking a job, an education or a training course; or just moving away from home to have more independence. Push factors force some young people out of the family home. These negative reasons for leaving often relate to unhappy family circumstances which may involve conflict and possibly violence or sexual abuse, or perhaps simply poverty and a lack of space and privacy.

The more predominant are the push factors in a young person's decision to leave home, the more problematic the transition into an independent household is likely to be. There are several reasons for this. Young people who leave home for negative reasons tend to leave at an early age, particularly young women, and so are less likely to have the emotional and practical resources and the skills and knowledge to make a successful transition (Jones, 1993). Another factor is that family conflict, although usually long-term in nature, is liable to flare up suddenly and so leaving home is undertaken with little preparation.

When I left, I left in a bit of a rush. I didn't have time to plan anything. I did have it in the back of my head to leave, but the situation at that time was such that I just had to go. Because everything happened so fast I didn't even have time to pack anything. I just grabbed a jacket and a couple of shirts, put them in a bag, and I was off. (Young homeless person in Glasgow, quoted in Bannister *et al.*, 1993, p. 15)

It is worth emphasizing the earlier point, that for many young people the process of leaving home is a very extended one in which they receive considerable practical and emotional support and may sometimes return to the family home for periods. For people who are fleeing family conflict this parental support is less likely to be forthcoming. Jones (1995) has argued that young people who leave home because of family problems, particularly those who leave at a very early age, are also less likely to attract societal support for their transition because their move is considered to be less 'legitimate' than young people who leave for traditional reasons, such as to get married or to start a course. They are therefore less likely to receive assistance from the state in the form of access to housing or income. This point is most clearly illustrated by the withdrawal of benefit entitlement from 16- and 17-year-olds. Without the safety nets of family or state support, the transition into independent living is likely to be very hazardous for these young people and they face much greater risks of homelessness.

Young people with difficult family backgrounds may also have suffered negative experiences in childhood which make them particularly vulnerable to homelessness:

The young peoples' problems, including homelessness, can be seen in the majority of cases, as a continuation of disruption and problems commencing long before they came into contact with agencies. . . . The lesson is that if children and young people are unsettled early in life, the style of life is likely to continue the same in adolescence. (Stockley *et al.*, 1993, p. 2)

There is a wealth of evidence that care-leavers, young people from stepfamilies and those who have suffered violence or sexual abuse are disproportionately represented among the young homeless (Caskie, 1992; Jones, 1993; Thornton, 1990). All of these groups are likely to embark on independent living at a particularly young age, in difficult circumstances and without family support.

These points are, of course, generalizations and, as such, do not hold in every case, but the factors outlined above did figure prominently in our sample of young homeless people in Glasgow. However, the most important point from this discussion is that the process of leaving home can have a profound influence on the subsequent housing pathway followed.

## The research

The pathways approach will be illustrated through research undertaken among homeless young people in Glasgow. This was a qualitative study of the experiences of young homeless people from a peripheral housing scheme in Glasgow called Drumchapel. There were three stages of fieldwork. First, eight group interviews were conducted with young people living in Drumchapel who were contacted through schools, housing, social work and youth agencies in the scheme. These focus groups were used to sharpen the research questions and to recruit young people for later stages of the research. The main stage of fieldwork consisted of 25 biographical interviews with young homeless people aged 16 to 19 years who were living in, or originated from, Drumchapel. Young people were contacted both through the service network in Drumchapel and through the city-wide homeless network in Glasgow, in order to represent as broad a range of experiences as possible. The final stage of fieldwork was a follow-up study of these 25 young people one year later. This exercise was successful in obtaining some information about the progress of almost all of these young people. In all, 53 young people were interviewed in the course of the research.

The small scale and located nature of the study, together with the opportunistic sample selection, mean that these findings should be viewed primarily as a basis for formulating hypotheses which should be tested more widely in later research. We believe the research offers fresh insights into the nature of homelessness among young people, which are worthy of further investigation. It should be noted that Drumchapel was selected as the location of the study because it is very similar to many other large housing schemes in Scotland, and the available statistics indicate that these areas yield particularly high levels of youth homelessness. We have no reason to suppose that these young people's experiences are atypical.

## Six pathways

The biographical interviews with young homeless people were used to construct six pathways which characterized the general experience of the sample. The pathways were based on three main variables. The first factor was whether the homelessness could be categorized as official or unofficial. In other words, whether the young person was staying in the network of accommodation provided by housing or homelessness agencies or had made their own informal arrangements. The second was the physical location of the pathway. That is, whether young people were homeless in their local area of Drumchapel or whether they had migrated to the city centre or elsewhere in Glasgow. It should be noted that Glasgow has a city-wide network of youth accommodation, including hostels and supported scatter flats, and Drumchapel has a local provision of supported cluster and scatter flats for young people. The third factor was the stability of the pathway, that is whether the accommodation and circumstances varied widely and often. The six pathways were as follows.

### Unofficial homelessness in the local area

A key characteristic of this pathway was that young people were in and out of the family home 'like a yo-yo', frequently walking out or being thrown out. Reliance was then placed on other family and friends, or more accurately the parents of friends. However, these arrangements were usually very short term and so the young people were often 'jumping about fae hoose to hoose'. Staying with family or friends was often punctuated by periods sleeping rough in the local area, when the young person had left it too late at night to make arrangements or had became embarrassed to ask for help. They would normally sleep rough for only a night or two in a row, but some young people had slept rough in Drumchapel for several weeks or even months at a time. They would usually sleep out in their own neighbour-hood, sometimes in their family's close, but would often try to hide their homelessness from family and friends. Their homelessness was also hidden from the appropriate agencies and these young people did not use any official homeless or young persons' accommodation, nor were they recor-ded as homeless. The lack of official help reflected a fear of being compelled to stay in hostels outside their local area, and they all emphasized their desire to remain in Drumchapel. This strong local attachment was shared with young people on the next two pathways below. A few of this group had spent time in other cities, but none had slept rough or used homeless services in the centre of Glasgow. Many young people started out on this pathway when they left home and quickly moved on to other types of homelessness, but others were unofficially homeless in their local areas for very considerable periods of time.

The young people on this pathway were often very young and rather immature, and the process of leaving home had often started for them at the age of 14 or 15 when they walked out or were thrown out after arguments. Most of these young people had a history of truanting from school, and this was the case for virtually all the young homeless people interviewed. Many of this group had been involved with social work services, but they generally had not experienced residential care. Few of these young people appeared to have suffered severe parental abuse in childhood, but there were often tensions within the family home created by difficult step-relationships, parental drink or drug problems, or simply poverty and unemployment. Many of the young men were involved in theft and other minor criminal activity from early adolescence and were heavy users of alcohol or drugs. These long-term problems were often at the root of the family conflict which led to them leaving or being thrown out of their home, but they were exacerbated by a lack of income when they could not get a job or training at the age of 16, or lost their training place. Many of these young people then had no source of income and placed immense strain on a family budget which often relied on social security payments. Despite these difficulties, there was usually not a complete breakdown in the family relations of young people in this pathway and they often received practical support such as baths and food from their parents when homeless.

The follow-up study demonstrated that there was not a universal or inevitable decline in the position of these young people. Some began using the local homelessness services, so moved onto the next two pathways below, or gained their own mainstream tenancy. In a couple of cases, young people reported a moderation of their behaviour with drink or drugs and a repairing of the relationship with parents, allowing them to settle back into the family home on a more permanent basis. But others had made little progress and were still in very unstable accommodation in their local area a year later. They may have had employment for a short period but were unable to keep it. None of the young people in this pathway had gravitated to the city centre to use homelessness services or to sleep rough in the intervening period.

*Unofficial/official homelessness in the local area*

Young people in this pathway differed from the group above in that they achieved access to the official network of young persons' accommodation in their local area. However, this was not a stable situation and was mixed with periods at home, staying with friends or sleeping rough. They left the official system either because their circumstances changed, thus allowing them to return home for a while, or they were evicted for reasons such as bringing drugs or alcohol into the cluster flat complex. Some found it difficult to cope with running their own flat even with the help they were given in the scheme.

These young people were slightly more mature than those on the first pathway, but tended to have worse relations with their parents because of poor step-relationships, parental drug addiction or physical abuse. A number of young people in this pathway had spent some time in residential care as children. However, most of them maintained some contact with their family after they left home.

Many of the young people on this pathway were still in the same position a year later, but some had moved on and stabilized their situation either to return home or to settle within the local official network. A couple of these young people had moved onto the city-wide official network of accommodation, but none had slept rough in the city centre.


*Stable in local official network*


In this pathway, young people are in a stable position in the local provision in Drumchapel. Some got there from spending some time unofficially homeless in the local area before approaching the official system. Others went straight into the official system, often because they did not have family and friends to turn to for accommodation.

Young people in this pathway were older and more mature than those in the previous two pathways and so were able to sustain a place in the hostel or a scatter flat. Once secure within this system, their lives seemed to stabilize more generally. Most young people on this pathway maintained contact with their families. There were the same strains as were evident in the family relationships of people on other pathways, but there seemed to be more extensive and mutual support between these young people and their parents. Emotional and financial assistance frequently passed both ways, and the young women in particular often still performed major roles in the family, for example looking after younger children. It should be noted that excessive childcare and domestic responsibilities were often important factors which drove young women to leave home, although their departure did not necessarily mean that these tasks ended.

When approached a year later, most were coping well in scatter flats and had had no further experience of homelessness. The majority had been working during the year, some for considerable periods of time, and those who were again unemployed were enthusiastically looking for work. They had all remained in contact with their families. The favourable experience of people in this group partly reflects the selection process in the local area system, where the most vulnerable young people are not accepted. Nevertheless, it does show that appropriate intervention can be successful for some people.


*Alternating between unofficial homelessness in the local area and the official city network*


Only one person in the sample was in this pathway. He had been thrown out of the family home at the age of 16 by his mother for fighting with his brothers. He stayed in a city centre hostel for a few weeks and then returned home. There followed a period of unofficial homelessness in the local area, sometimes staying with friends, sometimes staying at home, which he was regularly told to leave because of his behaviour, and sometimes sleeping rough. This was interspersed with stays in the official city network of homeless accommodation, but he never slept rough in the city centre. He was then offered a furnished flat by the council in his local area, but was evicted for causing damage. During this time he took drugs and sometimes sold them. He was in trouble with the police for breach of the peace, stealing a car and blackmail and had spent time in prison on remand. He had had a number of jobs but found it difficult to keep them.

He decided to move out of the local area because of problems with drug dealers, and applied for and was offered a place in a hostel in the city network. Here his behaviour caused some problems and when attempts were made to contact him a year later it was found that he had been forced to leave the hostel after 'a major incident'.

*Official city network*

Young people in this pathway are staying in the official city network of homeless accommodation on a relatively long-term basis. They may be settled in one particular hostel or they may move around the circuit of hostels. A distinction must be drawn between those who are living in youth residential projects and those living in adult hostels. The former group of young people were staying in small, specifically designed projects where attempts were generally being made to prepare them for independent living, whereas the latter group seemed to have been dumped in large-scale, institutional hostels on a more or less permanent basis.

All of the young people in this pathway had particularly difficult childhoods. Most had suffered physical abuse and there were a host of other problems such as death of a parent, destructive step-relationships, offending behaviour and drink and drug addiction on the part of the young person and/or their parents. Many had spent some of their childhood in residential care. They left home because of these serious family problems. Few of these young people had regular contact with their parents, but most tried to maintain some relationship, however irregular and difficult, with at least one member of their family, usually their mother or a sibling. They generally expressed less attachment to their local area than young people in the previous pathways.

These young people's social networks tended to become limited to other homeless people they met in the hostels as they lost their friends from their local community. Some of the young people in the adult hostels rarely left the institution. There was evidence of severe personal problems resulting from the difficult childhoods and social isolation in the hostel. Heavy drinking, depression and suicide attempts were evident among the most damaged people. Some were receiving extensive support in the young people's hostels, but those in the adult hostels received virtually no formal support.

A year on, very little information was gained about the circumstances of the residents of the young persons' hostels as all of them had moved on. However, all those in adult hostels were still there one year later and their lives did not appear to have progressed. Most seemed to be institutionalized and were resigned to living in the hostel despite being only 20 years old. They were still unemployed, had if anything even less contact with the outside world, and seemed to suffer from deteriorating mental health, including depression as well as drug and alcohol abuse.

*City centre homeless*

Young people on this pathway are the group most visible to helping agencies and to the public at large. However, this research suggests that they are a very distinct, and probably relatively small, subgroup of the young homeless population. These young people are in a very unstable situation, with periods of rooflessness interspersed with stays in hostels, drug rehabilitation units or prison. They sleep rough in the city centre, some of them alone and some in groups, and may combine this with begging during the day. This is the group who are most often mobile, moving between different towns and cities.

These young people often spent long periods sleeping rough when they did not have access to the official accommodation system. This could be because of challenging behaviour, which meant they were banned from the hostels, or a lack of knowledge of provision, or sometimes because they were under-16 runaways who did not want to be returned to home or care. Some were 'out of towners' with no local connection to Glasgow and so were not accommodated by the local authority. Others were not officially categorized as homeless, either because it was felt they had a home to go to, or because they were deemed to be intentionally homeless.

For the young people on this pathway, their homelessness was simply a continuation of a long history of disruption, insecurity and trauma. They had all suffered physical abuse as children and had spent time in residential care. Most had alcoholic parents and/or poor step-relationships. They regularly truanted from schools to the extent that they were rarely there, and many had repeatedly run away from home or care. Several developed drug or alcohol dependencies before they were 16, and one young man entered prostitution at the age of 14. All became homeless at an early age, one girl saying she had been homeless since the age of 13.

Young people on this pathway were the group most estranged from their families and all were angry with them for the way they had been treated. Only a few retained any contact with their parents, but most kept in touch with a member of their wider family or siblings. Most of their social relationships were with other young homeless people and so they had little contact with ordinary communities or with people with stable lifestyles.

These young people had sometimes gravitated towards the city centre because they were afraid of their family or other people in their own area, or because they were under 16 and seeking anonymity to escape from being sent back home or into care. Some already knew people in the city centre rough sleepers' community, usually by meeting them in children's homes. Others were there because they had no local connection with Glasgow. Young people on this pathway exhibited least commitment to their local area out of all the groups of young people interviewed.

The position of young people in this group was generally not much improved a year later. Some were still in the same position and lived chaotic lives dominated by continuing homelessness, drug problems, suicide attempts and spells in prison. Others had settled into the city-wide hostel system and seemed set to become long-term hostel dwellers. However, one person did make good progress and had moved into her own mainstream tenancy one year later and was coping well.

**Two biographies**

In order to bring the pathways to life the experiences of two young people interviewed in the Glasgow research will be given. Again the pressures of space dictate that only two pathways can be illustrated in this way and only a small fraction of the information gained from the interviews can be used. The two young people chosen illustrate some of the differences between city centre and local homelessness, but it must be remembered that the experience of every young person is unique in many ways and so there is no such thing as a representative biography. Some details, including the young person's names, have been changed to protect their anonymity.

*Keith*

Keith and his younger sister were brought up by their parents in Drumchapel. Eight months before we interviewed Keith, his father had left home after arguments with his mum, but he still kept in touch with them all. Keith's father worked in a factory and his mum did not have paid employment.

Keith's education was hampered by his truancy which started by missing odd days in primary school and got worse in secondary school where he stayed off for six months at a time.

I didnae like school, it was crap. The teachers; the teachers didnae like me. Just didnae get on with them cause I was too cheeky. I started uproars in class.

Keith truanted with a group of friends who hung around the shops. According to Keith, he never had a social worker and his parents did not bother about his truanting. At the age of 14, he left home for a couple of nights and stayed with his gran after an argument with his parents over tampering with his dad's car. He said that he got on well with his parents until he left school, when rows started about getting a job. He gained two standard grades at school and got a Youth Training (YT) place one month after leaving under some pressure from his parents.

Just kept telling me tae get work; 'go oot and look for a job'. I just got a YT tae shut them up.

His YT lasted two months, because 'the money was crap' and 'you never done anything'. He then had no income. He went on to explain:

Then it started. Flung me oot, back in. Flung me oot, back in.

The longest period he spent out of the house was three months when he stayed at his friend's mum's house. He didn't plan leaving home, but just walked out as he was getting 'hassle' from his parents for not working, for taking drugs and for stealing. He went back home eventually because he was uncomfortable living in someone else's house.

He stayed at home for eight months, but relations with his mum were difficult. There were the usual arguments about his behaviour and his mum complained about him not contributing any money and that he was 'eating too much'. He started getting into trouble with the police, and when we interviewed him he was due to appear in court for stealing cars, breaking into garages and serious assault.

He left home again one month before our interview and was sleeping rough in Drumchapel with a friend. He had decided he could not take the fighting at home any more. He had no formal income and made some money from begging at the local shops and stealing. He still went home for a bath and 'just to see if they're awright'. His belongings remained at home and he thought he would go back there in the cold weather.

When we interviewed Keith a year later, we learned that he had gone back home for six months, but had to sleep rough for a few nights when he was thrown out. He managed to get a place at the cluster flat complex and received severe hardship payments, but he was forced to leave after money problems. He then moved into his friend's mum's house and had been living there for two months.

*George*

George's mum and dad brought him up until he was nine years old, when he was taken into care. George had two sisters and one brother. His father was in the army until George was five and after that he worked as a part-time lorry driver. His mum worked as a cleaner.

George said he was taken into care because 'I was abused by my father' who 'booted fuck oot me aw the time'. His father was an alcoholic and also hit his mum and brother. George attacked his father with a knife when he was eight years old during a fight. He stayed in a children's home for two years and then was placed with foster parents near his own parents in Drumchapel for six months when he was 11. At this time, he would pass his mother in the streets without a word between them. He then decided that he wanted to go back into a children's home again and he lived in a succession of these until he was 14. George rarely attended school.

At the age of 14, George ran away to the city centre 'to noise the staff up' and slept rough and stayed in squats with a group of young people he knew. He was caught after five months and returned to the children's homes, but was then moved to a secure unit because 'I was a junkie by that time'. He tried to commit suicide by overdosing 'just for attention'.

When George was 16 years old, it was arranged for him to take up a job looking after old people in Manchester. He shared a house with two other YTs and loved the independence. He also managed to make a lot of friends.

Everything was goin' great for me, and then I was just missing everybody up in Glasgow so I came back and fucked everything up for maself.

George wanted to go back into care, but the Children's Panel decided he was too old and he was placed in a young person's hostel. He moved around the youth network of hostels in Glasgow and was evicted and barred from each one for behaviour such as using drugs, throwing televisions out of the window, fighting and stealing cars. He was moved on to the adult hostels, but was also thrown out of most of these. When asked why he behaved in this way he replied:

A lot of people ask me that and I cannae gie them an answer . . . you just want a good laugh . . . when I start I don't know when tae stop.

When we interviewed George, he was sleeping rough, but spending some nights in a hostel. He had recently tried to commit suicide by overdosing and said this was largely because he had nowhere to stay.

When we traced George a year later he had overdosed again and was in a hospital unit, from where he was transferred into a detoxification unit. His social worker said that he was still homeless and leading a chaotic lifestyle.

## Some general issues

The pathways identified in this chapter reflect the experiences of some young people over a period of time and allow a dynamic analysis of the factors which have shaped their experience. The pressures of space preclude the inclusion of more from the wealth of information gleaned through the interviews. Similarly, not all of the aspects of the framework described above and adopted in this research could be elaborated on in the chapter. For example, the structural forces which shape young people's opportunities, their use of 'strategies' and 'coping mechanisms' as well as the interaction between young people's housing and homelessness pathways and other aspects of their lives were only touched upon in the accounts of the pathways and illustrative biographies. The intention is further to develop these themes and other findings emerging from the research in future publications. We can, however, indicate here some of the benefits of the dynamic approach taken, and highlight a few of the main factors affecting young people's pathways through homelessness.

These six pathways represent an attempt to show the often unstable current situations of some young homeless people and to indicate how they reached this position, and also to trace their progress by engaging in the difficult task of re-contacting them a year later. However, the pathways are simple abstractions from a very complex reality. It is extremely difficult to impose a valid and meaningful structure on the mass of detail which makes up each individual's life. However, this effort does reap rewards. For example, one of the major findings to emerge from the research was the sharp distinction between local and city centre homelessness in Glasgow. This divergence could only be discerned by tracing people's experiences over a period of time. This finding has particular policy relevance because most homeless agencies concentrate their activities at city centre locations, partly because this is the most visible aspect of homelessness and it is given most attention politically. However, underlying this focus is the belief that it will result in catching most homeless young people eventually. The evidence of this research is that this is not necessarily the case, as a substantial group of homeless people do not gravitate to this location at any stage of their pathways.

A key benefit of this pathways approach has therefore been to help break down the image of young homeless people as a homogeneous group with similar experiences. The homelessness pathways charted here were complex and did not all conform to the general picture of a deepening homelessness crisis which moved through well-defined stages, eventually leading, for those who were unable to exit, to 'chronic' homelessness characterized by long-term hostel residence or rough sleeping. The research did support the findings of previous research that the incidence of institutional living increased as the homelessness experience lengthened

(Hutson and Liddiard, 1994; Jones, 1993). This was often due to the difficulty in sustaining unofficial homelessness for a long period of time. In particular, young people were more likely to be staying in adult hostels or prison later in their homelessness pathway. However, these trends may be attributable to their increasing age rather than length of time homeless, because access rules mean that young people are likelier to be channelled into adult rather than young persons' hostels once they reach 18 and their criminal records tend to lengthen as they get older, which increases the likelihood of a prison sentence. There was no evidence that rough sleeping or mobility between cities increased as the homelessness pathway lengthened. These events could happen at any point, even right at the beginning of the homelessness experience as the family home was left, sometimes very suddenly. The city centre homeless, at whatever stage, were most likely to experience these situations.

'Territoriality', that is level of attachment to local area, was one of the most important factors identified in the research which influenced the pathway that a young person took. This concept is explored in more detail in an article by one of the authors which focuses particularly on young homeless people who remain 'hidden' in their local communities (Fitzpatrick, 1998).

As has been mentioned above, this was a small-scale project in a particular community, and research is required in other locations to test how widely this pathways framework may be applied. It would be very interesting, although difficult, to monitor young homeless people's progress over a period longer than a year, and to trace in greater detail pathways which take them further afield than the centre of their nearest city. Finally, the pathways framework could usefully be applied to other homeless groups to gain insights into the causes and processes underlying their situation.

## References

Anderson, I. and Quilgars, D. (1995) *Foyers for Young People: Evaluation of a Pilot Initiative*, York: Centre for Housing Policy, University of York.

Bannister, J., Dell, M., Donnison, D., Fitzpatrick, S. and Taylor, R. (1993) *Homeless Young People in Scotland: The Role of the Social Work Services*, Edinburgh: HMSO.

Caskie, K. (1992) *Young People, Social Work Care and Homelessness*, Edinburgh: Shelter (Scotland).

Caskie, K. (1993) *Some Change – Some Chance! Scottish Local Authorities' Response to Homelessness and Housing Need among Young People*, Edinburgh: Shelter (Scotland).

Clapham, D., Means, R. and Munro, M. (1993) 'Housing, the life course and older people', in S. Arber and M. Evandrou (eds) *Ageing, Independence and the Life Course*, London: Jessica Kingsley.

Coles, B. (1995) *Youth and Social Policy: Youth Citizenship and Young Careers*, London: UCL Press.

Crow, G. (1989) 'The use of the concept of strategy in recent sociological literature', *Sociology*, vol. 23, no. 1, pp. 1–24.

Fitzpatrick, S. (1998) 'Hidden homelessness amongst young people', *Youth and Policy*, special edition, 'Youth homelessness and social exclusion', no. 59.

Forrest, R. and Kemeny, J. (1984) *Careers and Coping Strategies: Micro and Macro Aspects of the Friend Forwards Owner Occupation*, mimeograph, Bristol: University of Bristol.

Forrest, R. and Murie, A. (1991) 'Housing markets, labour markets and housing histories', in J. Allan and C. Hamnett (eds) *Housing Markets and Labour Markets: Building the Connections*, London: Unwin Hyman.

Giddens, A. (1984) *The Constitution of Society*, Oxford: Polity Press.

Hutson, S. and Liddiard, M. (1994) *Youth Homelessness: The Construction of a Social Issue*, London: Macmillan.

Jones, G. (1993) *Young People In and Out of the Housing Market*, Edinburgh: Centre for Educational Sociology, University of Edinburgh and Scottish Council for Single Homeless.

Jones, G. (1995) *Leaving Home*, Buckingham: Open University Press.

Jones, G. and Wallace, C. (1992) *Youth, Family and Citizenship*, Buckingham: Open University Press.

Leonard, D. (1980) *Sex and Generation: A Study of Courtship and Weddings*, London: Tavistock.

Pickvance, C. and Pickvance, K. (1994) 'Towards a strategic approach to housing behaviour: a study of young people's housing strategies in south-east England', *Sociology*, vol. 28, no. 3, pp. 657–77.

Randall, G. and Brown, S. (1993) *The Rough Sleepers Initiative: An Evaluation*, London: HMSO.

Stockley, D., Canter, D. and Bishopp, D. (1993) *Young People on the Move*, Guildford: University of Surrey, Department of Psychology.

Thornton, R. (1990) *The New Homeless: The Crisis of Youth Homelessness and the Response of Local Authorities*, London: SHAC.

# 10 More than community care: supporting the transition from homelessness to home

*Bridget J. Franklin*

## Introduction

It has been accepted, for a decade or more, that the stigma and consequences of homelessness may result in the need for support during the rehousing process. This issue of support has come to the fore with the recognition of the inadequacies of the implementation of the community care legislation of 1990 and the realization that many people, who should be provided for by the legislation, are falling through the net and becoming homeless. Similarly, many existing homeless people have unidentified community care needs or have refused to accept assistance through the community care route. However, just as with community care, the mistake should not be made of assuming that every homeless person, or every person falling within the terms of the community care legislation, either wants, needs or has to receive, assistance and support. As Morris (1993) has pointed out, there is a danger of fostering the perception of dependent and defective people who need care and who should be encouraged to conform to certain normative conventions. This point is also discussed in Chapter 11. Subscription to the belief that homeless people should be 'persuaded' into settled housing (Randall and Brown, 1993) through a 'resettlement' process conveys similar notions of the imposition of the standards of a dominant ideology. Such conformity denies the right to individuality. The rhetoric of independent living should be just that and should encourage self-determination and the choice to be different.

Despite the increasing recognition of the policy causation of homelessness there is still a tendency, by many, to view the homeless as inadequate, in some cases defiant and deserving of condemnation. This intensifies feelings of stigma and ostracism. The received view is that every normal person should have a home – so those who do not are failing to conform. In addition, such transgressors stir contradictory emotions, from disgust and contempt, to concern and shame at the failings of society to provide for visibly vulnerable people. How much more comfortable it would be if these people were swept out of view and put in their proper place, leaving our streets and urban spaces clear for their intended use and projecting an image of an ordered, safe and cohesive society.

The mere provision of a proper place, of a roof over the heads of the homeless, is not alone the answer to the problem, either at the institutional level or the individual one. It is inadequate to assume that the provision of shelter is, in itself, the end of the problem for a homeless individual, on the basis that this person is now no longer *homeless*. There is a much more complex process at issue – which involves, not only rehousing, but also a progression through the stages whereby an individual comes to feel *at home* – a progression which is too easily taken for granted by those who have a safe, secure and predictable pattern to their lives:

. . . whilst housing is supposedly the permanent solution to homelessness there are so many other factors within that and we are talking about the creation of a home, not just 'houselessness', if you like, it's '*hom*elessness'. (Local Authority Policy Officer, quoted in Pleace, 1995, p. 77; emphasis added)

At the intuitive level this is understood. At the level of policy and practice it is more convenient to ignore the wider context and adopt a minimalist response. Such an approach, however, offers at best a partial solution; at worst, it is a recipe for failure in which the underlying needs of the individual are subsumed within the presumption that any accommodation is better than none and that the recipient should be grateful and make the best of it.

This chapter is concerned with approaches to a more supportive response to the rehousing of homeless people and argues for a better understanding of the impact of the homeless experience and an acknowledgement that the management of the rehousing process may be crucial to the ability of the individual to make the transition from homelessness to home. Particular attention will be paid to a holistic approach and to an adequate identification of the support needs of homeless people and the requirement for mechanisms which meet those needs. Attention will be drawn to the difficulties inherent in the present arrangements for the provision of support in the rehousing process, in particular the uncertainties over agencies' responsibilities and the consequences of these for the effective delivery of services.

## Whose responsibility?

The support needs of homeless people may not differ markedly from those identified in the context of community care (see Clapham and Franklin, 1994a; Watson and Conway, 1995). Homelessness *per se*, however, is not a category under the legislation of the NHS and Community Care Act, 1990 and, furthermore, the categories of vulnerability are not the same as those which are used by local authorities in considering entitlement to housing under the homelessness legislation. The community care legislation speci- fies four priority categories – older people with particular needs, people with mental health problems, people with learning difficulties and people with physical disabilities or sensory impairment – but it suggests that other groups, such as people with drug or alcohol problems and people with progressive illnesses such as AIDS, can also be included within the remit of the Act. A homeless person may indeed fall into one of these groups but, as noted above, that does not necessarily mean that they will receive any help under the provisions of the Act or that they will be willing to accept it.

Analysis of a survey of self-reported health problems (Bines, 1994) shows that homeless people suffer from ill health to a much greater extent than the general population. For example, they have rates two or three times as high in regard to musculo-skeletal, skin, digestive and chest disorders. Furthermore 60 per cent of rough sleepers have multiple health problems, with some 40 per cent reporting themselves as suffering from mental health symptoms such as depression, anxiety and 'nerves'. The incidence of mental illness is of particular concern, being eight times more prevalent among people in hostels and bed and breakfast accommodation and 11 times more prevalent among rough sleepers than it is in the general population. One in four of those who reported themselves as having a mental health problem (depression, anxiety or 'nerves') had been in a psychiatric hospital at some point in their lives, yet two thirds were receiving no treatment at the time of the survey. Other evidence supports this finding. For example, Anderson *et al.* (1993) found that one in eight people in hostels and bed and breakfast hotels, one in five in day centres and one in six people on soup runs had stayed in a psychiatric hospital at some time. However, very few homeless people are rendered homeless immediately on discharge from psychiatric hospitals, which suggests that the problem is related more to issues of care in the community, in terms of both support and housing. It appears that people with mental health problems often find it difficult to keep accom- modation, do not understand the housing system, and are frequently not accessing any support services at all.

It is an unfortunate fact that homeless people are either unable or unwilling to register with a G.P. and do not make appropriate use of primary health care. One consequence of this is that recourse is had to accident and emergency (A&E) departments of hospitals. North *et al.* (1996) have studied the use of an A&E department in London, and have shown that over half the visits made are inappropriate. Ten per cent of those attending were doing so for mental health reasons, this being the highest cause after accidents and injuries. Both psychotic and depressive illnesses are common, often resulting in repeated visits to A&E departments, yet fewer than a third of those with a history of psychotic illness have any contact with a psychiatrist or other mental health worker. North *et al.* (1996, p. 4) conclude: 'For many, "care in the community" has not worked.'

There is therefore growing concern about the situation of homeless people with community care needs and even though guidance has been sent to health authorities, social services departments and housing organizations on the necessity for joint planning and co-ordination (Department of Health, 1993), it does not appear to have achieved much improvement in terms of outcomes. Two health reports, one from the Royal College of Physicians (Connelly and Crown, 1994), the other from the Standing Conference on Public Health (Knight, 1994), have both called for improved access to housing and health services for homeless people, with a particular emphasis on a review of the role played by community care. The Mental Health Foundation (1994) endorses this approach, following a survey that showed that almost a quarter of homeless people with mental health problems had become homeless after the breakdown of a tenancy with a local housing authority or housing association.

The main responsibility for the delivery of community care lies with social services departments, but the central involvement of health authorities is also explicit. The significance of housing in community care is now acknowledged to have been marginalized, with little recognition of the fact that the provision of appropriate housing is crucial in achieving successful independent living and minimizing the level of additional support. The lack of clear boundaries between responsibilities both at the level of joint planning and of delivery has created confusion and uncertainty in terms of the support of vulnerable tenants and has all too often resulted in housing management having to provide support by default (Clapham and Franklin, 1994b; Gregory and Brownill, 1995). Social workers are reluctant to have any significant degree of involvement and appear to find it difficult to identify with the problems facing housing managers in providing support for increasing numbers of tenants struggling to sustain a tenancy.

This situation has led to housing organizations devising a number of strategies to address the situation. Some employ specialist workers such as tenancy support workers and resettlement workers. Others have accepted that the generic housing officer role should include activities which go beyond the basic landlord function. More in the spirit of the community care legislation have been those who have sought to improve relations with other agencies, fostering joint working and a team approach. By contrast, others have adopted a denial strategy, either refusing to house 'difficult' tenants, or leaving them to their own devices and resorting to eviction with no exploration of alternative solutions.

If this unsystematic and precarious situation pertains for those who, nominally at least, are provided for under the community care legislation, how much more unsatisfactory is the position facing the homeless with no such similar statutory status. While the assumption should not be made that support is always needed, the evidence suggests that in most cases it is, even if only in the form of a friendly visit and the knowledge that there is someone 'on call' in a crisis. Those leaving institutions or hostels under a supervised programme are likely to have support workers or key workers who will facilitate the resettlement process. For those rehoused through the homelessness procedures of the local authority, where the duty is only to rehouse and not to provide support, the receipt of any form of support, for any period at all, is something of a lottery.

## The need for support

Anderson (1994) and Pleace (1995) have both argued that there is inadequate research into the support needs of homeless people as well as little agreement about what these needs are, how they should be met, and who might benefit from continuous support. Some surveys of the support needs of homeless people exist, although these have concentrated on the single homeless. For example, among those surveyed in a study of the Rough Sleepers Initiative (Randall and Brown, 1993) it was found that three quarters would need some support – 10 per cent of these would need support to a minimal degree, two thirds would need a reasonable amount, reducing over time, and one quarter would need long-term or permanent support. This is endorsed by the study of the single homeless by Anderson *et al.* (1993), where it was reported that two thirds would require some form of support when provided with their own home. The earlier research of Dant and Deacon (1989) suggested that nearly two thirds of those in a rehousing project in Leeds would need 'sensitive housing management', one third would require low-level support, while a small minority could only have their support needs met through remaining in long-term hostel care. Similarly, Garside *et al.*'s report (1990) on hostels stated that over half the sample felt they would want continued support in move-on accommodation.

Quantifications such as these, without further definition, while giving a general impression, are inadequate in determining what forms of support should be delivered in practice and by whom. Anderson (1994) has attempted to distinguish 'support' from 'care', with the latter being seen as the type of care embodied as 'care in the community'. This is separated into social care delivered by social services and medical care delivered by the health service. The implication seems to be that there is thus no need for housing services to concern themselves with 'care' needs but only with a fairly limited support role. This overlooks the fact that, in many cases, community care help is either unforthcoming or rejected.

Pleace (1995) has attempted to devise a more systematic approach, dividing the needs of vulnerable single homeless people into five categories: housing need; support needs, which include health care and personal support (cooking, washing, emotional support and welfare benefits); daily living skills; financial needs; and social needs (for relationships and activity). While this represents a move in the direction of a bottom-up rather than a top-down approach, it is lacking in refinement and its practical application is unclear.

From empirical studies of homeless people, including those mentioned above and others such as Dix (1995) and Duncan and Downey (1985), it is possible to extrapolate a range of issues identified either by the homeless people themselves or by the staff working with them, in regard to potential areas where support might be needed. These areas of support can then be grouped in a way which demonstrates the progression or transition, from the acceptance of shelter through the development and application of daily living skills to the consciousness of being 'at home'. Such a progression marks a move from a more passive to a more self-directed position and represents also a transition from a place-centred to a person-centred perspective. In this it is reminiscent of the theory of human motivation and needs fulfilment devised by Maslow (1970). Maslow conceptualizes needs as starting from the lowest level of physiological needs and, once those are met, progressing through a hierarchy of security needs, belongingness and love needs, esteem needs and finally to the higher level of the need for self-actualization.

The following represents an attempt to address all those areas where support might be needed. It is not intended to be either prescriptive or patronizing but to make suggestions and raise awareness. For some homeless people all levels of support might be appropriate, for others none. The majority will be likely to need assistance in some of these areas but not all.

## The rehousing process

The rehousing process is the first, and also the most crucial, step, signifying the end of a period of homelessness; it encompasses the allocation of a property, equipping it, moving in and accepting its possible limitations.

The evidence is that the majority of homeless people who want to be rehoused would prefer self-contained accommodation, in an area perceived to have a good image, or with which there is familiarity. The importance of this is stressed in Chapter 11. The idea of any ability to choose is, however, somewhat hollow. Where local authority rehousing is concerned, there is often a policy of one offer only and, if more than one offer is made, refusal of the first may result in the applicant being returned to the bottom of the list. The residualized nature of the remaining housing stock means that any property that is available is likely to suffer some drawback in terms of location, condition or suitability. Furthermore, it is rare to find an authority where much effort is made to match the applicant with the property. Housing associations have the reputation of a more sympathetic approach, but this may change as the role which has been thrust upon them directs them to increasingly pragmatic considerations. This creates the danger that, in the future, their stock may be as problematic as some of the worst local authority stock (Page, 1993).

Even with restricted choice, there are ways in which the rehousing process can be rendered supportive and increase the prospect of successful rehousing. For example, there should be discussion as to the advisability of self-contained accommodation, with attention drawn to the potential of isolation. Applicants can be encouraged to widen their geographical preference by discussion of areas they may not have considered, if necessary by being taken to visit them. This may be particularly relevant for those who have suffered domestic violence or other forms of abuse and harassment as well as for those leaving institutions for the first time, including care-leavers. It may be appropriate to consider whether former hostel or supported accommodation dwellers are best housed near a continuing source of support or at a more distant location in order to discourage dependency. It may be helpful to introduce a homeless person gradually to the new area, in order to try and establish familiarity and the beginnings of a social network before the final move is made. An additional consideration is that some, particularly those who have never had their own home, will need help in deciding whether a property that they have viewed is suitable for their needs or whether it is not.

Most studies identify the provision of furniture and other household goods as a major obstacle in establishing independent living. While some authorities and housing associations have second-hand furniture stores, many do not, and new tenants have to rely on charities, community care grants or inadequate social fund loans. The latter option means that a tenant is in debt from the outset. However, if at least minimal furniture is not supplied, the likelihood of abandonment is increased. Where prospective tenants are in the position of having to select and purchase their own furniture, assistance may be required to accomplish this.

The process of moving and settling-in has been identified as inadequately supported. It involves the transport of possessions (if any), the disposition of furniture (if any), the location and operation of items such as power points, meter cupboards, stop taps, water heaters, and the signing of tenancy agreements. The symbolic significance of possessing keys, perhaps for the first time, may only be diminished by the sudden realization of all the implications of being alone. One of these implications relates to security, particularly if the new tenant concerned has experienced harassment, theft or violence. Hutson (1994b), for example, has found that the provision of locks and alarms was felt to be particularly important to young homeless people. The ability to make the transition to successful independent living should ideally be monitored in the first few weeks, with regular visits, which do not, however, give the impression that a test of competence is being undertaken.

Given the lack of real housing choice that exists for any low-income householder, let alone the homeless, it is likely that the eventual home will be inadequate in some respects, whether in terms of size, condition, layout, neighbours or location. An accompanied viewing should mean that these deficiencies have been prepared for, but it is often only in the fullness of time that they become a source of frustration. If serious, they may lead to abandonment of the tenancy. The reality of 'home' may be far removed from the image the homeless have formed of their ideal home, and accommodating the reality to the image could prove an insurmountable task if the need for realistic compromise is not appreciated and accepted.

## Functional skills

The use of the phrase 'functional skills' denotes the development of the ability to function effectively in a geographic sense, in relation to the locality and its facilities, and in the sense of understanding 'the system', in terms of officialdom and available public services.

As noted in the previous section, the location in which a previously homeless person finds himself or herself may be far from ideal, in regard not only to its physical or geographical situation, but also in its social location in terms of distance from known social networks, employment opportunities or being in identified areas of crime or drug dealing. If this is the case, more on-going support is likely to be needed than if the location were more appropriate. For some, the facilities of the area will be more important than for others, and this will relate to levels of dependency, mobility, need for health care and so on. It is important to establish that a rehoused person knows the position and means of access to the facilities they need or might wish to use and is aware of the services they can offer, including, for example, schools, adult education services, job centre, post office, lunch clubs and social clubs. This will involve the ability to orientate and navigate one's way around, including an awareness of public transport routes. Without the development of these abilities and the confidence to get about unaided, the tendency may be to remain indoors and isolated, which is not in itself problematic if a person *prefers* to remain indoors and isolated.

In terms of understanding 'the system' it is important to know the rights and duties of the ordinary citizen – for example voting rights, the payment of taxes, and the right to appeal against apparently unjust decisions by state agents. In addition, it is necessary to know something of the services offered by such agencies as the DSS, social services, the various branches of the health service, relevant voluntary agencies and the police, as well as the right method and the appropriate circumstances for approaching each agency for assistance.

## Financial skills

Financial problems have been identified as one of the main difficulties in establishing independent living. Initial assistance with claiming benefits and maximizing income often need to be supplemented with detailed help in budgeting for household and other bills. Given the low level of benefits, this is difficult to do in a realistic way. Young people under 25 are often faced with training allowances or income support levels of only £30 a week (at 1996 rates) and the apportioning of such inadequate amounts among items of necessary expenditure could stretch the imagination of the most expert adviser. Bills can be outfacing for those who are not accustomed to them and so are unprepared for the regularity with which they arrive. For some, there will need to be an explanation of how a bill is drawn up, how to check readings with the meter, when and where to pay the bill, and which 'bills' are only statements. Alternatives, such as pre payment coin or card meters, stamps, direct payments from income support, all need to be explained and the benefits and drawbacks for each individual described. In the short term, there may be competence in this area, but as other financial demands arise and resolution weakens, it is often a case of borrowing from one pot of money to pay into another, leading to problems in the longer term. The concept of saving for future need may be alien, especially for those who have relied in the past on daily rather than weekly sources of money.

## Household skills

Some people who have come from institutions, hostels, or the street may have little appreciation of the running of a home, and be unaware of the need, purpose or process of regular cleaning, laundry as well as other domestic and practical tasks. Similarly there may be a lack of skills in shopping, knowing where to go, what to buy, how to prioritize items on a low budget, how to choose between items, amounts to purchase, how to read a label, how long different foods will keep and how to store them. Cooking skills may also be lacking or poorly developed, with little awareness of quantities, use of utensils, following and adapting recipes, cooking times, balanced meals and so on. However, it is important not to make assumptions in regard to the presence or lack of such skills. Studies of young homeless people, including care-leavers, have shown that they often feel competent in basic household skills which they have absorbed as children in their families of origin (Hutson, 1994a).

On-going practical problems in connection with the property include coping with simple maintenance tasks, such as changing light bulbs and plugs, adjusting heating systems, decorating, reading meters, noting when repairs are needed, assessing their severity, and knowing whom to contact. The management of, and responsibility for, common spaces such as stairs and landings are a potential source of conflict and misunderstanding, as are the perennial problems of litter and rubbish collection. Gardens, as well as the access and use of other open spaces, are additional problem areas. In order to facilitate upkeep, some associations and housing authorities have organized tool-hiring facilities or employed decorating, handyman and gardening services.

## Personal skills

These include personal hygiene, taking regular meals, and health care, especially administering medication. People need to be able to recognize when they are ill, when they are ill enough to need assistance and when to call an emergency service. Research has shown that single homeless people, especially if they have spent a period living rough, often have multiple health problems, both physical and mental, for which regular treatment may be required. Without regular supervision, medication may not be taken, leading to a relapse, inability to cope, hospitalization and ultimately failure of a tenancy. Help may also be needed in coping with a history of drug or alcohol dependency, both in relation to its after effects, and in terms of maintaining control or abstinence.

Personal management also extends to the ability to adopt normally accepted lifestyles and to integrate into the community. To some extent this is a matter of personal choice as people have the right to be different. On the other hand, people should be enabled to choose from a basis of knowledge and, where skills are lacking, to receive some support in terms of how to present themselves in regard to dress, appearance, cleanliness, and appropriate behaviour. In addition, they should be enabled to engage in those areas of activity which mainstream society takes for granted such as making friends, having relationships, developing literacy and numeracy, advancing one's knowledge through education, and finding meaningful

occupation whether paid or not. The issues of personal contact and con-
nectedness are important. People who are vulnerable, and perhaps
desperate for companionship, are all too easily exploited by others. There is
then a risk of being beguiled into illicit or nefarious activities, from petty or
even serious crime to substance abuse. Loneliness and isolation are frequently cited as reasons for the lack of success of independent living and
there may be a desire to return to the relative companionship and structured living of a hostel or supported accommodation.

In this connection, a common problem which is reported by agencies
housing young homeless people is the serious difficulties which can occur
between them and their neighbours (Hutson, 1994a). Fears of troublesome
behaviour can lead to opposition from neighbours to the siting of hostels in
residential neighbourhoods and such fears may still exist where people are
scattered in properties across a wider area, but with central support (see
Chapter 11). Difficulties can be exacerbated where the newly rehoused
person's friends and acquaintances, who have not themselves been
rehoused, seek to avail themselves of the facilities of the property on a
temporary or a more permanent basis.

## Self-actualization

At a remove from the personal and community integration skills mentioned
above is the development of identity and self-worth, being at ease with
oneself and one's surroundings, attachment to place, fulfilment, self-
direction and the achievement of individual potential. Although these are
more nebulous concepts than those dealt with so far, they may have a more
significant part to play in sustaining independent living than is perhaps fully
understood. It is in this regard that emotional support and counselling can
help to increase feelings of self-worth and the ability to make decisions.
These skills may never have been developed, may have been erased in the
experience of institutional living, or effaced through oppression by a
parent, partner or carer:

... helping people to settle is less about whether they can manage in the home as
about whether they feel they are in the right place, whether they can identify with
their place as a home and whether they can maintain a lifestyle congruent with
having a settled home. (Dant and Deacon, 1989, p. 71)

Research on the meaning of the home has shown the extent to which
personal identity can be bound up with place identity (Cooper Marcus,
1995). The symbolic and emotional importance of home is rarely acknowledged in policy debates and is overlooked by those who see support as
ending at the mechanistic level. However, an understanding of this deeper
level is what is needed in order to enable someone to develop an awareness

of what being 'at home' can be. Even at its most superficial, there are certain conventions associated with being 'at home' and, for those who have never had a home of their own, the experience of relating to that home, of feeling at ease in it, of seeing it as a place of freedom where they make the rules, is a novelty which may be both alien and awesome:

> You'd forget that you can make a brew, you sit and think 'God I am thirsty' and forget that you could just get one. . . . You also have to come down to being in a house, it's weird to sit in a chair, when I first come in here and sat in that chair next to that fire in me coat, I sit in my coat for days because I was not used to taking my coat off. (Woman in her 20s, quoted in Pleace, 1995, p. 29)

At the deeper level of the meaning of home are those aspects referred to by Després (1991), such as home as reflection of one's ideas and values, home as permanence and continuity, home as relationship with family and friends, home as acting on and modifying one's dwelling, home as the centre of activities. These meanings, and others, may only be achieved with the fullness of time.


## Providing supportive solutions

In the light of the analysis above, it is apparent that the allocation of a suitable property and the provision of appropriate support should not be discrete activities. The one crucially impacts on and reinforces the other. The provision of housing and support should therefore be seen as *one* process, not a sequential one in which a property is allocated and support is given as an add-on extra or where a support need is identified and a place in a scheme allocated because that level of support is available. Unfortunately, this is all too often how the process is perceived, both in community care as a whole and in the rehousing of the homeless. This is a consequence of the fact that different agencies have responsibilities for what are perceived as two very different areas of work. One is charged with a technical and administrative function in the allocation and management of property (the bricks and mortar) and the other is charged with a welfare and person-centred function in the support and care of people. The lack of understanding of each other's work that exists between these agencies, housing organizations and social care agencies is, moreover, seemingly deliberately fostered by the desire to carve out and maintain professional boundaries and distinctiveness (Franklin and Clapham, 1997). A salutary consequence of the new demands imposed by the community care legislation has been that it has required agencies to work more closely together, and there have been attempts either to overcome traditional hostilities or to embrace new aspects of work which will facilitate the 'seamless' service for which the legislation calls.

This move has been of benefit, not only in the community care context, but also to homeless people who require support. In recognition of the need, many local housing authorities have adopted specific homelessness strategies, in some cases over and beyond their statutory obligations. There are also a number of housing associations which have focused their attention on the homeless, generally because they recognize the lack of available options, especially for the single homeless and those with significant support needs. Looking at specific examples of how the housing and support issue is managed, however, it would appear that it is still a case of a housing and care divide, rather than a seamless service.

In one Scottish city the housing department has established a homelessness strategy revolving round three groups – homeless families, young people and adult single homeless (see Clapham and Franklin, 1994b). The unit responsible for this strategy is a more or less autonomous concern and located away from those responsible for other housing department functions. The families and individuals concerned are deemed to have relatively low support needs, with the support geared to the transition period rather than being for the long term. Families are usually placed in temporary accommodation from which they will have to move in due course. Individuals are offered furnished flats where they will be able to stay once they have demonstrated that they can manage a tenancy. Support is provided by the housing department through caseworkers who advise on housing options and the requisite level of support as well as through family welfare officers for families and youth housing workers for young people. In addition, the social work department provides homemakers to support the single homeless. Although the housing department and the social work support provide similar services, offering help with budgeting, claiming benefits and giving advice on community activities, the emphasis is subtly different, with the support of the former being oriented to managing the property in a manner acceptable to the housing department and the support of the latter orientated to the person's ability to cope in a manner acceptable to that person. Indeed, the homemaker service is scathing about the ability of the homelessness service to offer support in the real meaning of the word. Aside from the actual process of referral, there is no contact between the two departments over a case, unless a problem occurs. What is interesting about this situation is that both the homelessness service and the homemaker service, working at the boundaries of their traditional areas of work, operate in isolation to the central work of their departments and are seen as marginal and peripheral.

'Floating' support, in which an agency provides support and care for a period of months or years to a tenant in a mainstream tenancy managed by a different agency, is a model which is growing in popularity. Part of the rationale is that it allows people with more intensive support needs, who would previously have been more likely to be housed in temporary group accommodation, to be allocated self-contained accommodation in which they can remain long term. With the best of intentions, ambitious projects have been set up which aim to help very difficult client groups, such as young people with challenging behaviour, to live independently, as described by Hutson (1994a; 1994b). In this case, the housing associations felt that the support was either inadequate or rejected by the person concerned, which left the housing association to deal with problems of trashed or abandoned properties, and disaffected neighbours. Experiences such as these lead housing associations to screen prospective tenants to ensure that only those likely to accept support will be nominated, thus undermining the objectives of the project. Housing officers and support workers may share the same overall objectives of housing vulnerable people but, in actuality, their approaches and perspectives are quite different; this can lead to frustrations and conflict. It is the client who is then caught in the crossfire. The housing officer has to consider the wider needs of the property, the other tenants, and the neighbours, and is not prepared to tolerate behaviour which puts these in jeopardy, even in the short term, while the support worker is focused on the needs of the client, the rights of self-expression and the progression to self-management. One consequence of this situation is that support workers may feel disinclined to pass on to housing officers all the information about a case for fear that this may put the client at risk of not being accepted for a tenancy or of being evicted. This can cause difficulties later.

These examples illustrate a fundamental difference in approach to the issue of what support should be about – in this case, a lack of communication and defensive attitudes between agencies. While the move to the employment of specialist workers within the social care agencies, be it social services or specialist support agencies, may be a step forward in terms of assisting people in the rehousing process, it still appears to create some of the same tensions that have been demonstrated more generally between housing workers and social workers in the management of mainstream tenancies in the community care context (Franklin and Clapham, 1997; Clapham and Franklin, 1994a; 1994b). Here, it is reported that while social workers have defined support roles, they do not have the resources, or in some cases the statutory obligations, to fulfil them. This can leave housing officers with inadequate preparation and training to pick up the pieces where they are willing and able to do so. However, in some cases this can mean that their only recourse is to evict the tenant because there is no way to provide the necessary support to sustain the tenancy. On the other hand, specialists within housing organizations are often charged by professional social workers with inadequate awareness of problems and their resolutions, which can potentially be harmful. The inevitable prejudices and frustrations can only be overcome through a process of change, achievable by more joint working, training and discussion and, above all, by better resourcing. Until then, the service provided will be inadequate to meet even the most basic of needs, and will certainly not assist those who are most vulnerable to achieve personal fulfilment through their housing situation.


## Conclusion

The process of rehousing the homeless should involve the provision of a responsive, sympathetic and non-stigmatizing service which ensures that the concept of blame and the need for self-justification do not enter the debate. The aim should be that those desirous of secure permanent housing are enabled to receive it and those who need and wish for support in this achievement have access to a person-centred progression towards independent living. Ultimately, the issue is less one of which particular agency provides the support but rather how effective this support is, who is best placed to provide it, and the relationship of this agency with the others involved. This may vary from one locality to another. The ideal situation would seem to be that where one agency only is involved, as this avoids confusion for all concerned and makes it less likely that a gap will appear between the responsibilities of different agencies through which clients all too easily fall. It is therefore essential that there is transparency between agencies as to where the responsibility of each begins and ends. This may take the form of precise guidelines or contracts between agencies which delineate, for example, which agency has responsibility for which element of the support continuum developed earlier in this chapter. It is also crucial that the individual homeless person is involved in discussion of the various support elements and has an understanding of who will provide what.

Housing departments are increasingly likely to succumb to the pressures of having to adapt to a more competitive environment, to reduce costs and to comply with performance targets, with the result that the scope to provide what are perceived of as welfare services will be further curtailed. Housing associations have, in the past, been in a position to offer more supportive management than housing departments and have been aided in this by the availability of Special Needs Management Allowance (SNMA) to offset the costs of additional support to certain categories of tenant. However, new financial arrangements, including threats to SNMA, are forcing them too to be more competitive, and their role in taking over new general needs provision from local authorities may prove to be at the expense of their special needs work. Threats to withdraw service charges which cover a support element from housing benefit eligibility are a further concern to all service providers.

The model of a specialist support agency may have much to commend it. As an agency with a specific remit for support, it can build an identity around this rather than support being regarded as either an optional extra or a peripheral activity. Relations with other agencies also benefit from this transparency of function. A further benefit is the circumventing of the traditional hostility between social work and housing departments. However, such agencies must ensure a complete understanding of the services of the housing organizations with which they work, of the demands on and limitations of housing officers and develop personal contact and workable networks across their area of operation. Ultimately support arrangements, from whatever agency, will not succeed without secure long-term funding, enabling a solid base for forward planning and enduring partnerships.

## References

Anderson, I. (1994) *Access to Housing for Low Income Single People*, York: Centre for Housing Policy, University of York.

Anderson, I., Kemp, P. and Quilgars, D. (1993) *Single Homeless People*, London: HMSO.

Bines, W. (1994) *The Health of Single Homeless People*, York: Centre for Housing Policy, University of York.

Clapham, D. and Franklin, B. (1994a) *Housing Management, Community Care and Competitive Tendering*, Coventry: Chartered Institute of Housing.

Clapham, D. and Franklin, B. (1994b) *The Housing Management Contribution to Community Care*, Glasgow: Centre for Housing Research and Urban Studies.

Connelly, J. and Crown, J. (eds) (1994) *Homelessness and Ill-Health*, London: Royal College of Practitioners.

Cooper Marcus, C. (1995) *House as a Mirror of Self: Exploring the Deeper Meaning of Home*, Berkeley: Conari Press.

Dant, T. and Deacon, A. (1989) *Hostels to Homes: The Rehousing of Single Homeless People*, Aldershot: Avebury.

Department of Health (1993) *Community Care Services for Homeless People*, London: Department of Health, Community Care Support Force.

Després, C. (1991) 'The Meaning of Home: Literature Review and Directions for Future Research and Theoretical Development', *Journal of Architectural and Planning Research*, vol. 8, no. 2, pp. 96–115.

Dix, J. (1995) *Assessing the Housing, Health and Support Needs of Single Homeless People Living in Hostel Accommodation in Cardiff*, Cardiff: City Housing Department.

Duncan, S. and Downey, P. (1985) *Settling Down: A Study of the Rehousing of Users of DHSS Resettlement Units*, London: HMSO.

Franklin, B. and Clapham, D. (1997) 'The social construction of housing management', *Housing Studies*, vol. 12, no. 1, pp. 7–26.

Garside, P., Grimshaw, R. and Ward, F. (1990) *No Place Like Home: The Hostels Experience*, London: HMSO.

Gregory, S. and Brownill, S. (1995) *The Housing/Care Divide: Community Care and the Management of Single Person Housing in Oxford*, Oxford: Oxford Brookes University.

Hutson, S. (1994a) *Monitoring and Evaluating Network with a Focus on Housing and Support*, Cardiff: Welsh Office (Housing).

Hutson, S. (1994b) *Monitoring and Evaluating Network with a Focus on Young People's Interviews*, Cardiff: Welsh Office (Housing).

Knight, M. (ed.) 1994 *Housing, Homelessness and Health*, London: Nuffield Provincial Hospitals Trust for the Standing Conference on Public Health.

Maslow, A. (1970) *Motivation and Personality*, 2nd edn, New York: Harper Row.

Mental Health Foundation (1994) *Creating Community Care*, London: Mental Health Foundation.

Morris, J. (1993) *Community Care or Independent Living*, York: Joseph Rowntree Foundation.

North, C., Moore, H. and Owens, C. (1996) *Go Home and Rest? The Use of an Accident and Emergency Department by Homeless People*, London: Shelter.

Page, D. (1993) *Building for Communities: A Study of New Housing Association Estates*, York: Joseph Rowntree Foundation.

Pleace, N. (1995) *Housing Vulnerable Single Homeless People*, York: Centre for Housing Policy.

Randall, G. and Brown, S. (1993) *The Rough Sleepers Initiative: An Evaluation*, London: HMSO.

Watson, L. and Conway, T. (1995) *Homes for Independent Living: Housing and Community Care Strategies*, Coventry: Chartered Institute of Housing.

# 11 The experience of 'homeless' accommodation and support

*Susan Hutson*

Underlying this chapter is the view that homelessness is an issue which is socially constructed by a number of involved agents in a public arena (see Chapter 1). In many other chapters, the emphasis has been on the official and legal constructions of homelessness. Here the views of people who experience homelessness on a day-to-day basis will be set out, views which normally have little impact on either policy or practice. The chapter focuses on what homeless people have to say about temporary accommodation and the support which can accompany it. It looks particularly for discrepancies between the views of homeless people themselves and the more official versions of the situation. To do this, quotations are used from a number of reports (Murie and Jeffers, 1987; Garside *et al.*, 1990; Pleace, 1995; Dix, 1995) and from accounts given to the author by young homeless people between 1988 and 1997.[1]

Because of the shortage of affordable housing and the legislative restrictions, particularly for single people, temporary accommodation has been a common experience for homeless people. The Department of the Environment figure (1996) for those people who are accepted as homeless and in temporary accommodation is 41,000 – a figure which has dropped from a peak of 58,000 in 1992. No comparable figures are collected officially for single homeless people, but Shelter gives an estimate (1991) of 60,000 such people in hostels (Burrows and Walentowicz, 1992, p. 8). The Department of the Environment stated that there were 31,000 hostel bed spaces in 1989 (Garside *et al.*, 1990, p. 8). This discrepancy may be explained by different methods of calculation. It must also be remembered throughout that many homeless people are not able to access the kinds of temporary accommodation and support covered here.

Since the 1977 Housing (Homeless Persons) Act, temporary accommodation has been provided differently for those who were deemed to be 'in priority need', principally women and children, and those who were not. Local authorities are responsible for those in 'priority need' whereas provision for 'non priority', or generally single homeless people, is left to the voluntary sector. Although the 1996 Housing Act removed the duty to rehouse anyone permanently, homeless families continue to have priority over single people and are still provided for differently. There have been some remarkable changes in the type of temporary accommodation offered and, in the last decade, the giving of support has played a part in this provision. Let us firstly summarize the changes in temporary accommodation.

## Continuity and change in temporary accommodation

From 1834, workhouses were set up to provide basic shelter for the poor. Conditions were deliberately less attractive than those which could be purchased by the lowest wage. The aim was to deter all but the most desperate from becoming dependent on the state. Philanthropy was mixed with the desire to correct the behaviour of the unsettled and malingerers. As late as the 1980s, many of these workhouse buildings were still operating as hostels for people 'without a settled way of life' (Minister for Social Security, 1985, in Oldman, 1993, p. 4). They were described as 'large, institutional, direct access hostels ... offering mostly poor, overcrowded dormitory accommodation to currently 1,400 homeless people, mostly men' (Oldman, 1993, p. 3). Many were closed from 1985 onwards by the government. Pressure from campaigning groups such as CHAR may have been influential, but the move to transfer control from central government to the voluntary sector was in line with the political ideology of that time. Nevertheless, voluntary agencies were required to design smaller units in line with ideas of good practice which also played their part in moves towards community care.

Prior to 1977, homeless women and children were accommodated in single-sex hostels. It was the media which drew attention to the physical conditions and the resulting suffering in the TV drama documentary *Cathy Come Home* (1966). Although the 1977 Housing (Homeless Persons) Act gave access to permanent housing for some, many still had to wait for this in temporary accommodation for months or even years. Throughout the 1980s, private sector bed and breakfast hotels were widely used for such families. Complaints about conditions reached the press. This, together with their high cost, played a part in their being run down from a peak of 13,550 in 1991 to 4,550 in 1996 (Department of the Environment, 1997). The placing of families in properties leased from the public by local authorities became a more popular type of temporary accommodation, both for the families and the authorities. A deliberate alternative to such state provision were the refuges for women fleeing domestic violence set up by the National Women's Aid Federation from 1971, which had a distinctive type of self-help organization.

The numbers of younger homeless people looking for emergency and temporary accommodation rose steeply after the benefit restrictions of 1988. It was felt that the older single-person hostels were unsuitable for them because of the mental health and alcohol problems of some of their older clients. Children's charities, such as Barnardos, moved into this field of work, providing longer-term accommodation and support in young people's projects. Many projects began as shared houses but, as the difficulties of sharing became apparent, were converted into self-contained bedsits. In the 1990s, independent flats with peripatetic support became the preferred model. It must always be remembered that the development of these projects was patchy and many people had no access to accommodation at all. In the mid-1990s, a number of foyers were set up. Following the French model of *foyers pour jeunes travailleurs*, training and employment schemes are linked to hostels with central catering and staff ratios lower than those in the young people's projects. Against this background, let us look at accounts of living in different types of temporary accommodation.

**Homeless families in bed and breakfast accommodation**

As the pressure on temporary accommodation rose in the 1960s and 1970s, local authorities, particularly in London, turned to using private sector bed and breakfast hotels to accommodate homeless families. Their use first came under fire in the 1980s from health visitors, and this emphasis on health issues has continued. There were reports of the poor health records of children and mothers in the cramped conditions (Drennan and Stearn, 1986) and of high levels of infections among children using shared washing facilities. High rates of accidents to children and delayed developmental progress were also of concern. The following account conveys the experience of living in a bed and breakfast hotel and the implications for health:

There were no chairs and the little girl had her meals in her push-chair while her mother sat on the bed. On the floor, among the children's toys, was an electric cooking plate with a tin kettle on it. . . . There was a laundry basket and a string of wet baby clothes drying between the wardrobe and a nail on the wall. (Bonnerjea and Lawton, 1987, p. 31)

Health issues have legitimacy, in part because they are measurable. However, questions of cost were probably more persuasive. The National Audit Commission (1989) estimated that it cost an average of £288 a week or £15,000 a year to keep a family in bed and breakfast accommodation in contrast to only £8,200 for supplying a new council house. The same report described the standard of accommodation in many of these hotels as 'totally unsuited to family life'.

In the personal accounts, many fears were expressed about living closely with strangers. For example, a Sikh woman speaks of Bengali residents:

Their children throw their rubbish on the floor, you see the stairs are very unclean you know, sometimes they get scary for children, they slip on the stairs, they're concrete stairs, they can knock their teeth out or whatever ... I don't allow my children out of this room, the youngest was accused of throwing stones, I know he wouldn't. (Murie and Jeffers, 1987, p. 19)

These, and other accounts, show that living in such temporary accommodation was creating problems over and above those which had triggered the initial loss of a home.

## Single people in hostels

If temporary accommodation is fraught with dangers for homeless families, then what is the situation of single homeless people, few of whom qualify for permanent housing? It had always been assumed that hostels were sufficient and appropriate for single people, but concerns were expressed by CHAR and other agencies in 1985 about the physical conditions in them. The appearance of increasing numbers of *younger* homeless people drew further attention to these conditions. The two following accounts show the dangers facing young homeless people in such hostels. One young man (21) said:

I only stayed two hours. I couldn't handle it. The people are anything from alcoholics to people who've come out of nick for G[(revous] B[odily] H[arm]. It's just benches and pea soup. (Hutson and Liddiard, field notes, 1990)

Another man (20) fears for his future:

... but it's not a place to live in. There's all sorts here and listening to them and that sometimes it gets to you like – Am I going to turn into one of these like, you know what I mean? (Hutson and Liddiard, field notes, 1990)

Accounts from a recent report of hostels for all-age single homeless people continue to document the dangers of communal living and make alarming reading. A man in his sixties explains the situation:

What the staff know and what the staff don't know, there's a very thick concrete line in between. The things that go on, shall we say, upstairs, are not known by the staff downstairs, because there's this famous word, grassing. (Pleace, 1995, p. 25)

A staff manager of a mixed hostel describes the hostel:

... we've had people chucking themselves out of windows here, we've had people setting fire to the skip outside, we've had people stabbing people, we've had people drug dealing, we've had everything. (Pleace, 1995, p. 25)

Pleace concludes that hostels, particularly all-male ones, were regarded by many single people and hostel staff as being unsafe environments. Crime was associated with harassment and bullying as well as violence both between inmates and towards staff. He suggests that, although major incidents may occur only months apart, these are remembered and become often-told stories. Such stories, when combined with the constant noise and verbal abuse of hostels, can make them threatening places in which to live. In all-women's hostels, the violence tends to come from the outside, with male partners breaking in or threatening staff as they leave. Self-directed violence, in terms of suicide, had taken place in most of the hostels visited. Pleace comments:

When individuals in distress did not direct violence at either themselves or other people in the hostel, it was quite frequently the case that they would smash fixtures and fittings. (Pleace, 1995, p. 26)

Such violence and crime necessarily lead to frequent evictions. Stays in such hostels can become only a matter of a few weeks or even days (Hutson, 1993). The finding that 40 per cent of rough sleepers would not accept a hostel bed, if one was available, is understandable and the fact that reasons such as 'behaviour of other residents' and 'don't feel safe there' top the list corroborate the material above (Randall and Brown, 1996). The dangers of sharing accommodation with people who are not known dominate accounts of hostels and, as we saw above, were also a feature of bed and breakfast hotels.

These dangers of temporary accommodation need to be seen in the light of more positive accounts. A number of reports, all of hostels with older residents, indicate some satisfaction with hostel life. For example, Duncan *et al.*, (1983, p. 22), in a study of hostel residents with an average age of 55, report:

They often spoke of the hostel as a clean, comfortable or warm place, where there was no need to bother about housekeeping. The beds were made, the sheets changed, there was no shopping to do and no electricity bill to worry about. Things were done for you, everything was laid on.

In a later study (Garside *et al.*, 1990), 88 per cent overall were satisfied with the way the hostels were run, although some complaints are recorded – about noise, petty pilfering between residents and external threats of violence in women's hostels. The report concludes that residents generally get what they need and that this is provided at a reasonable cost. Thomas and Niner (1989) found that people were satisfied with a standard of accommodation which was often poor, as did Kemp and Rhodes (1994) in a study of commercial hotels in Glasgow.

An interesting situation is described by Dix (1995). In a survey of single homeless people living in city centre hostels, she found that a minority did not want to move out. They considered their hostel their home and did not consider themselves to be homeless. These were all men and all over 40. They had no mental health or other problems which might prevent them from moving out. The staff, however, described them as having become 'institutionalized'. The hostel worker attributed it to lack of self-confidence, saying:

It's almost a self-fulfilling prophecy. 'I'm not going to succeed' and they seem to do something in order not to have to go. We have had people that have run away on the day they are supposed to move out. (Dix, 1995, p. 73)

In this way, a legitimate desire to stay in a place to which one is accustomed is described as a pathological condition, thus creating a discrepancy between the views of agency workers and tenants.

How can these statements of satisfaction be squared with the earlier negative accounts? It may be significant that all those satisfied with their accommodation were middle-aged or older. The most critical comments in this chapter come from young people. It is also likely that people are more positive about accommodation into which they have been settled for some time. Interestingly, the workers above felt that it took a year for someone to become accustomed to hostel accommodation or 'institutionalized' (Dix, 1995). I have also found people being more positive when looking back on their past accommodation than when assessing their current place, where difficulties are more immediate (Hutson, 1994a). It is important to realize that differences may be generated by methodology in that a questionnaire may illicit more positive answers than an in-depth interview where some of the 'stories' mentioned above may be recounted. It should also be noted that the reports with the positive conclusions were mostly written for the Department of the Environment. With cost levels in some of these hostels at only £56 a week (Garside et al., 1990, p. 70), there could be strong reasons for stressing client satisfaction.

Homeless people are, of course, heterogeneous, in terms of age, gender and ethnicity as well as in their immediate experiences and objectives (Hutson and Liddiard, 1994). It is to be expected that, on every topic covered in this chapter, there will be differences of opinion. However, in nearly a decade of research with homeless young people, I have nearly always been given negative reports of larger hostels, particularly in terms of the danger and violence which arise.

## Single people in shared houses

It was the difficulties of hostel living, expressed above, which led in part to the use of more self-contained units in shared houses. Depressingly, although standards of accommodation undoubtedly improved, reports of the dangers of sharing continue. A man in his forties explains:

... if you've got a mental condition sitting in with just four walls, just like in one room, you're eating, sleeping and you're sharing a bathroom and you don't know who you're sharing your bathroom with, and I mean, could have been junkies. (Pleace, 1995, p. 27)

The following complaints come from shared housing in a young people's project reported to the author. The dangers which were highlighted are familiar – namely the physical dangers of sharing accommodation and mixing vulnerable people. One young man felt that it was:

... a waste of time and money putting a bunch of kids in [a shared house] ... It puts teenagers together. It adds up to trouble. It was people there and their friends, people coming in all hours. Giving them drugs ... It was a public house. (Hutson, 1994a, p. 5)

The scene painted by this young woman was no more positive:

If you didn't open the door, it got kicked in. It wasn't safe, there were drugs there. They were injecting speed. Chucking out needles. I was in the middle of it all. ... Everyone calling round. Can I stay? That makes more trouble. Friends, boyfriends, girlfriends. They used to call. Crash down. It was difficult. It gave you hassle. (Hutson, 1994b, p. 32)

While the negative views of the older hostels came from the majority of users, these depressing accounts of shared houses were common but not always in the majority. Although I have been told by workers that shared houses can work well, I have not come across one where there were not complaints, sometimes serious, from residents. The fact that there have been moves towards further self-containment indicates that there are difficulties. Projects have cut down on communal areas and turned shared houses into bedsits. Although some problems were solved, there were still complaints, both between tenants and between tenants and neighbours. The introduction of Special Needs Management Allowance (SNMA) to housing associations in England and Wales in 1990 encouraged the move to self-containment and the scattering of tenancies.

### Single people in permanent accommodation

Many felt that the solution to the problems in hostels and shared houses would be solved by the provision of independent housing. It is clear what homeless people themselves want. Surveys (Dix, 1995; Hutson and Jones, 1997; see also Chapter 8) and qualitative interviews show that most homeless people, even 16- and 17-year-olds, want self-contained, unfurnished flats – not hostels, shared housing or bedsits.

There is no doubt that good-quality accommodation can make a difference in the lives of vulnerable people. For example, this 18-year-old girl felt that she was able to make a fresh start in a new housing association flat away from the city centre. In the new flat her safety, her health and her control over her life increased. She explains:

It's a safe address. I'm trying to stay out of trouble. New people don't know anything. It's a fresh start . . . I've got a lot better. I've stopped hanging round with 'the crowd'. The flat is more important. If my mother comes in, I don't want drugs or drink. It's connected with the flat. If you've got a place of your own, you want it to look smart. I want to keep myself smart. I'm eating properly. (Hutson, 1997, p. 53)

What people liked best about self-contained housing was 'independence'. As a 17-year-old coming out of care into a permanent flat on a project said:

It's more like home here. It's the freedom . . . I've my own time, my own space, not people telling me, you know. It's quiet and peaceful. (Hutson, 1995a, p. 36)

This term 'quiet' came up again and again. 'Quiet' means being away from trouble, away from danger or crime and sometimes even being away from old friends, the 'crowd' whose company draws them into trouble. The new home is the opposite to the city centre hostel – of which people and trouble were an integral part. The safety of the area is particularly important, as is internal security in terms of locks or entry systems. The importance of locality comes out again and again in accounts and is further indicated by the high number of people who apply to transfer to a preferred area immediately on gaining accommodation (see Chapter 7).

However, some single vulnerable homeless people find that even the independent housing they gain after their stay in temporary accommodation is also unsafe. A woman in her fifties reports:

I don't go out any more. I only go to the paper shop and come back. It's about as far as I dare go. (Pleace, 1995, p. 44)

As some single homeless people are, at last, being offered flats in the community, it is depressing that there are reports of serious prejudice from neighbours. This is particularly strong against young people who are 'associated with crime against property, physical violence or extreme noise whether or not they actually did anything' (Pleace, 1995, p. 45). Ironically, complaints may be becoming more common following good practice policies of scattering vulnerable tenancies across residential areas rather than concentrating them in hard-to-let areas.

These kinds of difficulties were prominent in one project which housed the 'most challenging' young people from care (Hutson, 1994b). Complaints came particularly from neighbourhoods with long-established tenants and the complaints made housing associations unwilling to offer properties to other tenants from this project. Such difficulties are described, in another project, by an estate manager:

Tenants say 'When we moved in here twenty-five years ago, this was a prestige council estate and look at all these scum that you are moving in now' . . . They [the tenants] are not very understanding about people with any lifestyle other than their own. (Pleace, 1995, p. 45)

It is ironic that, in leaving behind the dangers of shared accommodation, some homeless people fear dangers in the community. Moreover, it is depressing that some homeless people are seen as dangerous by their neighbours and that, because of grassroots pressure from these majority tenants, housing associations and local authorities are finding it difficult to house them. Let us now turn to the issue of 'support', which is seen by some to be a solution to some of the problems outlined above.

**The question of support**

Although the logical end solution to homelessness is housing, support is currently seen as the missing element which will lead to the successful housing of young single homeless people. This emphasis on support has a particular origin. In the mid-1980s, children's charities moved into youth homelessness as child residential care was being run down because of costs and 'better practices' such as fostering. These charities brought with them support skills. After the Children Act in 1990, some social service departments set up after-care teams to work with the care-leavers who were increasingly being seen in the homelessness hostels. They too had support skills. In youth homelessness, a new area of work was created. In homeless youth projects, the aim was to provide clients with more than the basic provision of a bed and food, namely to teach them the skills of independent living. Terms such as individual 'empowerment' and 'networking' the young person into further support networks were associated with such work. It is important, in the debate about support, to realize who is defining the issue and to acknowledge that it is likely to be defined so that it emphasizes the skills and the economic interests of those in control (Scott, 1970).

There are other reasons for this emphasis on support. First, with the increasing numbers of homeless 16- and 17-year-olds, support was felt to be necessary because of their age. Second, the resettlement of older homeless people out of the hostels necessitated a new kind of work, namely support in the community, which also meant the teaching of independence skills. Lastly there was a need to explain the failure of some of the tenancies which were being given to single homeless people. Lack of support has become a main explanation of trouble and failure in rehousing (Pleace, 1995). The solution to a wide range of housing management problems such as rent arrears, damaging or abandoning a property, noise or neighbour complaints is felt to be the provision of support. The difficulties of supplying support in a housing context is explored in Chapter 10. Interestingly, this current emphasis on support echoes attitudes towards homelessness under the 1948 National Assistance Act (Nelson *et al.*, 1982, p. 23) which stated that:

The problem of homelessness was still seen to be one of idleness. Temporary accommodation was only afforded the homeless by the State on condition that they work ... doing many more hours supposedly as *preparation for life in the world outside* (author's italics)

Although the programmes of work which make up the 'support' offered today differ in content and name from the 'work' mentioned above, the current teaching of 'life skills' today has a similar element of preparation and control.

When single homeless people register their needs themselves, support is consistently a minority request. In a recent survey (Hutson and Jones, 1997), 71 per cent said that they did not need support if they were given tenancies. Of those who did request support, this was for sorting out benefits and budgeting. Only eight per cent requested more intensive support such as help with cooking and shopping. These figures were identical with two earlier surveys (Hutson, 1993; 1994c). They, and other interviews (Hutson, 1994a), show that most homeless people feel that they are in control of their lives but that their finances are problematic.

What do people say about the support which they have received? Not surprisingly, there are a number of different views. Some are appreciative of support. In a study of leaving-care schemes (Biehal *et al.*, 1995, p. 188), all the quotes from the young people are positive. For example:

Cos if I didn't have [the scheme] I would have been out on the street. I wouldn't know what to do, who to go to and it has been helpful, you know ... I think they've given me everything that they need to give, they've bent over backwards for me, that's the way I see it anyway.

Many are, however, more critical consumers. This young man, while acknowledging the financial help, feels that the project should have kept better control:

They [project workers] help me with my money and give me £40 a month. Sometimes they can interfere. Instead of saying 'do this, do that' they should suggest 'Here's an idea'. They should give warnings [to stop houses being closed down]. There was noise all the time. They should have stopped it happening. (Hutson, 1994a, p. 5)

This young woman is more negative. She advises others to:

Keep to yourself. Don't tell them your business. Try and get on living like you were living if you weren't here. (Hutson, field notes, 1993)

These comments come from a significant minority of young people. They show a lack of fit between the project's support and the young people's lives. This lack of fit is also shown by the number of people who miss support visits. In one project the numbers out of touch with their support workers for months on end caused difficulties with the tenancies. The take-up of support improved when the original target group of young people involved in offending and embedded in a peer group was changed to young people with mental health problems or learning difficulties who were more socially isolated. They had little peer group contact and were more eager for formal support.

However, if a project only accepts those who will take support and are likely to succeed, then the most needy will be left out. One street homeless young man (Hutson and Liddiard, 1994, p. 120) spoke of being turned away from a project. He said: 'I was homeless. I went to a homeless hostel and I was told I couldn't have a place in a homeless hostel.' Speaking to the manager of what she had told him, he said: 'You said you didn't feel that I'd benefit from it. But if you're on the street, you've got nowhere to sleep like, how can you not benefit from a bed?' The manager replied that this project was about a lot more that just having a bed, namely a programme of work which this young man was unlikely to complete. Such decisions, which are necessary in management terms, illustrate further the lack of fit between some young people's lives and what is on offer from projects in terms of support.

Just as many homeless applicants do not stay the course (see Chapter 7), a number of young people failed to make the expected course in projects (Hutson, 1995a). Some were evicted, others chose to leave because of changed relationships or objectives. In one scheme, offering permanent self-contained flats, it was expected that the length of stay would be two years. Over three years, the average stay was eight months and the turnover rate 50 per cent. This again indicates a lack of fit between public routes and private strategies. At a revenue cost of £350 per person per week, is this value for money?

The emphasis on support can play a part in turning a mainstream housing problem into one of personal pathology. Carlen (forthcoming) points out that the language of 'priority need' in itself suggests to young homeless people that there is 'something amiss in their lives'. This leads to officials seeing homelessness as a symptom of another problem, such as drug taking, which the young person must deal with by going on a programme before housing can be considered. She suggests that homelessness has been defined so as to exclude and pathologize ordinary young people who are merely requesting housing. Depressingly, this view corresponds with that of homeless people themselves who so often blame themselves for their situation. As Stuart (aged 21) said:

I'm a fool to myself as well like. I've got to admit that. I have had some problems and some I have brought on myself because I'm stupid. (Hutson and Liddiard, field-notes, 1990)

Lack of support, either in its provision or its uptake, can be a reason for not housing people. Support is expensive and so may not be obtained. There is a danger that an emphasis on support will place the blame for homelessness on the individual. It is interesting that homeless families, who have greater access to housing through legislation, are not generally seen to be needing support. This poses the question – does child-bearing suddenly increase the capacity of a person no longer to need support?

## Homeless people and informal support

There is a danger that this expansion of professional support can lead to informal networks being ignored or undermined. Although it is clear that a lack of family support is a major factor behind homelessness, particularly for care-leavers, and that breakdowns in family relationships are major triggers for homelessness, there are factors in policy, research and practice which tend to overlook or undermine family support networks (Hutson, 1995b). In a recent survey (Hutson and Jones, 1997) it was clear that, although most of the young homeless people had had some family difficulties in the past, many were in fact using occasional family accommodation or family contacts to ease their homeless situation. For example, while sleeping rough, several had used female kin for occasional overnight stays, meals and washing. This use of family and informal networks is well described in Chapter 9 for those who are 'unofficially homeless in the local area' . Ironically, official regulations, such as DSS and tenancy arrangements, can restrict the extent of this support. For example, bureaucratic routes may require a denial of family relationship. The following quote is from a young woman in a homelessness hostel for mothers and babies waiting to be rehoused. She is aware that too close contact with her mother might disqualify her from help:

If you get caught going to your mother all the time, they'll tell you to go ... They think that if you stay there all day, you can stay there all night ... There's one girl in here and she was up her mother's every day because her mother was ill and people 'phoned the council and said: 'Why is she in a homelessness hostel when she's at her mother's all day?' She had a worry then. (Hutson, 1995b, p. 344)

Informal support can be overlooked. For example, in two projects studied, although half the young people were sharing with boyfriends or partners, there was no acknowledgement of this. There are obviously legal and management reasons for dealing with the person as single but, again, a lack of fit between the life of the young person and the image of the project is illustrated. As Brandon *et al.* (1980, p. 192) points out:

The homeless are presented as more hapless and hopeless than our study would indicate ... The annual reports and campaign documents of the voluntary societies stress their own centrality in efforts to 'solve' homelessness.

In the same way, and for the same reasons, young people's involvement in the informal economy does not appear in official accounts. However, the very real loneliness which is reported by some young people, the difficulties in making stable relationships, the failure of family contacts as well as the difficulties of getting a job, even 'off the books', should not be overlooked.

## Financial support is the key

It is clear that the main problem facing homeless people and the main reason for failed tenancies is lack of money which, in turn, rests on lack of employment. The reduction of income support levels to those under 25 and the removal of this benefit from 16- to 18-year-olds triggered youth homelessness in the late 1980s. Jobs and even training for young people who leave education early have disappeared so far from view that this state of affairs is taken for granted. While people in homelessness surveys are a heterogeneous group in many respects, one feature which they share is near universal unemployment. Lack of finance can, moreover, affect informal support, particularly for men, who tend to socialize in venues where money is required, such as pubs, betting shops and leisure centres (Dix, 1995, p. 74). Problems with finances are particularly acute in self-contained properties where average expenditure on bills and food leaves only £1.10 disposable income out of an average benefit of £35 (Dix, 1995, p. 80). Ironically, finance enters into the literature less often than the question of support. While support or the models of accommodation can be altered and refined, broader economic polices have proved harder to alter. One may, however, speculate that £20 a week as direct payment into the pocket of a homeless person on top of benefit might enable them to pursue their own lives more effectively than the maintenance of a team of support workers which can cost £350 per person per week.

## Foyers

In response to concerns about employment, the most recent model of accommodation for young people is foyers, where training schemes and employment are linked to the provision of accommodation. The failure of so many independent tenancies and their cost had brought about some dissatisfaction with self-contained accommodation. It appears here, as before, that if a problem with accommodation is difficult to solve, a common response is to move on to a new model. Whether or not foyers will succeed, they represent a new name and a new image. In addition, foyers bring in new agencies such as the Employment Service and the TECs.

Initially, there were fears that the building of large hostel-type accommodation would mean a return to the problems associated with shared accommodation. There were also debates as to whether lower staffing ratios would create difficulties if long-term homeless, and so vulnerable, people were accepted. In reality, of the first seven foyers in the pilot initiative set up in 1992, only two were newly built while, in the other five, employment facilities were attached to existing YMCA hostels. This determined the characteristics of the clientele in being predominately male and white with relatively high measures of vulnerability, as measured by previous rough sleeping, court convictions and long-term health and literacy problems.

In relation to the themes of this chapter, a reading of the evaluation of the pilot initiative (Anderson and Quilgars, 1995) indicates some lack of fit between, on the one hand, the 'official linear route of assessment, action planning and training or job search towards secure employment and then independent housing' and, on the other, the actual routes of young people who often move out of the foyers, through eviction or choice, before any work is secured. This lack of fit was illustrated by the moves, in two hostels, to get young people to sign action plans prior to moving into the foyer, 'as it proved difficult to track people down and get their commitment to the action plan once they were in the hostel' (Anderson and Quilgars, 1995, p. 27). A scepticism of training is seen in the following statement from a young person:

I was a bit wary about it, because there are so many projects and government kind of schemes and everything that are basically a waste of time. (Anderson and Quilgars, 1995, p. 37)

However, the blocks to success lie, not with the young people, many of whom searched for jobs enthusiastically, but with the paucity of appropriate jobs or training. As one young person commented (Anderson and Quilgars, 1995, p. 43):

It's not the foyer that needs improving, it's the government that needs to improve things.

**Conclusions**

In this chapter, I have outlined the marked changes which have occurred in the patterns of accommodation and support offered to homeless people since the 1977 Housing (Homeless Persons) Act. Underlying such changes have been moves to privatize services, moving them from central government to the voluntary sector. Cost has been a driving factor in, for example, the rundown of bed and breakfast accommodation, and changes in funding have made it possible for some hostels to place tenants into self-contained scattered units. Management difficulties, which are so often associated with shared accommodation, lead to new models being tried in the hope that the difficulties of the former accommodation type will be overcome. Innovation is an essential element in competitive bids for funding. Although there is a strong sense of good practice in many of these changes, too many resources seem to go into professional pockets rather than to those who are homeless because they lack resources. Moreover, the responses of the voluntary sector are limited to temporary schemes because of the lack of permanent housing, which is held in the statutory sector. Since the bed and breakfast scandal and the closing of many resettlement units, temporary accommodation has not been an issue of public concern. This may be because conditions have improved. It may also be because its structure is complex and its provision so diverse. Rough sleeping can be so much more easily presented.

However, a predominant theme which runs through all the accounts presented here is of the dangers of temporary accommodation. These dangers, particularly acute in hostels, come from the shared aspect of living and fears of mixing with others who are not known. These dangers can continue in shared accommodation even when conditions are much improved. Ironically, when, and if, homeless people are eventually housed into permanent accommodation, some face prejudice as they themselves can become the perceived danger. Housing has a particularly territorial aspect and fears of living near undesirable others has always shaped residential patterning. The recent use of probationary tenancies and the ability of the local authority to review tenants with criminal records can further exacerbate fears within the neighbourhood. If formalized, such fears can go so far as to block housing, particularly to single homeless men. The observations in this chapter suggest that moves to run down shared temporary accommodation should be continued and that serious efforts should be made to house people in the areas of their choice where they feel safe.

This chapter also looks at personal accounts of support. Support has been seen by the agencies as the secret ingredient essential for the successful housing of homeless people, and the lack of this support can be used to explain tenancy failures. This emphasis on support can be explained by the role of voluntary agencies in creating a new area of work within youth homelessness. Ironically, support is not felt to be an issue in housing homeless families, although there may be little difference in age between the young people involved (see Chapter 6). With single people, lack of support can be used as a reason for not rehousing, but its use can imply that homeless people cannot manage their lives, thus turning homelessness into a question of personal pathology. Professional support can also play down informal support networks. Young people often do not take up the support offered and this can lead to eviction. All this indicates a lack of fit between official routes and individual pathways. These observations suggest that public policies should be aimed at creating structures which better enable individuals to take their own routes and to use their own informal support networks. Reasonable benefit levels for under-25s, bond boards and some form of direct payment so that homeless people could purchase their own support would all improve the current levels of destitution which are so damaging. Easier access through the bureaucracies of benefits and housing, which may be offered in 'one-stop shops', is clearly needed. Giving people choice in housing and encouraging flexibility through transfers would enable better use to be made of informal support.

Throughout this chapter, discrepancies between official constructions and what some homeless people have said have been highlighted, particularly in the area of support. The following views on survival illustrate a further discrepancy which runs through this chapter between professional and informal structures. In relation to the two quotes below, it is not that one is true and the other is not. It is that they are very different, and so, if we take only one view as being true, then the complexity of a homeless situation will be misunderstood. The first statement is from a study of leaving care projects. It states that:

It is unrealistic to expect young people with fundamental insecurities about themselves, with few links and difficulties in making and managing relationships, to make a smooth transition to the adult world. (Biehal et al., 1995, p. 203)

Against this, a young man speaks of how he learnt his 'life skills':

And on the streets, you don't get taught. You have to learn how to look after yourself ... You've either got to be very fast or very good at fighting ... Moving in and out of flats all the time and like getting a job and finishing jobs, things like that, teaches you all about DSS. (Hutson and Liddiard, field notes, 1989)

These two statements say different things about the nature of youth homelessness and what should be done about it. The first justifies the formal project route and links extreme vulnerability with professional support. In making a bid for further resources, it can imply that young homeless people are unable to live their lives on their own. The latter statement indicates that young people do live their own lives and, moreover, that survival skills can be learnt informally. The young man stresses learning from experience, but this is an experience which is not always acknowledged or facilitated by professional agencies. It is important that informal or 'private' pathways and networks should be acknowledged by, incorporated into and strengthened by public policies.

### Notes

1.   These statements come from: young homeless people interviewed around Wales in 1988–91 with Mark Liddiard; care-leavers from all counties of Wales, 1992–5; homeless people in Rhondda Cynon Taff, 1997, with Stuart Jones. For

these studies, I am grateful for funding from the Rowntree Foundation, the Welsh Office, Barnardos and Rhondda Cynon Taff Borough Council.

## References

Anderson, I. and Quilgars, D. (1995) *Foyers for Young People: Evaluation of a Pilot Initiative*, York: Centre for Housing Policy, University of York.

Audit Commission (1989) *Housing the Homeless: The Local Authority Role*, London: HMSO.

Biehal, N., Clayden, J., Stein, M. and Wade, J. (1995) *Moving On: Young People and Leaving-Care Schemes*, London: HMSO.

Bonnerjea, L. and Lawton, J. (1987) *Homelessness in Brent*, London: Policy Studies Institute.

Brandon, D., Wells, K., Francis, C. and Ramsay, E. (1980) *The Survivors: A Study of Homeless Young Newcomers to London and the Responses Made to Them*, London: Routledge and Kegan Paul.

Burrows, L. and Walentowicz, P. (1992) *Homes Cost Less than Homelessness*, London: Shelter.

Carlen, P. (forthcoming) 'The governance of homelessness: Legality, lore and lexicon in the agency-maintenance of youth homelessness', *Critical Sociology*.

Department of the Environment (1997) *PIE Quarterly Homeless Returns*, London: Department of the Environment.

Dix, J. (1995) *Assessing the Housing, Health and Support Needs of Single Homeless People Living in Hostel Accommodation in Cardiff*, Cardiff: City Housing Department.

Drennan, V. and Stearn, J. (1986) 'Health visitors and homeless families', *Health Visitor*, vol. 59, no. 20, pp. 340–2.

Duncan, S., Downey, P, and Finch, H. (1983) *A Home of their Own: A Survey of Rehoused Hostel Residents*, London: HMSO.

Garside, P., Grimshaw, R. and Ward, F. (1990) *No Place Like Home: The Hostels' Experience*, London: HMSO.

Hutson, S. (1993) *Housing and Support Needs of Single Homeless People*, Neath: Neath Borough Council.

Hutson, S. (1994a) *Marlborough Road Projects: Report of the Second Round Interviews*, London: Barnardos.

Hutson, S. (1994b) *Monitoring and Evaluating Network with a Focus on Housing and Support*, Cardiff: Welsh Office (Housing).

Hutson, S. (1994c) *Snapshot Survey of Single Homelessness in Swansea*, Swansea: Swansea Borough Council.

Hutson, S. (1995a) *Monitoring and Evaluating Network: The Final Report – Taking the Model Forward*, Cardiff: Welsh Office (Housing).

Hutson, S. (1995b) 'Children without families? Young homeless people and young people from care talking', in J. Brannen and M. O'Brien (eds) *Childhood and Parenthood*, London: Institute of Education University of London.

Hutson, S. (1997) *Supported Housing: The Experience of Care-Leavers*, London: Barnardos.

Hutson, S. and Jones, S. (1997) *Rough Sleeping and Homelessness in Rhondda Cynon Taff*, Pontypridd: University of Glamorgan.

Hutson, S. and Liddiard, M. (1994) *Youth Homelessness: The Construction of a Social Issue*, London: Macmillan.

Kemp, P. and Rhodes, D. (1994) *The Lower End of the Private Rented Sector: A Glasgow Case Study*, Research Report 35, Edinburgh: Scottish Homes.

Murie, A. and Jeffers, S. (1987) *Living in Bed and Breakfast: The Experience of Homelessness in London*, Bristol: SAUS.

Nelson, J., Sternberg, A. and Brindley, E. (1982) *Avoiding Institutions*, London: Nelson's Column Publications.

Oldman, J. (1993) *Broken Promises: A Survey of Resettlement Unit Replacement Packages*, London: CHAR.

Pleace, N. (1995) *Housing Vulnerable Single Homeless people*, York: Centre for Housing Policy.

Randall, G. and Brown, S. (1996) *From Street to Home: An Evaluation of Phase 2 of the Rough Sleepers Initiative*, London: Stationery Office.

Scott, R. (1970) 'The construction of conceptions of stigma by professional experts', in J. Douglas (ed.) *Deviance and Respectability: The Social Construction of Moral Meanings*, London: Basic Books.

Thomas, A. and Niner, P. (1989) *Living in Temporary Accommodation: A Survey of Homeless People*, London: HMSO.

# Conclusions

*David Clapham*

A key theme of this book is the contested nature of the concept of homelessness. In his chapter on homelessness in Europe (Chapter 3), Harvey shows that the term has different meanings in different countries, which makes any generalization difficult. For example, it is very difficult to ascertain how many homeless people there are in Europe because there is no common basis for the collection of national statistics. The statistics match the different ways the concept of homelessness is socially constructed within the societies.

The understanding of homelessness, as a socially constructed phenomenon, is a theme which runs throughout the book. It is argued that the dominant definition of homelessness in Britain has changed over time and this is reflected in the discourses which surround it, whether in policy documents, political speeches, administrative procedures or media coverage. In Chapter 1, Jacobs, Kemeny and Manzi argue that the 1977 Homeless Persons Act was a watershed in the definition of homelessness in Britain. Before this, the dominant construction was what they term a 'minimalist' definition, in which the causes of homelessness were assumed to be rooted in individual pathologies. Homelessness was held to be a private trouble which was primarily the responsibility of the individual to deal with. The role of the state was to provide support and correction through social work intervention with the individual and family in order for them to be able to cope within the existing system.

The 1977 legislation encapsulated a different construction, which Jacobs, Kemeny and Manzi term the 'maximalist' definition. Here, there is an underlying assumption that there are systemic influences on the existence of homelessness. In particular, homelessness is viewed as resulting, in large measure, from a shortage of housing caused by endemic failures in the housing system, such as a shortage of private rented accommodation and a lack of investment in public rented housing. Homelessness is therefore defined as the result of a defect in public policy which it is the duty of the state to put right. Homeless people have the right to expect the state to use public policy to solve their problems.

Somerville, in his analysis of the making of the 1977 legislation (Chapter 2), shows that this construction of homelessness was supported by media representations (most notably through the television programme *Cathy Come Home*), as well as key political figures and government agencies. Nevertheless it was resisted by some Conservative politicians and some local government interests. They succeeded in restricting the scope of the change of definition by including the concepts of vulnerability, intentionality and local connection in the legislation. These concepts clearly had their roots in the minimalist construction and were designed to ensure that there were procedures to exclude the 'undeserving' from help and to perpetuate concepts of individual pathology in homelessness policy and discourse.

Somerville shows how these cracks in the application of the maximalist construction were exploited to lessen its impact incrementally and to re-establish the primacy of the minimalist, individual pathology construction. The centralization of policy in the central government, the depoliticization of housing in general and homelessness in particular, and the deregulation and marketization of the housing system, all created the conditions in which legislation could be introduced in 1996 to re-instate firmly the minimalist construction.

The dominant image of homelessness in Britain in the 1990s has become that of the roofless rough sleeper who is there because of mental illness, alcoholism, drug abuse or family breakdown. These people are presented as a nuisance, making city centres dirty and tawdry and representing a threat to public order through 'aggressive begging'. The appropriate public response is to sweep them off the streets into hostels designed to offer shelter and correction. Ford (Chapter 5) shows how this dominant construction has not been challenged, even by the increase in homelessness caused by the rising levels of mortgage default in the late 1980s and early 1990s. This was caused primarily by instability in the private housing market caused by the management of the national economy and the government-promoted expansion of the owner-occupied sector. Nevertheless, the primary discourse was of faulty household decisions and personal misfortune rather than of government or housing system failure. Although mortgage repossession is endemic, the resolution of it is left to the market, through the actions of mortgage lenders, rather than through public policy. Those households in mortgage debt blame themselves, are isolated and take their own individuated routes back into housing.

The general deregulation and marketization of the housing system since the 1980s has created the conditions in which any form of housing problem is constructed as a personal trouble rather than a public policy failure. Thus, housing in general and homelessness in particular have been effectively depoliticized. At the same time, the ability of public agencies such as local authorities to provide accommodation for homeless people has been undermined by the same trends which have led to a shortage of public rented housing.

Even before the 1996 legislation the minimalist construction had resulted in profound difficulties in the implementation of the homelessness procedures. Evans (Chapter 7) shows how the objective of weeding out the 'undeserving' has resulted in a complicated and cumbersome bureaucratic process which many homeless people view as alienating and hostile. Moreover, the result is that only 20 per cent of applicants are housed through the statutory route. There is no difference in the housing need of those included and those excluded. The difference is in whether they are considered to be 'deserving' or 'undeserving'. The deserving group has been women with dependent children. However, the growing numbers of single-parent families have begun to dominate this group, leading to the 1996 legislation which can be construed as a clear attempt to recategorize this group and to restrict their rights to housing. The undeserving group has largely been young single people who are constructed as work-shy and as leaving home unnecessarily.

The social construction of homelessness and of homeless people is closely tied into general constructions of groups within society. Smith examines, in Chapter 6, the social construction of gender differences and their impact on the experiences of homeless people. Anderson, in Chapter 8, describes the position of young single people in the employment market and their treatment in a wide range of public policies such as education and social security. The key point is that the construction of homelessness cannot be viewed in isolation from more general constructions which are closely linked to political ideologies.

### Examining competing social constructions

The examination of the experiences of homeless people through personal biographies can shed light on the factors which are associated with homelessness. For example, Fitzpatrick and Clapham (Chapter 9) show that, in their sample of young single people, the causes of homelessness were very complex. Homeless young people tended to leave home early and were often pushed out of the home by the circumstances there rather than being pulled by external opportunities. The family circumstances which caused problems included the difficult and sometimes violent behaviour of parents towards their children, or to each other, as well as the challenging behaviour of the children themselves, such as inability or unwillingness to find work, drug or alcohol abuse and criminal behaviour. The homelessness pathway often started early in the young person's life and was linked to difficulties at school, including truanting. All these factors meant that young people received little help from parents and others on leaving home. Of course, individual circumstances varied substantially and the degree of support received from family and friends was a major influence on the nature, frequency and extent of homeless episodes.

At first glance, this analysis would seem to re-inforce the minimalist construction of individual and family pathology as the root cause of homelessness. The strength of the pathways approach is that it shows the dynamic nature of homelessness and highlights the individual experiences, decisions and circumstances which lead to and structure the homeless experience. It also shows the complex array of factors which interact in the individual biography to shape the housing pathway. However, the disadvantage of the approach is that, used on its own, it can highlight individual differences while hiding general similarities. It also focuses attention on the immediate causes of homelessness rather than on the underlying factors.

Family breakdown plays a key role in the homelessness of the young people interviewed in the course of Fitzpatrick's research reported in Chapter 9. The question is why this breakdown occurred. In the minimalist construction the answer would be found in the internal structure and dynamics of the individual families. Individual inadequacy and moral degradation would be seen as the heart of the problems and the appropriate focus for any curative intervention. Jacobs, Kemeny and Manzi focus on a version of the maximalist construction during the 1970s which placed emphasis on the shortage of housing as being the root cause of homelessness. However, a shortage of housing by itself is unlikely to lead to the breakdown of family, identified in the experiences of some young people. The maximalist construction can also include other public policies and structural factors. Examples are policies of education which leave some schoolchildren with an alienated experience which leads to poor motivation and achievement and to uncontrolled truancy; social security policies which do not provide for some younger people and create stresses within the family; as well as housing policies which make it difficult for young people to afford or to access good-quality housing as well as economic policies which do not provide opportunities for work to large numbers of young people. To these can be added de-institutionalization and community care policies which result in some people living without appropriate shelter and support.

A common thread in the biographies of young people was the material poverty of the families and their communities. In Chapter 8, Anderson draws attention to the social exclusion of many young people and the communities in which they live. In Fitzpatrick and Clapham's sample of young people (Chapter 9), many families were put under strain by the difficulty of supporting a young person who brought no income into a household which was dependent on state benefits. This not only created material hardship but also created emotional tensions and difficulties in the creation of identity and self-worth for the young person.

These difficulties were shared by many families living in the communities concerned which showed the well-recorded signs of excluded communities. Private hardship was closely associated with poor, or absent, public facilities, substandard housing and a depressing environment. Private troubles become public ones as crime and other forms of anti-social behaviour plague families already struggling to cope. In these circumstances, private troubles are more likely to occur and families are less likely to have the material and personal resources to cope with them. Therefore the process of leaving home for young people in these families and communities is more likely to be problematic and lead to episodes of homelessness. Young people facing personal and family difficulties need to draw on external support networks for help. Where this is forthcoming, from families or friends or public agencies, homelessness episodes may be short and relatively unproblematic. Some young people survived for many years, living with friends and in local hostels and drawing support from the wider family. Where this support did not exist, homelessness episodes could be more extended and could lead to rough sleeping in city centres and the dangers which this poses to safety and to good health.

In addition to processes of social exclusion, are the elements of what Beck (1992) has called the 'risk' society. A key element of this is labour market flexibility including widespread unemployment, a growing number of part-time and short-term jobs, as well as a growth in self-employment. This is coupled with social trends, such as rising divorce rates, the growing number of single-person households, later marriage and cohabitation. The implications of this trend can be seen in the rise in mortgage arrears and repossessions and the consequent homelessness. Because of factors outside the control of individuals, such as interest rate increases, employment restructuring or house price reductions, households can find themselves at risk of homelessness.

## Analysing homelessness

The individual chapters of this book have been written from different and sometimes conflicting standpoints. Nevertheless, an approach can be identified which brings together the analyses in the different contributions to offer a coherent approach to the study of homelessness. One important element of this approach is the concept of a housing pathway built around the research method of biographical interviewing. As we argued earlier, this approach has the strength of grounding analysis in the experiences of individuals and their reaction to the complex interactions of the many influences which shape their lives and their housing pathway. Through this device homelessness can be seen as one or more episodes in a dynamic housing and life experience. Individuals move into, and usually out of, homelessness and without a recognition of the dynamics of this process it will not be fully understood.

The pathway approach offers unique insights into the experience of homelessness and accords primacy to the voices of those who are undergoing the experience. It provides a framework for analysis of the interactions of individual personality and lifestyle as well as the many and varied factors which influence the situation in which individuals find themselves.

Nevertheless, as we argued earlier, *by itself*, the approach could lead to an overemphasis on the actions of individuals and a corresponding lack of emphasis on the causes which shape the environment in which those actions are taken. Therefore, it is crucial that a pathways analysis is combined with a study of the nature of that environment. This book has pointed the way to appropriate methods of such an analysis through the emphasis on the way the environment is socially constructed. Changing social constructions of homelessness shape both the attitudes of homeless people themselves to their situation, and also the attitudes of others towards them. Social constructions also form the basis of public policy and shape its legal framework and institutional structure. A good example of this given in the book is the way that minimalist constructions of homelessness shaped the 1977 legislation through the introduction of the concepts of intentionality, vulnerability and local connection. In turn this influenced the nature of the bureaucratic processes which served to exclude many homeless people from access to permanent housing and to influence strongly the nature of the experience which homeless people had and the way they were treated by employees of the public agencies. Of course this in turn will influence the attitudes and behaviour of homeless people themselves.

The analysis of the social construction of homelessness should not be undertaken in isolation from the wider social constructions which shape attitudes, actions and public policy. For example, the way that the position of homeless young people is constructed should not be viewed in isolation from the constructions of young people generally, which is influenced by their position in relation to the labour market as well as by the social constructions of the family. Another example is the position of homeless single mothers, which can only be understood in relation to moral debates about the nature of the family. Dominant social constructions reflect the power structures in society and the ability of different groups to have their definitions of the world accepted. This may seem to have moved a long way from a discussion of homelessness, but the important point is that there are many different levels of analysis and an adequate understanding of the nature of homelessness must take into account all these levels.

## Models of intervention

Social constructions of homelessness structure the way that public policy intervenes to deal with homelessness. For example, the minimalist construction, with its emphasis on individual pathology and the division between those who are deserving of help and those who are not, has structured the statutory homeless procedures with their emphasis on exclusion of the undeserving. It has also influenced the forms of help which are provided. In Chapter 11, Hutson examines the provision of hostels and other forms of accommodation for young homeless people. She argues that these forms of provision reflect the individual pathology construction in that their form and nature correspond with the view that young people are undeserving of their own house. This becomes evident if the alternative ways in which help could be provided to young homeless people are examined. If the assumption is that the main reason for homelessness among young people is the difficulty of access to housing, then the obvious policy approach would be to improve access to permanent housing, either through changes to the allocation priorities of social housing agencies or through improving their access through the statutory homeless procedures.

If the main assumption is that the major cause of homelessness is individual pathology, then provision will be shaped by the need to alter what is defined as inappropriate behaviour and to ensure that inappropriate behaviour is not rewarded through the provision of the 'prize' of permanent housing. The predominant form of provision for young homeless people at present tends towards the latter model with the provision of hostels and other forms of 'special' shared accommodation which is not popular with young people and invokes echoes of the 'less eligibility' of the Poor Law. Many young people find hostels threatening and demeaning places to stay. For example, in Fitzpatrick and Clapham's sample in Chapter 9, some young people slept rough rather than return to hostels which were situated away from their support networks and away from the locations where they felt safe. The concept of special forms of shared living is also often supported by the homelessness industry because it re-inforces the idea that special expertise is required in planning and running such provision which only they are held to possess.

Alternative models of provision for young homeless people are available. For example, access to mainstream housing can be made easier for young people and, if needed, support can be provided in flexible ways in their homes. Where young people do not want, or would find it difficult, to cope in this situation, housing and support can be provided in non-institutionalized ways which are in the local area and are not threatening or demeaning. Franklin, in Chapter 10, draws attention to the support needs which some homeless people may have and the different ways in which they can be met.

However, these forms of intervention are curative in that they are aimed at dealing with homelessness once it has occurred rather than attempting to prevent it occurring. By placing emphasis on intervention with individual homeless people they implicitly reinforce the view that the causes of homelessness are located at this level. Of course, whatever the causes of homelessness, there is a place for emergency intervention with individuals once it has occurred. Nevertheless, if the assumption is that homelessness has its roots in social exclusion and the risk society, then intervention could be pitched at this level. There is no space here to spell out what such a strategy would look like, but it would clearly have as its basis a challenge to the individual pathology construction of homelessness and models of intervention based on this view.

### Towards a maximalist construction

Most of the contributions to this volume have either implicily or explicitly adopted and advocated a maximalist construction of homelessness which is at odds with the current dominant construction in Britain. The key questions to be addressed here are what a maximalist construction would look like in practice and how and whether it could become dominant in the British context.

In my view, a maximalist construction is not in direct opposition to an individual pathology approach because of the wide range of factors which influence homelessness, including individual and family problems. The young people in Fitzpatrick and Clapham's sample in Chapter 9 were involved with or subjected to violence, drug abuse and crime and some suffered from mental health problems. In one or two cases, access to housing had been provided, but the young people were unable to cope without intensive support. Therefore a maximalist approach cannot deny the importance of individual and family pathology and the efficacy of intervention at this level, but it does not restrict analysis to this level. It looks at the wide range of factors which can influence family and individual functioning and seeks to intervene at this level as well.

Examples of the kind of issues involved have been given in the course of the book. These include: a social security policy which does not create family tensions and force young people on to the streets; job opportunities for young people; an education system which provides adequate training for employment and life and deals effectively with alienation and truancy; effective systems for controlling crime and drug abuse; a system for dealing effectively with mental health problems; and so on. Perhaps, most importantly, these are all related to questions of social exclusion of individuals, groups and communities and to the insecurities generated by the risk society. A maximalist construction would link these issues with home-lessness and provide a framework for intervention at this level.

Writing at the beginning of a new Labour government in Britain, the prospects for the growing power of this maximalist construction seem brighter than for many years. Social exclusion is being openly discussed and expressed as a priority target for public policy, although it is rarely linked in public debate to issues of homelessness. The general 'problem', of excluded young people, has been brought to the fore of public policy and is being tackled through educational, social security and training reform. At this stage it remains to be seen how effective this will be in preventing home-lessness.

There are three major concerns at present in the construction of home-lessness. The first is the general lack of visibility of homelessness as a political issue. It played little or no part in the recent general election campaign. The second concern is the construction of young homeless people in particular as a threat to social order and as aggressive and anti-social. The provision of help through training is being combined with the rhetoric and practice of social control. Finally, the stated aim of public policy intervention is being circumscribed by the government-imposed limits on the overall level of public expenditure. Therefore it is difficult to see how the problem of inadequate investment in rented housing can be effectively addressed in the near future.

**Reference**

Beck, U. (1992) *Risk Society: Towards a New Modernity*, London: Sage.

# Name index

# Subject index